Designing Web Interfaces

ISBN 0-13-085897-8

90000

9 780130 858979

THE ADVANCED WEBSITE ARCHITECTURE SERIES

DESIGNING WEB INTERFACES
Michael Rees
Andrew White
Bebo White

SUPPORTING WEB SERVERS
Benay Dara-Abrams
Drew Dara-Abrams
Trevor Peace
Bebo White

ANALYZING E-COMMERCE & INTERNET LAW
J. Dianne Brinson
Benay Dara-Abrams
Drew Dara-Abrams
Jennifer Masek
Ruth McDunn
Bebo White

Designing Web Interfaces

Michael Rees

Andrew White

Bebo White

Prentice Hall PTR
Upper Saddle River, NJ 07458
www.phptr.com

Library of Congress Cataloging-in-Publication Data available

Editorial/production supervision: *Jessica Balch (Pine Tree Composition)*
Project coordination: *Anne Trowbridge*
Acquisitions editor: *Karen McLean*
Developmental Editor: *Ralph Moore*
Editorial assistant: *Richard Winkler*
Manufacturing manager: *Alexis R. Heydt*
Marketing manager: *Kate Hargett*
Cover design director: *Jerry Votta*
Interior designer: *Meryl Poweski*

 © 2001 Prentice Hall PTR
Prentice-Hall, Inc.
Upper Saddle River, NJ 07458

Prentice Hall books are widely used by corporations and government agencies for
training, marketing, and resale.

The publisher offers discounts on this book when ordered in bulk quantities.
For more information, contact: Corporate Sales Department, Phone: 800-382-3419;
Fax: 201-236-7141; E-mail: corpsales@prenhall.com; or write: Prentice Hall PTR,
Corp. Sales Dept., One Lake Street, Upper Saddle River, NJ 07458.

All products or services mentioned in this book are the trademarks or service marks of their
respective companies or organizations.

Printed in the United States of America
10 9 8 7 6 5 4 3 2

ISBN 0-13-085897-8

Prentice-Hall International (UK) Limited, *London*
Prentice-Hall of Australia Pty. Limited, *Sydney*
Prentice-Hall Canada Inc., *Toronto*
Prentice-Hall Hispanoamericana, S.A., *Mexico*
Prentice-Hall of India Private Limited, *New Delhi*
Prentice-Hall of Japan, Inc., *Tokyo*
Pearson Education Asia Pte. Ltd.
Editora Prentice-Hall do Brasil, Ltda., *Rio de Janeiro*

To Margot, for her support and understanding, and for sacrificing many boating weekends.

—M.R.

To my family for their ongoing support and encouragement.

—A.W.

My contributions to this book series are dedicated to my loving and supportive family—Nancy, Andrew, and Christopher—whose tolerance for patience is always severely tested whenever I take on a book project. We did it again!

—B.W.

CONTENTS

CHAPTER 2   Introduction to Human-Computer Interaction   71

CHAPTER 3 Human-Computer Interaction Principles   **107**

CHAPTER 4 Human-Computer Interaction Design   **163**

CHAPTER 5   Human-Computer Interaction for the Web   209

CHAPTER 6   Web Page Navigation   233

CHAPTER 7 Overview of Multimedia Formats   279

FROM THE EDITOR

As the Internet rapidly becomes the primary commerce and communications medium for virtually every company and organization operating today, a growing need exists for trained individuals to manage this medium. Aptly named *Webmasters,* these individuals will play leading roles in driving their organizations into the next millennium.

Working with the World Organization of Webmasters (WOW), Pearson PTR has developed two book series that are designed to train Webmasters to meet this challenge. These are *The Foundations of Website Architecture Series,* and *The Advanced Website Architecture Series.*

The Webmaster who masters the materials in these books will have working knowledge of Web site management, support, maintenance, organizational strategy, electronic commerce strategy and tools, as well as legal issues surrounding the Web. The Webmaster will be able to implement sound Web site design, navigation and HCI (Human-Computer Interaction) practices. Webmasters will also have a solid understanding of networking, Web servers, Web programming, and scripting, as well as supporting supplementary technologies.

The goal of *The Advanced Website Architecture Series* is to provide an advanced Webmaster training curriculum. *The Advanced Website Architecture Series* offers in-depth coverage of the content, business, and technical issues that challenge Webmasters.

Books in this series are:

> *Designing Web Interfaces*
> *Supporting Web Servers*
> *Analyzing E-Commerce & Internet Law*

The Foundations of Website Architecture Series is designed to introduce and explain the technical, business, and content management skills that are necessary to effectively train the new Webmaster.

Books in *The Foundations of Website Architecture Series* include:

> *Understanding Web Development*
> *Mastering Internet Protocols*
> *Administering Web Servers, Security, & Maintenance*
> *Exploring Web Marketing & Project Management*
> *Creating Web Graphics, Audio, & Video*

Thank you for your interest in *The Advanced Website Architecture Series,* and good luck in your career as a Webmaster!

Karen McLean
Senior Managing Editor
Pearson PTR Interactive

EXECUTIVE FOREWORD

Within the next few years, you will think about the Internet in the same way you think about electricity today. Just as you don't ask a friend to "use electricity to turn on a light," you will assume the omnipresence of the Web and the capabilities that it delivers. The Web is transforming the way we live, work, and play, just as electricity changed everything for previous generations.

Every indication suggests that the explosive growth of the Web will continue. The question we need to address is, "How can we deliver the most value with this ubiquitous resource?" Today, most of the world's Web sites were created and are maintained by self-taught Webmasters. Why? Because there were limited opportunities to receive formal standards-based education. Quality, accessible, affordable education will help provide the broad range of knowledge, skills, and abilities to meet the demands of the marketplace.

Over the last three years, the World Organization of Webmasters (WOW) has worked with colleges and universities, business and industry, and its own membership of aspiring and practicing Web professionals to develop the Certified Web Professional (CWP) program. Our three-part goal is to provide:

- Educational institutions with guidelines around which to develop curricula.
- An organized way to master technical skills, content development, business proficiency and personal workplace ability.
- An assessment standard for employers to measure candidates.

The Foundations of Website Architecture Series and *The Advanced Website Architecture Series* grew organically from the communities they will serve. Written by working professionals and academics currently teaching the material, and reviewed by leading faculty at major colleges and universities and the WOW Review Board of industry professionals, these books are designed to meet the increasingly urgent need for Web professionals with expertise in three areas: technical development, design and content development, and business.

There is a huge increase in demand for qualified Web professionals, with the number of Web sites projected to grow from about 5 million today to about 25 million by the year 2002. Web professionals with business, technical, design, and project management skills are, and will continue to be, the most in-demand and will receive the highest compensation.

On behalf of WOW and its members, we wish you the best of success and welcome you to this exciting field.

William B. Cullifer
Executive Director-Founder
World Organization of Webmasters
bill@joinwow.org

INTRODUCTION

WHAT YOU WILL NEED

A networked PC with access to the Internet. The faster the connection, the less time you spend on the "World Wide Wait."

A Web browser with as many plug-ins as you can support (to experience as much marketing media as possible) and an e-mail account. In your browser preferences, please enable cookies.

HOW THIS BOOK IS ORGANIZED

In this book, and the others in this series, you are presented with a series of interactive labs. Each lab begins with Learning Objectives that define what exercises (or tasks) are covered in that lab. This is followed by an overview of the concepts that will be further explored through the exercises, which are the heart of each lab.

Each exercise consists of either a series of steps that you will follow to perform a specific task or a presentation of a particular scenario. Questions that are designed to help you discover the important things on your own are then asked of you. The answers to these questions are given at the end of the exercises, along with more in-depth discussion of the concepts explored.

At the end of each lab is a series of multiple-choice Self-Review Questions, which are designed to bolster your learning experience by providing opportunities to check your absorbtion of important material. The answers to these questions appear in the Appendix. There are also additional Self-Review Questions at this book's companion Web site, found at http://www.phptr.com/phptrinteractive/.

Finally, at the end of each chapter you will find a Test Your Thinking section, which consists of a series of projects designed to solidify all of the skills you have learned in the chapter. If you have successfully completed all of the labs in the chapter, you should be able to tackle these projects with few problems. There are not always "answers" to these projects, but where appropriate, you will find guidance and/or solutions at the companion Web site.

The final element of this book actually doesn't appear in the book at all. It is the companion Web site, and it is located at http://www.phptr.com/phptrinteractive/.

This companion Web site is closely integrated with the content of this book, and we encourage you to visit often. It is designed to provide a unique interactive on-line experience that will enhance your education. As mentioned, you will find guidance and solutions that will help you complete the projects found in the Test Your Thinking section of each chapter.

You will also find additional Self-Review Questions for each chapter, which are meant to give you more opportunities to become familiar with terminology and concepts presented in the publications. In the Author's Corner, you will find additional information that we think will interest you, including updates to the information presented in these publications, and discussion about the constantly changing technology Webmasters must stay involved in.

Finally, you will find a Message Board, which you can think of as a virtual study lounge. Here, you can interact with other *Advanced Website Architecture Series* readers, and share and discuss your projects.

NOTES TO THE STUDENT

This publication and the others in *The Advanced Website Architecture Series* are endorsed by the World Organization of Webmasters. The series is a training curriculum designed to provide aspiring Webmasters with the skills they need to perform in the marketplace. The skill sets included in *The Advanced Website Architecture Series* were initially collected and defined by this international trade association to create a set of core competencies for students, professionals, trainers, and employers to utilize.

NOTES TO THE INSTRUCTOR

Chances are that you are a pioneer in the education field whether you want to be one or not. Due to the explosive nature of the Internet's growth, very few Webmaster training programs are currently in existence. But while you read this, many colleges, community colleges, technical institutes, and corporate and commercial training environments are introducing this material into curriculums worldwide.

Chances are, however, that you are teaching new material in a new program. But don't fret, this publication and series are designed as a comprehensive introductory curriculum in this field. Students successfully completing this program of study will be fully prepared to assume the responsibilities of a Webmaster in the field or to engage in further training and certification in the Internet communications field.

Each chapter in this book is broken down into labs. All questions and projects have the answers and discussions associated with them. The labs and question/

answer formats used in this book provide excellent opportunities for group discussions and dialogue between students and instructors. Many answers and their discussions are abbreviated in this publication for space reasons. Any comments, ideas, or suggestions to this text and series will be would be greatly appreciated.

ACKNOWLEDGMENTS

From Michael: I would like to thank

- The fathers of human-computer interaction generally, and Jakob Nielsen in particular, for giving us the foundation on which to build a usable and successful Web browser interface.
- My fellow authors for helping me keep up the momentum of writing, and to Bebo especially, who knows how to persuade without pressure.
- The editors and staff at Prentice Hall and Pine Tree Composition, whose support was invaluable, even from the other side of the world.

From Andrew: My thanks to

- Apple Computer for continuing to provide in the Macintosh a superb platform for multimedia.
- Countless Web content providers whose work made my research manageable and tolerable.

From Bebo: I am grateful to

- Robert Cailliau and Tim Berners-Lee who let me share their visions a decade ago and have continued to support me.
- My book co-authors who worked tirelessly to make this book series the best that it could be.
- Bill Cullifer of WOW for finding in Prentice Hall, a publisher not interested in just another book series on the Web, but a series that dares to address many of the Web management issues that have been previously overlooked or ignored.
- Karen McLean of Prentice Hall for a patient, yet firm, hand that pushed this project to completion.

ABOUT THE AUTHORS

Michael Rees is currently an Associate Professor in Computer Science at Bond University in Australia, where he lives with his wife, Margot. He currently teaches and undertakes research on the Internet and the World Wide Web. In addition, he teaches programming with Java, JavaScript, and Visual Basic. He has over thirty years of teaching experience in programming, operating systems, human-computer interaction, electronic publishing, and the Internet.

Educated in the United Kingdom, Michael obtained his Bachelor degree in Mathematics at the University of Birmingham. At Oxford University, Pembroke College, he was one of the first students to gain a Postgraduate degree in Programming Languages. He gained his PhD at the University of Southampton in incremental language compiler design.

Coming to Australia in the mid-1980s, Michael established research groups in human-computer interaction at the University of Tasmania and at Bond University. He concentrated on user interface design for electronic mail systems and subsequently on collaborative systems such as chat systems and electronic meetings. This research work naturally utilized the World Wide Web, and from 1993, Michael has gained experience of user interface design in this medium. His work is published in many journal and conference papers.

He is co-author of two previous books from Addison-Wesley (*Text Processing with troff,* with D. W. Barron, 1985, and *Practical Compiling with Pascal-S,* with D. J. Robson, 1988).

Andrew White has been involved in Web and multimedia development for over eight years. His accomplishments include the production of independent video for public access television, the development of Web-based action games, and the administration of an online newspaper. His current interests include technologies for the reliable and secure delivery of online content to wireless devices. He presently works as a software consultant in Seattle.

Bebo White is a member of the technical staff at the Stanford Linear Accelerator Center (SLAC), the high-energy physics laboratory operated by Stanford University. He also holds academic appointments at the University of California, Berkeley, the University of San Francisco, and Hong Kong University.

He was fortunate enough to become involved with WWW development quite early while on sabbatical at CERN in 1989. Consequently, he was a part of the team instrumental in establishing the first non-European web site at SLAC in December 1991.

Bebo has authored and co-authored multiple books and articles. He has lectured and spoken internationally to academic and commercial audiences and has been particularly involved with two major international conference series: the Computing in High Energy Physics (CHEP) Conference and the International World Wide Web Conference. He served as Co-Chair of the Sixth International World Wide Web Conference, co-hosted by SLAC and Stanford University.

In 1996, Mr. White was added to the Micro Times 100 list of those making outstanding contributions to personal computing. He is a member of the IW3C2 (International World Wide Web Conference Committee), a fellow of the International World Wide Web Institute (IWWWI) and is cited by the World Wide Web Consortium.

CHAPTER 1

UNDERSTANDING HYPERTEXT SYSTEMS

Technical descriptions of the Web are filled with references to *hypertext*. *HyperText* Markup Language (HTML), *HyperText* Transport Protocol (HTTP), and *hypertext* reference (href) are but a few. Even in a formal definition, the WWW is categorized as "a networked *hypertext* system."

Before we say what hypertext is, it is perhaps more important to say what it isn't. A popular quote in the hypertext community is, "Hypertext is *not* simply linear text with links, any more than television is simply radio with a picture." Likewise, many authors' interpretation of hypertext is that "hypertext is more than point and click."

Hypertext is an authoring and reading paradigm that long predates the Web and for which a substantial body of research exists. Thanks to the success of WWW, hypertext has also become a new medium of expression and should be used accordingly. A new medium not only dictates who the audience is, but also defines what the content should be and how it should be presented.

In this chapter you will learn the fundamental concepts of hypertext and hypertext systems. The goal is to illustrate the unique communication medium that hypertext represents and how it can best be used by content authors/providers and users/readers. We will also discuss how some basic hypertext techniques can be used in the development of Web-based content and how these techniques address some of the fundamental Web-authoring issues. All along we will be evaluating the effectiveness of WWW as a hypertext system with emphasis on what the technology provides and what an author must provide.

LAB 1.1

DOCUMENT MARKUP FUNDAMENTALS

LAB OBJECTIVES

After this lab, you will be able to:

✔ Explore the Concept of Document Markup
✔ Apply All Five Types of Document Markup to HTML
✔ Define a Document Tagset
✔ Explore the Issues Surrounding HTML Page Conversion

A discussion of document markup is relevant to Web content development because markup is a critical component of the authoring process. Most Web authors are familiar with document markup using HTML (the HyperText Markup Language) and maybe XML (eXtensible Markup Language); however, few are familiar with the fundamentals of document markup and the types of markup that have been defined.

By definition, document markup is not a part of the intellectual content of a written work, but instead provides information about how that work is structured and how it should be interpreted, read, presented, or displayed. Although independent of a work's content, markup can change a reader's interpretation of that content.

In the planning phase of document development, an author must make a conscious decision to separate content and structure from presentation.

- Content is "what" you say.
- Structure is how you organize what you say.
- Presentation is how what you say and how you organize the information appears, feels, or sounds to your audience.

Five types of document markup are used to help make these distinctions:

1. Punctuational
2. Presentational
3. Procedural
4. Descriptive
5. Referential

Each of these types will be discussed and examples will be given.

TYPES OF DOCUMENT MARKUP

PUNCTUATIONAL MARKUP

Punctuational markup consists of the use of a well-defined set of punctuation marks to provide syntactic or rhetorical information about how some body of text will read. Punctuational markup requires some level of agreement on how the markup is appropriately used.

■ FOR EXAMPLE

There are precise literary rules surrounding the use of the comma. Probably very few of us know these rules and use the comma when "it feels right," or when a pause should occur during reading. It is clear that the omission or incorrect use of a comma can change the interpretation of a sentence dramatically.

PRESENTATIONAL MARKUP

In presentational markup, an author introduces elements intended to make the organization of the work clearer to a reader. These elements are often visual or structural in nature.

■ FOR EXAMPLE

Examples of presentational markup are page layout definitions (horizontal and vertical space and margins) and page breaks to occur during printing. Markup that supports structural definitions such as chapter, section, subsection, and so on could also be viewed as presentational.

PROCEDURAL MARKUP

A procedural markup system consists of a collection of commands that allow an author to specify how text and other document components are to be formatted. Procedural markup can, and often does, replace presentational markup.

■ *FOR EXAMPLE*

Good examples of procedural markup are the T$_E$X and LaT$_E$X systems. For example, in LaT$_E$X, a fraction in a mathematical expression is "marked up" by an author as \frac{numer}{denom} where numer and denom are the values of the fraction's numerator and denominator respectively.

DESCRIPTIVE MARKUP

In descriptive markup, document authors identify the element type of text tokens or collections of text. The scope of these types is then tagged in order to insure that the affected text is presented in the desired manner.

■ *FOR EXAMPLE*

It should be fairly obvious that HTML and XML are good examples of a descriptive markup system. As is familiar to all HTML and XML authors, *tagsets* (e.g., <H1> and </H1>, <OL> and </OL>) form *containers* that indicate how the enclosed text and/or objects are to be presented/rendered by a Web browser. Some tags have no scope (e.g., <BR>) because they indicate an immediate action and do not contain text or objects.

REFERENTIAL MARKUP

Referential markup allows an author to insert external entities into a document. This is accomplished by including references within the document that result in the replacement with the entity when the document is processed.

■ *FOR EXAMPLE*

Once again, HTML contains examples of referential markup. Since browsers are designed to "collapse" strings of "white space" (e.g., spaces or tabs), an author who deliberately wants to include three spaces in some text cannot just type in three spaces. It would be necessary for that author to enter the entity   (nonbreaking space) three times. Another entity example would be á if the author needs an acute accented "a." Therefore, the   reference results in the inclusion of three spaces when the text is rendered and the á entity results in inclusion of the appropriately accented "a."

The HTML <IMG> tag is referential markup in that it specifies the necessary parameters for the inclusion of an external entity (i.e., an image) into a page.

EXAMPLES OF MARKUP LANGUAGES USED IN WWW

In our discussion of the types of markup languages, it can be seen that each of the described types addresses particular author needs and/or concerns. We've also seen that a markup language such as HTML does, in fact, include multiple markup features. A Web author would want to have access to as many markup features as possible in order to create the richest and most visually "correct" document. It is well known that HTML is a weak markup tool—its major advantage is that it is easy to learn. It is also ubiquitous and highly portable. However, HTML is unable to adequately express or contain structures (e.g., chapters), nor is it easily tailorable for different users, contexts, or media. Considerable effort is underway to enhance the descriptive "power" of HTML.

In this section we will discuss three markup systems that also have particular relevance to Web authoring:

- SGML—Standard Generalized Markup Language
- XML—Extensible Markup Language (or eXtensible Markup Language)
- MathML—Mathematics Markup Language

Chapter 7, Overview of Multimedia Formats, includes a brief description of VRML, one of the technologies for bringing virtual reality to the Web. VRML does *not* stand for Virtual Reality Markup Language, but rather Virtual Reality *Modeling* Language. VRML is used to describe and model virtual environments through which Web users can navigate.

SGML

In terms of Web/Internet years, SGML has been around for a long time. It is an international standard (ISO 8879) that defines, in general, an interchange format for electronic documents. One of the key features of SGML is reusability. This means that it allows the definition of a document that is platform (computer) and operating system independent. It also means that the version of a document used for reading online can also be used by a publisher for a printed version.

SGML is actually a meta-language (a language used to define languages) capable of defining an infinite (theoretically) number of document types. That means that you can use SGML to describe layout unique to a brochure or a newspaper/newsletter or a billboard. A particular document type is defined in a Document Type Definition (DTD) written in SGML. The DTD defines the permissible markup tagsets.

SGML was in widespread use for document description at CERN (the European Laboratory for Particle Physics) when Tim Berners-Lee invented the World Wide

Web (WWW) there. He realized that he would need a markup language capable of defining the elements unique to hypertext pages. So, he wrote an SGML DTD that included those elements. That SGML DTD is HTML. HTML and other DTDs are known as SGML *instances*.

A document of an SGML-based type references the DTD defining its tagset. For example, the <!DOCTYPE> tag that HTML authors *should* include at the top of their page files (but usually don't) is actually an SGML tag specifying the version of the HTML DTD to be used in processing the file.

XML

As the Web has gained more widespread use, authors have demanded greater control over document layout and structure. It has become increasingly clear that HTML is unable to provide the precise control desired. So, why not put SGML on the Web, since it offers infinite control?

Given the extent of its capabilities, it should be no surprise that SGML is quite complex. Writing an SGML DTD is a sophisticated task. Bringing SGML to the Web would conflict with the "ease of use" of HTML that has allowed so many authors to publish on the Web.

In 1998, a committee of the World Wide Web Consortium (usually called the W3C) released a definition for XML (Extensible Markup Language or sometimes eXtensible Markup Language). XML has been described as "SGML-lite" because it has stripped away the "heavy elements" of SGML and concentrated on those features most relevant to Web authoring.

Like SGML, XML *schemas* describe specific document types. But unlike SGML, these instances/DTDs are easier to define. XML also addresses other Web-specific issues such as providing an expanded capability for program use of XML files (e.g., search applications that can retrieve and exchange information). It also supports internationalization efforts that will allow Web pages to be displayed not only in languages other than English, but in languages using other than the Latin-Roman alphabet (e.g., Chinese, Arabic, Hebrew).

 While there are numerous books and articles about XML, future study should begin at the W3C website—http://www.w3.org/XML/.

MathML (MML)

Since the Web was developed in a scientific environment, there has been a desire since the beginning for support of mathematical formatting. Early efforts were unsuccessful. Scientific authors have used various (and nonstandard) methods for including mathematical formulae in their pages. Mathematical expressions are often included by means of graphical images produced by other applications such as T$_E$X or Mathematica. Some authors have used third-party multimedia applications that require browser plug-ins. While such methods have enjoyed limited success, pages using them are usually limited to readers with graphical (i.e., non-linemode or text) browsers or with access to the required plug-in.

MathML is an XML-defined schema for describing mathematical expressions. The same description will display appropriately on both graphical and linemode browsers. In addition, applications are being developed that will allow readers to "cut and paste" MML expressions directly into mathematical software for calculation and/or graphing.

MathML efforts are in a continuous state of flux. In the meantime, several other technologies have been introduced to support mathematical formatting.

As with most Web technologies, the first stop for future study (and progress reports) on MathML should be the W3C website— http://www.w3.org/Math/.

HTML CONVERSION

The "rush" to get on the Web has led to the development of numerous tools to support the conversion of existing documents to HTML. Examples of such tools are:

- LaT$_E$X2HTML—for converting LaT$_E$X documents to HTML
- rtf2HTML—for converting Rich Text Format (RTF) files to HTML
- ps2HTML—for converting PostScript files to HTML

We have also seen word-processing and text-processing applications (e.g., Microsoft Word) begin to offer a "Save as HTML" option. Word processor formats as well as other markup formats such as LaT$_E$X offer a much greater range of formatting options as compared to HTML. In addition, you have much finer control over the formatting that HTML provides.

LAB 1.1 EXERCISES

1.1.1 EXPLORE THE CONCEPT OF DOCUMENT MARKUP

a) Compose a sentence where punctuational markup (e.g., the use of commas) actually changes the meaning or interpretation.

_____

_____

b) What appearance aspects of a book would be considered the result of descriptive markup?

_____

_____

1.1.2 APPLY ALL FIVE TYPES OF DOCUMENT MARKUP TO HTML

We have described HTML as containing components corresponding to all five types of document markup—punctuational, presentational, procedural, descriptive, and referential.

a) Give examples of HTML for each of the five types of markup.

_____

_____

1.1.3 DEFINE A DOCUMENT TAGSET

We have indicated that part of the power of SGML and XML is the ability to describe a markup tagset unique to a specific type of document. Suppose you are an entrepreneur and you want to define a generic description for an online billing invoice.

a) What are the common elements of an invoice that could be defined by a presentational tagset (e.g., <amountdue>)?

_____

_____

1.1.4 EXPLORE THE ISSUES SURROUNDING HTML PAGE CONVERSION

The availability of tools to convert other formats can present dilemmas for the Web author. Authors constantly ask themselves if they should convert an existing document to HTML or reauthor that document in HTML. Take a word processor that can store in both RTF and HTML (for example, recent versions of MS-Word or Corel WordPerfect). Create a fairly complex document with various fonts and format elements (e.g., tables, headers, and so forth).

a) Load the HTML page into a browser and compare the appearance to what is in the word processor. What differences do you see?

_____

_____

b) Load both the HTML page and the RTF page into a text editor such as Notepad. Try to figure out where the text elements are that you included as well as the markup components. What can you say about each?

_____

_____

c) Comparing the contents, what issues arise when deciding whether to author directly in HTML or convert text from another format?

_____

_____

LAB 1.1 EXERCISE ANSWERS

1.1.1 ANSWERS

a) Compose a sentence where punctuational markup (e.g., the use of commas) actually changes the meaning or interpretation.

Answer: There can obviously be an unlimited number of answers to this question.

For example, these sentences are identical in content but have different meanings due to their punctuational markup:

"Tom," says Tim, "is wrong."

Tom says, "Tim is wrong."

Although less obvious, HTML provides punctuation markup to a limited extent. For example, the <QUOTE></QUOTE> tag set would be used to change the appearance of the text indicating it would be a quote from someone. Without this markup, the text may be considered part of the document and not coming from a different source, for example. Note that in the context of HTML, this is also procedural markup because it tells the browser to change its behavior when displaying the text.

b) What appearance aspects of a book would be considered the result of descriptive markup?

Answer: In the lab, we discussed the <H1></H1> tag set as being a "container," because it contains certain text. In this case, it is also describing that text as a level 1 header. Books also have similar contents and therefore similar markup. Other aspects of a descriptive mark would be the subheading contents, illustration captions, and so forth. If you change the appearance associated with the description "Chapter Heading," all of the chapter headings change.

As an interesting side note, Corel WordPerfect enables you to see and manipulate the markup directly. Therefore, you can much more easily see why certain text is being displayed they way it is (and not the way you want it).

1.1.2 ANSWER

a) Give examples of HTML for each of the five types of markup.

Answer: There is no one specific answer to this question, but the following offer some examples. Compare your answers to the types of HTML tags given.

- ***Punctuational:*** *HTML does not contain any tagsets that could uniquely be described as punctuational markup. HTML authors are free to include punctuation (e.g., periods, commas, etc.) wherever they choose.*

- ***Presentational:*** *The HTML tag <HR> is presentational in that it specifies the inclusion of a construct (a horizontal rule) whose sole purpose is to separate document/page content.*

- ***Procedural:*** *The HTML <FORM> and <TABLE> tagsets are procedural in that they support unique page/document components. Certain collections of tags (e.g., <INPUT>, <TD>) can only be used within these components.*

- ***Descriptive:*** *Most of the HTML tagsets are descriptive. For example, the header tags (<H1>, <H2>, etc.) specify how specific text is described with respect to other text in the document/page.*

- ***Referential:*** *The HTML 4.0 <SCRIPT>, <OBJECT>, <STYLE>, and <LINK> tags can "refer" to external entities that help to form a total description of the page/document that contains them.*

1.1.3 ANSWER

a) What are the common elements of an invoice that could be defined by a presentational tagset (e.g., <amountdue>)?

Answer: The following are some of the data entities you would expect to find on a billing invoice:

```
<invoicedate>
<orderdate>
<invoicenumber>
<customerlastname>
<customerfirstname>
<customertitle>
<customerorganization>
<organizationaddress>
<amountdue>
<productorservice>
<duedate>
```

Note here that since these are parts of a tagset, there is a closing tag indicating the end of the element. For example, there would be an </invoicedate> and a </duedate>, as well.

Although one could create tags and tagsets that are short, and therefore easier to type, the ones listed here intuitively tell us what elements they describe. We could then create

*a template using these tags and have an external program (such as a Web browser)
load the template and then pull the real values from a database, for example.*

*The DTD that described this particular document could go so far as to say that particular tags are required (like <invoicenumber>), whereas others are optional, like
(<customertitle>). Take a look as the tags available for HTML and see which ones are
required and when.*

1.1.4 ANSWERS

a) Load the HTML page into a browser and compare the appearance to what is in
the word processor. What differences do you see?

*Answer: Depending on your document, the original document will have a much more
varied appearance, which will probably be closer to the way you had envisioned the
original document. The HTML conversion of the word processor may not be able to assign HTML tags to all of the elements you chose or in the way you chose them and
may either make "guesses" or leave things out.*

b) Load both the HTML page and the RTF into a text editor such as Notepad. Try
to figure out where the text elements are that you included as well as the
markup components. What can you say about each?

*Answer: Depending on your document, there will be a lot of information in the RTF file
in the header (at the top of the file), which may cause "information overload." If you
look carefully you will find your text elements in there. With the HTML file, the textual
information is much easier to find, and interpreting what each of the tags does is generally much easier. Looking at these two documents, it should be clear why people do not
typically edit RTF files directly, but rather use a word processor.*

c) Comparing the contents, what issues arise when deciding whether to author directly in HTML or convert text from another format?

*Answer: Conversion tools usually involve "stepping down" from a "richer" document description format (e.g., RTF) to a "poorer" description format (HTML). No matter how
good the tool is, compromises must be made. These compromises usually affect presentation at some level. Some tools have been known to use tricks (e.g., using HTML tables
for layout) or browser-dependent tagsets. The resulting HTML files may therefore have
limited usability.*

*These tools may be good for small documents, in which case the author can still
"tweak" the HTML markup if necessary. Editing HTML directly does not appeal to
everyone, but even programs that are specifically designed to create HTML documents
often do not allow constructs that can be created by editing the documents directly as
well as displayed in every browser. Some examples I have encountered are tables within
forms or bulleted headers.*

LAB 1.1 SELF-REVIEW QUESTIONS

In order to test your progress, you should be able to answer the following questions.

1) HTML and XML are instances of SGML.

a) _____ True
b) _____ False

2) Procedural Markup always implies a programming language like JavaScript or Active Server Pages.

a) _____ True
b) _____ False

3) HyperText is so named because it transmits the data across the "hyper media" of the internet.

a) _____ True
b) _____ False

4) DTD stands for which of the following?

a) _____ Data Transmission Document
b) _____ Document Transmission Definition
c) _____ Document Type Definition
d) _____ Document Transmission Data

5) Which of these is not a reason for using a "rich" text document (such as MS-Word) as compared to HTML?

a) _____ Finer control of the appearance
b) _____ Wide range of formatting elements
c) _____ Ability to have "forms"
d) _____ Document easily read and changed by hand

6) Tags that describe the appearance of the document are known as which of the following?

a) _____ Punctuational
b) _____ Presentational
c) _____ Procedural
d) _____ Descriptive
e) _____ Referential

7) Tags that refer to a characteristic of a particular elements are known as which of the following?

a) _____ Punctuational
b) _____ Presentational
c) _____ Procedural
d) _____ Descriptive
e) _____ Referential

Quiz answers appear in the Appendix, Section 1.1.

LAB 1.2

HYPERTEXT CONCEPTS

Spoken language is a series of words, and so is conventional writing. We are used to sequential writing and so we come easily to suppose that writing is intrinsically sequential. It need not be and should not be.

Many people believe these forms of writing [hypertext] to be new and drastic and threatening. However, I would like to take the position that hypertext is fundamentally traditional and in the mainstream of literature. Customary writing chooses one expository sequence from among the possible myriad; hypertext allows many, all available to the reader.

—Ted Nelson, 1993

LAB OBJECTIVES

After this lab, you will be able to:

✔ Explore the Nonlinear Nature of Hypertext
✔ Identify Examples of Nonlinear Text
✔ Define Hypertext and Hypermedia

In 1965, Ted Nelson coined the term *hypertext* to describe "non-sequential or non-linear text." He defined it as "a body of written or pictorial material interconnected in a complex way that could not be conveniently represented on paper." Nelson (and others before him) was attempting to define an authoring and reading style that more closely approximates the way people think. In particular, written text (such as books or newspapers) are linear in nature. They are written sequentially and meant to be read sequentially. On the other hand, we do not think sequentially—our thoughts often jump between multiple ideas, concepts, and references that our brain manages to bring together into a meaningful whole. Reading and writing processes are based on the nonlinear nature of thinking.

It is difficult to accurately represent the way we think using written text due to the limitations of the medium (paper). However, specific literary styles and conventions have evolved that attempt to address (in part) the nonsequential issue. For example, the table of contents and index of a book allow the reader to "jump" into the middle of the text in order to locate specific information. They allow books to be used nonsequentially (imagine having to find something in a book by searching all pages in order!). Footnotes allow an author to provide additional information "out of the usual document flow." To read a footnote, the reader interrupts a linear reading process. Reading a footnote is usually optional.

Other authoring styles that support nonlinear reading are more dramatic and not as well standardized as tables of contents or indices. Textbooks often have multiple sections that can be read or skipped based on the reader's level of expertise or interest. A popular children's series, "Choose Your Own Adventure," allows readers to choose alternative paths through a book, which may result in different story endings. Both of these examples place emphasis on the reading audience's thinking and learning styles.

 Those of you who are serious students of computer-based hypertext should be sure to read books by Ted (Theodor Holm) Nelson—The Literary Machine and Computer Lib/Dream Machines (1987) and Literary Machines 93.1 (1993). An excellent scholarly work on hypertext is Hypertext: The Convergence of Critical Theory and Technology by George Landow. This book is also available on CD so that it can be read in a "hypertextual" fashion.
Another great source for information on hypertext is the ACM Special Interest Group (SIG) SIGWEB (http://www.acm.org/siglink/).

LAB 1.2 EXERCISES

1.2.1 EXPLORE THE NONLINEAR NATURE OF HYPERTEXT

We have described a book index as being a "weak" form of hypertext because it allows a user/reader to "jump" into a book nonsequentially. However, indices are by their very nature set up alphabetically. People don't think alphabetically and alphabets are a characteristic of the language being used.

a) Could there be a better way of providing index-type information more similar to the way we think?

_____

_____

1.2.2 IDENTIFY EXAMPLES OF NONLINEAR TEXT

Understanding how nonlinear text has been used can help to understand how it might be used. Ted Nelson cites numerous historical and religious examples of nonlinear literature (hypertext).

a) Either research Nelson's references or identify some examples of nonlinear literature yourself.

_____

_____

1.2.3 DEFINE HYPERTEXT AND HYPERMEDIA

Hypermedia brings the nonlinear associations to multimedia that hypertext brings to text. Hypertext that includes nontextual content (such as images or audio) is actually hypermedia.

a) Expand the definition of hypertext to include hypermedia and describe an example of hypermedia.

_____

_____

LAB 1.2 EXERCISE ANSWERS

1.2.1 ANSWER

a) Could there be a better way of providing index-type information more similar to the way we think?

Answer: A "hyper-index" might allow a user to identify relevant document content by supporting an interactive search of keywords, concepts, descriptions, and so forth. The user would then not be constrained by the alphabetical ordering of the index or by the arbitrary selection of index entries.

One existing text-based example would be the Encyclopedia Britannica, with its "Outline of Knowledge." Although information is listed alphabetically, it is broken down by concepts and not specific entries. Many technical documents online have hyperlinks that lead to other areas of the text, such as a detailed discussion of something simple being mentioned, glossaries, or additional information.

1.2.2 ANSWER

a) Either research Nelson's references or identify some examples of nonlinear literature yourself.

Answer: Nelson suggests that nonsequential writing has roots that extend into antiquity. The Talmud, with its use of annotations and nested commentary, is a classical example. The Indian epics such as Ramayana and Mahabharata are comprised of stories branching off to other stories.

William Dickey, a poet who works with hypertext, suggests that authors create links that offer several sets of distinct reading paths: "The poem may be designed in a pattern of nested squares, as a group of chained circles, as a braid of different visual and graphic themes, as a double helix. The poem may present a single main sequence from which word or image associations lead into sub-sequences and then return."

There is a whole study of hypertext literature, as well as nonlinear literature, on the Hyperizons Web page (http://www.duke.edu/~mshumate/hyperfic.html). This also includes things like collaborative literature. There are also a number of links at the Audiovisual Institute of Pompeu Fabra University in Barcelona, Spain (starting at http://www.iua.upf.es/ literatura-interactiva/eng/p5.htm). There are lots of interesting examples if you're inclined to research this. One particular example, found at http://192.211.16.13/ curricular/panopticon/student_projects/fiction/thread.htm, presents an interesting implementation of original collaborative hypertext fiction called CityThreads. It tells the story of a number of characters in the Seattle area on the same day. There is no beginning or ending—each story details the life of one of the characters and contains links to the other characters' stories whenever two characters meet. While each story may be read linearly, the reader will achieve the most enjoyment by exploring the story through the links.

1.2.3 ANSWER

a) Expand the definition of hypertext to include hypermedia and describe an example of hypermedia.

Answer: Hypermedia is an extension of the idea of hypertext that includes multimedia. Since text is one of the media types supported in a multimedia system, then hypermedia incorporates hypertext.

In a hypermedia document, the author creates links (or associations) between multimedia components. An example of hypermedia could be a textual description that links to an audiovisual presentation.

LAB 1.2 SELF-REVIEW QUESTIONS

In order to test your progress, you should be able to answer the following questions.

1) Hypertext is generally considered "nonlinear" because you can move the document in many different directions.

    a) _____ True
    b) _____ False

2) A footnote provides linear information because it appears on the same page as its reference.

    a) _____ True
    b) _____ False

3) Indexes provide hypertext-like features to written media because you can "jump" directly to specific text.

    a) _____ True
    b) _____ False

4) Which of the following would be nonlinear methods of accessing information?

   a) _____ index
   b) _____ Web Search engine like Yahoo
   c) _____ table of contents
   d) _____ all of the above

5) Which of the following would be not be a method to provide nonlinear content to a document?

   a) _____ hyperlinks
   b) _____ in-line images
   c) _____ scripting languages like JavaScript
   d) _____ search pages

Quiz answers appear in the Appendix, Section 1.2.

L A B   1 . 3

THE FUNDAMENTAL COMPONENTS OF A HYPERTEXT SYSTEM

LAB OBJECTIVES

After this lab, you will be able to:

✔ Identify the Difference Between the Concepts of Hypertext and a Hypertext System
✔ Explore Computer-Based Hypertext Systems
✔ Explore Web-Based Hypertext Systems

If human thought is basically nonlinear, then we can define the human learning and perceptual process as essentially organized as a semantic network in which concepts are linked together by associations. We learn and remember through nonlinear associations. Likewise, the fundamental components of a hypertext system are:

- Nodes—representing concepts
- Links—representing the relationships between nodes

Graphically, a particular (relating to a particular body of information) collection of nodes and links (a hypertext system) might be represented as shown in Figure1.1.

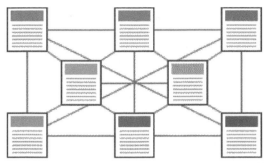

Figure 1.1 ■ An Example of a Hypertext System

In Figure 1.1, the pages represent the *nodes* and the lines represent the *links*. It is not clear from this graph the path that a reader would follow when "reading" this system.

NODES

A node is defined as a single concept or idea. As such, nodes can be virtually any kind of information. In human thought, a node might be a sound or a smell or an experience. In a computer-based hypertext system, a node can contain text, graphics, animation, audio, video, images, programs, and so on. Nodes can be "typed," indicating how they are used. For example, if a node in a Web-based hypertext system is designated as the "home page," there is the implication that that node will be used in a specific way to traverse that system (i.e., it is the node where readers will begin).

Finally, nodes are connected to other nodes with links. The node from which a link originates is called the *reference;* the node at which a link ends is called the *referent.* References and referents are also called *anchors.* The contents of a node are made available (viewed, remembered) by activating a link.

LINKS

The role of a link in a hypertext system is to connect related concepts or nodes. In general (though not in WWW), links are bidirectional, meaning that a reader can go backwards and forwards. The word *beach* could be a link invoking a vision of warm sand (a node/concept) and the sound of the surf (another node/concept). "Activating" a link "reveals" the content of a node.

Like nodes, links can also be "typed," illustrating features of the relationship of the nodes they connect. For example, a link might be simply a reference (like the word "beach" above) or actually reflect some relationship between nodes such as parent–child, chapter 1–chapter 2, and so on.

COMPUTER-BASED HYPERTEXT SYSTEMS

In general, computer-based hypertext systems contain the following elements: a user interface (UI), an authoring system, an information retrieval (IR) system, a hypermedia system, and a storage system. These systems should be used in determining the overall hypertext plan or roadmap to navigating through your Web site:

- A user-interface that assists the reader/user in moving (navigating) through large amounts of information; the user-interface provides the reader with the ability to activate links and read the contents of nodes/pages. This is often a Graphical User Interface (GUI).

- An authoring system providing tools to create and manage nodes (of multiple media) and links.

- Traditional information retrieval (IR) mechanisms such as keyword searches, author searches, and so on. There are also attempts to incorporate structure queries along with content queries—retrieving a part of the hypertext network based on some user-specified criteria.

- A hypermedia engine used to manage information (e.g., a database) about nodes and links.

- A storage system that can be a file system, a knowledge base, a relational database management system, or an object-oriented database management system.

LAB 1.3 EXERCISES

1.3.1 IDENTIFY THE DIFFERENCE BETWEEN THE CONCEPTS OF HYPERTEXT AND A HYPERTEXT SYSTEM

Lab 1.2 described hypertext concepts. This lab described hypertext systems.

a) Must "hypertext" always be delivered by a "hypertext system"?

_____

_____

In the "Choose Your Own Adventure" series, the book text is the "hypertext."

    b) What is the "hypertext system" of the "Choose Your Own Adventure" series?

_____

_____

1.3.2 EXPLORE COMPUTER-BASED HYPERTEXT SYSTEMS

Implementation of a "hypertext system" using computers and networks is well understood. However, one of the first (and best-known) hypertext systems—Memex—was based on microfilm. Research the work of Vannevar Bush and the Memex system.

    a) What was the Memex system intended to be?

_____

_____

    b) List and discuss existing computer-based hypertext systems.

_____

_____

1.3.3 EXPLORE WEB-BASED HYPERTEXT SYSTEMS

WWW is certainly the world's most famous and successful hypertext system. But how good is Web hypertext?

    a) Compare the Web's "hypertextual" features (e.g., node and link definition, navigation, and so forth) with some of its lesser-known predecessors and peers such as Xanadu, Zog, or Hyper-G.

_____

_____

Lab 1.3 Exercise Answers

1.3.1 Answers

a) Must "hypertext" always be delivered by a "hypertext system"?

Answer: When one thinks of a "hypertext system," normally there is the belief that some "device" delivers the hypertext to the user. However, the "Choose Your Own Adventure" series is one example where there is no "device" in the traditional sense. Simply, choices made by the reader determine the "path" the story takes. Looking at it abstractly, something like the Encyclopedia Britannica is a hypertext system as there is no requirement to traverse the information linearly and the reader is free to choose which links he or she follows.

b) What is the "hypertext system" of the "Choose Your Own Adventure" series?

Answer: The book chapters are the hypertext nodes. *The instructions for moving between the chapters are the* hypertext links. *The entire book is the* hypertext system.

1.3.2 Answers

a) What was the Memex system intended to be?

Answer: In 1945, Vannevar Bush, the Science Advisor to President Roosevelt during World War II, proposed Memex (Memory Extension) in a famous article in The Atlantic Monthly. *It was intended to be " . . . a device in which an individual stores his books, records, and communications, and which is mechanized so that it may be consulted with exceeding speed and flexibility." Memex was never actually implemented.*

b) List and discuss existing hypertext systems.

Answer: The World Wide Web is perhaps the most widely used and well-known hypertext system. Because it is an open standard, it has been implemented in one form or another on most every modern operating system. In addition to applications that are specifically designed to read and display the hypertext system of the WWW (HTML), there are a number of other types of applications that support this system, such as world processors, spreadsheets, e-mail applications, and so forth.

Another common system is the online help system used by Microsoft Windows. Although it enables quick access to important reference information, it is proprietary to Microsoft and not implemented on other operating systems.

LAB
1.3

Dynatext is similar to the help system used by MS-Windows and implemented by many vendors for both Windows-based and Unix-based applications. Unlike the help system in MS-Windows, Dynatext allows a single source of information, regardless of the client system.

1.3.3 ANSWER

a) Compare the Web's "hypertextual" features (e.g., node and link definition, navigation, and so forth) with some of its lesser known predecessors and peers such as Xanadu, Zog, or Hyper-G.

Answer: Some of the lesser known hypertext systems actually are "more true" to hypertext concepts than WWW. The hypertext system provided by HTML (and therefore the WWW) provides links in only a specific direction (from the reference to the referent). These other systems typically supported bidirectional links, "rich links" (links contain information about their referent), and link management systems.

**LAB
1.3**

LAB 1.3 SELF-REVIEW QUESTIONS

In order to test your progress, you should be able to answer the following questions.

1) Nodes are the endpoints in a chain of relationships.

   a) _____ True
   b) _____ False

2) Links represent a relationship between two or more nodes.

   a) _____ True
   b) _____ False

3) On the WWW, links are bidirectional connections between nodes.

   a) _____ True
   b) _____ False

4) "Typed" links provide some information about the relationship between the nodes.

   a) _____ True
   b) _____ False

5) Which of the following is not normally considered part of a computer-based hypertext system?

    a) _____ A user-interface that assists the user to navigate and access the information.

    b) _____ A tool to author and manage the hypertext system.

    c) _____ An SQL database containing the information displayed by the system.

    d) _____ Traditional information retrieval mechanisms such as keyword searches.

Quiz answers appear in the Appendix, Section 1.3.

**LAB
1.3**

LAB 1.4

THE GOLDEN RULES OF HYPERTEXT

> ## LAB OBJECTIVES
>
> After this lab, you will be able to:
>
> ✔ Apply the Rules of Hypertext to Hypertext Components
> ✔ Apply the Rules of Hypertext to Different Types of Documents

There are many WWW (and hypertext) evangelists who perceive this medium as the ultimate in online document delivery. Even Ted Nelson's Xanadu was planned as "a *docuverse* (document universe) of all human knowledge." "Put it on the Web" is often viewed as the ultimate online solution for books, documents, art, recordings, and so on.

In reality, not all information is suitably structured for the Web or any other hypertext system. As we discussed earlier, hypertext-appropriate content is that which reflects the way in which people think and learn. Determining whether content is suitable for a hypertext system is summarized in the "Golden Rules of Hypertext," which state that the use of hypertext is most appropriate when:

- The content of the material is a large body of information logically organized and structured into multiple units or fragments.
- These units or fragments are loosely associated with one another, though not necessarily in a sequential manner.
- A user or reader of the material only needs one unit or fragment of the content at any one time.

In the context of a hypertext system, the fragments or units correspond to concepts and nodes. The associations between fragments or units correspond to links. The third rule is more presentational. In the case of the Web, it suggests that a reader only has access to a single Web page at a time given the limitations of a Web browser.

Even if the decision to author a document in hypertext is a good one, poor design of the document can easily present major problems. Just because document content has been defined into fragments and linked does not ensure that it will be effective or attractive.

LAB 1.4 EXERCISES

**LAB
1.4**

1.4.1 APPLY THE RULES OF HYPERTEXT TO HYPERTEXT COMPONENTS

The "Golden Rules" primarily address fragments/nodes and usability.

a) What guidelines or restrictions should be presumed regarding use of links? *Hint: For example, does "fragments are loosely associated with one another, though not necessarily in a sequential manner," imply anything about number of or directionality of links?*

1.4.2 APPLY THE RULES OF HYPERTEXT TO DIFFERENT TYPES OF DOCUMENTS

Online/Web-based books have been a major topic of discussion.

a) Given the "Golden Rules of Hypertext," what types of books would be suitable candidates for hypertext and why? Fiction vs. nonfiction? Reference? Educational?

---

b) Some organizations feel as though all online documentation (e.g., online help systems) should/could be converted to hypertext and made viewable via systems such as the Web. Discuss the appropriateness of such a strategy.

_____

_____

LAB 1.4 EXERCISE ANSWERS

1.4.1 ANSWER

a) What guidelines or restrictions should be presumed regarding use of links?

Answer: The "Golden Rules" imply that all nodes must have (at a minimum) an "entry" and an "exit." This could be accomplished with either two unidirectional links or one bidirectional link. In addition to this minimum, nodes can have any number of additional links, depending upon how closely associated they are with other nodes. This basically means that there must be some way of getting to the node. For example, it would not be very efficient to have Web pages on your site to which there are no links or other ways to access them such as a keyword search.

1.4.2 ANSWERS

a) Given the "Golden Rules of Hypertext," what types of books would be suitable candidates for hypertext? Fiction vs. nonfiction? Reference? Educational?

Answer: Given the sequential nature of fiction, hypertext may only be suitable for fragments that are "visited" sequentially. However, portions of fictional text (e.g., alternate endings) may be better suited for hypertext.

Nonfictional works are good candidates for hypertext, depending upon the required relationships in the content. Reference books are typically very good candidates for hypertext since they would offer a user a broader range of reference and research possibilities.

Like fiction, educational books typically require sequential reading. However, nonsequential structure could allow for various knowledge and skill levels (as in "skip this section if …"). The "fragmentation" of hypertext content can lend itself well to educational material.

b) Some organizations feel as though all online documentation (e.g., online help systems) should/could be converted to hypertext and made viewable via systems such as the Web. Discuss the appropriateness of such a strategy.

Answer: A strategy of converting any documentation to a hypertext system should first involve a careful examination of that documentation and how well its content and structure can be described by "The Golden Rules of Hypertext." For example, an on-line reference system for the company's help desk would be a good candidate for conversion because of the relationship between all of the various pieces of information. On the other hand, a cookbook contains "multiple units or fragments" (the recipes), but there is little relationship between those fragments.

LAB 1.4 SELF-REVIEW QUESTIONS

In order to test your progress, you should be able to answer the following questions.

1) Using the "Golden Rules of Hypertext" helps to ensure that the document is effective as well as attractive.

   a) _____ True
   b) _____ False

2) Hypertext should be implemented for large documents where linear access is required.

   a) _____ True
   b) _____ False

3) Hypertext systems are best employed where the information fragments are related in some way.

   a) _____ True
   b) _____ False

4) Which of the following is not considered one of the "Golden Rules of Hypertext"?

   a) _____ The content of the material is logically organized and structured into multiple units or fragments.
   b) _____ These units or fragments are loosely associated with one another.
   c) _____ Associations between the units or fragments are nonlinear.
   d) _____ A reader of the material only needs one unit or fragment of the content at any one time.

Quiz answers appear in the Appendix, Section 1.4.

L A B   1 . 5

WWW AS A HYPERTEXT SYSTEM

**LAB
1.5**

LAB OBJECTIVES

After this lab, you will be able to:

- ✔ Apply Traditional Hypertext Concepts to WWW Content
- ✔ Evaluate WWW as a Hypertext System

While our description of hypertext systems can become very philosophical, we are primarily concerned with the organization and presentation of computer-based information using WWW. As such, a number of conventions are required.

WEB PAGE

A Web page corresponds to our hypertext system node. It is a single file and whatever resources (e.g., graphics, scripts, stylesheets, and so forth) it contains. Thus, it represents a single concept.

WEB DOCUMENT

A Web document is a collection of Web pages and the links between them. Therefore, we think of a Web document as an independent hypertext system. Given this definition, a Web site is a Web document like other information databases and information spaces. Since a Web document is a collection of Web pages, then Web documents can themselves contain other Web documents. That is, they can be compound structures. Using WWW terminology, a Web document is "entered" via such author-defined devices as *home pages, welcome pages, root pages, entry pages,* and *front pages.*

ADDING HYPERTEXT TO WWW CONTENT

Contrary to the conception of many, the World Wide Web is not the first hypertext system—although it is certainly the most successful. Systems with names such as Memex, Xanadu, Augment, and Zog do not have the household familiarity of the WWW. Research into hypertext/hypermedia systems has been going on for more than thirty years. Much of this research has led to tools and techniques that could (and should) be applicable to the Web. Many of what appear to be new problems are actually old problems that have resurfaced.

If you do additional reading on the background of and research in hypertext, you will discover that the WWW is a fairly limited hypertext system. Some of the earlier hypertext systems provided far richer tools for authoring and reading. However, most of these systems would only execute on a single computer running a specific operating system. The greatest strength of the Web is that it is a *distributed* hypertext system capable of linking multiple computers of many types running different operating systems over a network.

Examples of some of the "classical" hypertext features that the Web lacks natively are:

**LAB
1.5**

- Bidirectional links—the ability to follow links in both directions.
- Rich links—the ability to determine something (other than just the name or location) about the node a link leads to before activating that link.
- Link management—the ability to manage links such that they always work (i.e., no broken links).
- Publishing and version control—the ability to manage the accuracy or "freshness" of a node.

The WWW has moved some features from the author control to the reader/browser control. For example, the "back" button on a browser logically operates as a backward operating link. But what if the reader is using a browser without a "back" button?

Other hypertext features can be added to Web pages and documents using scripting and programming techniques. Hypertext features such as dropdown and expanding/collapsing menus and inclusion of "rich link" information can be accomplished with client-side scripting and the Document Object Model (DOM).

LAB 1.5 EXERCISES

1.5.1 APPLY TRADITIONAL HYPERTEXT CONCEPTS TO WWW CONTENT

a) Demonstrate how a bidirectional link between two Web pages may be emulated using HTML. *Hint: The "name" attribute of the anchor tag might be one way.*

_____

_____

b) How might you add "rich text" to a Web page?

_____

_____

1.5.2 EVALUATE WWW AS A HYPERTEXT SYSTEM

a) How might the problem of "broken links" on the WWW be addressed with today's technology?

_____

_____

b) Ted Nelson once told a Web conference, "Your future is my past." The implication was that the features he described for his Xanadu system should be incorporated into the WWW. Research some of Xanadu's features (e.g., "transclusion") and discuss how they might be a part of the next generation of WWW.

_____

_____

LAB 1.5 EXERCISE ANSWERS

1.5.1 ANSWERS

a) Demonstrate how a bidirectional link between two Web pages may be emulated using HTML.

*Answer: The following example illustrates the use of a "quasi-bidirectional" hyperlink between two pages. Use of the "Go Forward" and "Go Back" links on the respective pages enable a reader to "toggle" between the same locations (using the anchor **name** attribute) on the two pages.*

```
<HTML>
<HEAD>
<TITLE>Example of Bidirectional Link</TITLE>
</HEAD>
<BODY>
<H1>Example of Bidirectional Link</H1>
<A name= "Top" href="...End_2.html#Bottom">Go Forward</A>
</BODY>
</HTML>

<HTML>
<HEAD>
<TITLE>Example of Bidirectional Link</TITLE>
</HEAD>
<BODY>
<H1>Example of Bidirectional Link</H1>
<A name= "Bottom" href="...End_1.html#Top">Go Back</A>
</BODY>
</HTML>
```

b) How might you add "rich text" to a Web page?

Answer: Using the "onmouseover" attribute to many HTML tags, you could provide a small popup or text in the status bar of the browser that provides addition information about the link.

**LAB
1.5**

a) How might the problem of "broken links" on the WWW be addressed with today's technology?

Answer: For links to pages internal to your Web server, any scripting language that can traverse the directory tree and can file contents could be used. Each file is checked for HREF tags and then a check is made to see if the file is still where it supposed to be.

Some scripting languages like Perl even provide the ability to directly connect to Web servers and can therefore be used to check connectivity. Pages on your Web site could be checked for external URLs using Perl, and then Perl would check the connectivity to that page. Commercial products such as LinkScan will do this for you.

There are also a number of commericial Web development products (i.e., Alliare Home Site, Netobjects Fusion) that have site management functionality.

In addition, numerous technologies are under development that address the problem of "broken links"—link management. Research the work currently being done with URNs (Universal Resource Names) and Persistent URLs (PURLs). The following URLs can provide useful resources:

> URNs: http://www.w3.org/Addressing/URL/uri-spec.html
> PURLs: http://purl.oclc.org/

b) Research some of Xanadu's features (e.g., "transclusion") and discuss how they might be a part of the next generation of WWW.

Answer: The following URL provides an interesting overview of the Xanadu system: http://www.internetvalley.com/intvalxan.html

LAB 1.5 SELF-REVIEW QUESTIONS

In order to test your progress, you should be able to answer the following questions.

1) A page is node within the hypertext system of the WWW.

    a) _____ True
    b) _____ False

2) All hypertext systems are distributed.

    a) _____ True
    b) _____ False

3) The WWW is not a true hypertext system because it does not provide for an author defined entry point.

    a) _____ True
    b) _____ False

4) Which of the following is not an example of a "classical" hypertext features that the WWW currently lacks?

    a) _____ Rich links—the ability to determine something (other than just the name or location) about the node a link leads to before activating that link
    b) _____ Native multimedia support
    c) _____ Link management—the ability to manage links such that they always work (i.e., no broken links)
    d) _____ Publishing and version control—the ability to manage the accuracy or "freshness" of a node

5) Which of the following is one of the key strengths the WWW has over "traditional" hypertext systems?

    a) _____ Secure communication
    b) _____ Inherently distributed information sources
    c) _____ Support for a wide variety of operating systems
    d) _____ Multiple language support

6) Which of the following cannot be emulated using HTML or client-side scripting?

    a) _____ Bidirectional links
    b) _____ Version control
    c) _____ Link management
    d) _____ Rich links

Quiz answers appear in the Appendix, Section 1.5.

**LAB
1.5**

L A B 1 . 6

HYPERTEXT DOCUMENT ENGINEERING

People have very little patience with poorly designed WWW sites. As one user put it: "The more well-organized a page/site is, the more faith I will have in the information."

—Jakob Neilsen

LAB OBJECTIVES

After this lab, you will be able to:

✔ Define the Role of the Hypertext Document Engineer
✔ Apply HDE Techniques

Hypertext Document Engineering (HDE) is defined as the application of software design engineering (SDE) techniques to the design of hypertext/Web pages and documents. This is important and relevant because, at some level, the creation of Web pages and documents is similar to the design of a software application. For example:

- Both disciplines are likely to involve the coordination and inter-operation of multiple parts that may or may not have been developed by the same person or team.

- Critical to both efforts is the development of interfaces between component parts and users.

- Both disciplines are concerned about the efficiency and reliability of their component parts.

- HDE and SDE are both interested in issues such as version control and maintenance.

At a time when potential Web authors and information providers are told "teach yourself Web publishing in a week," why is Hypertext Document Engineering important? The simplicity of HTML often leads to spontaneous ("markup as you go") page and document design. From a software perspective, many of these pages are analogous to the "spaghetti code" produced by inexperienced programmers.

As has been discussed in previous labs, HDE also incorporates techniques unique to the support and development of hypertext documents. Many of these techniques have evolved from hypertext systems research and experience. In addition, HDE draws from research and experience in human-computer interaction (HCI) and online document authoring. Chapter 5 of this book focuses on HCI technology and the Web.

SDE AND HDE

Software engineering techniques facilitate the design of large and complex software projects. Components of these projects are often independently designed and coded modules produced by different programming staffs. A precise specification of how these modules are to function and their interfaces is what makes "engineered" software projects successful. The most obvious goal of software engineering is that the software produced meets the stated requirements. Four properties that are sufficiently general to be accepted as goals for the entire discipline of software engineering are:

- Modifiability—Is the software designed to be readily (not necessarily easily) modified? Can bug fixes and new features be efficiently added? Can the application evolve to meet new demands?

- Efficiency—Does the software execute efficiently? Is its response time acceptable? Does it make the best use of the resources it requires?

- Reliability—Is the software reliable? Does it fail often or give mysterious errors? Can it crash the computer on which it's executing?

- Understandability—Can the users of the software readily understand how to use it and how it was designed to be used?

In this list of SDE goals, try replacing the words "software" and "application" with "Web page" and/or "Web document" and you will see that the issues are

**LAB
1.6**

still applicable. There are, however, some important areas of involvement that make HDE quite distinct from SDE.

HDE requires additional skills of software design and programming. For example, the authoring process is a key component in the design of hypertext content. Likewise, the design of a hypertext document usually involves capturing and organizing a complex body of information and making that body of information accessible to readers/users. The scope of content is usually broader for developers of hypertext-based content. For example, the decision to include multimedia content presents special challenges.

Many Web authors would immediately have little patience with the suggestion to add an engineering paradigm, such as HDE suggests, to their authoring process. After all, publishing on the Web is supposed to be easy. Learning HTML is supposed to be easy.

In reality, HDE helps to address issues that no Web author can easily ignore. Such issues include:

- Page sizing—How big should a Web page be?
- User disorientation—How can a page author help keep a user/reader from feeling "lost in cyberspace"?
- User cognitive overload—How much information can a page realistically deliver to a reader/user without overwhelming him or her?
- Broken links—What Web site designer wants a visitor to encounter broken links (the dreaded error 404 message)?
- Dead-end pages—Transferring legacy information to the Web often leads to pages that contain no links (dead-end pages). A user/reader therefore must use browser navigation tools (e.g., the "back" button) in order to escape the page.

**LAB
1.6**

Who of us have not visited Web sites where we encountered such problems? Too often the problems could have been eliminated with careful page and document engineering.

In Lab 1.7 you will be introduced to three design methodologies that address the goals of HDE.

LAB 1.6 EXERCISES

1.6.1 DEFINE THE ROLE OF THE HYPERTEXT DOCUMENT ENGINEER

a) What is the relationship between the "hypertext document engineer" and the content developer/author?

_____

_____

b) What are some inherent problems with the "markup as you go" method of Web page development?

_____

_____

1.6.2 APPLY HDE TECHNIQUES

a) How might a Web page designer address the problem of "dead-end" pages during the development stages?

_____

_____

b) How can a Web page designer help keep a user/reader from feeling "lost in cyberspace"?

_____

_____

c) How can a Web page designer help prevent "information overload"?

_____

_____

d) Like printed media, a Web page design is concerned with how the material looks on the page. How might a Web page designer determine how big a page should be?

LAB 1.6 EXERCISE ANSWERS

1.6.1 ANSWERS

a) What is the relationship between the "hypertext document engineer" and the content developer/author?

Answer: The "hypertext document engineer" designs and maintains the structure of a hypertext document, which usually contains multiple hypertext pages. The hypertext pages that comprise a hypertext document are often written by multiple content developers/authors.

b) What are some inherent problems with the "markup as you go" method of Web page development?

Answer: Links can end up pointing to nowhere, pages may not be accessible from other pages, and it is extremely easy to lose track of the overall structure of the system. As with software development and "spaghetti code," you can end up with "spaghetti pages."

**LAB
1.6**

1.6.2 ANSWERS

a) How might a Web page designer address the problem of "dead-end" pages during the development stages?

Answer: Many commercial Web management products have the ability to create templates that can then be applied to each page. The template would include some kind of navigational aid such as a toolbar with links to specific pages or at the very least a link to the home page.

On some sites, I have utilized the Web server's ability to include specific HTML code at specific locations (such as the top and bottom of each page). I can then include a navigation bar that I can change as I need to without having to edit each file individually. An excellent reference on developing your site with these techniques is The UNIX Web Server Administrator's Interactive Workbook *by James Mohr, also from Prentice Hall.*

b) How can a Web page designer help keep a user/reader from feeling "lost in cyberspace"?

Answer: One important characteristic of any Web site is a consistent look and feel. If a Web site were constantly changing format between pages, you would quickly become just as disoriented as with a book that changes format between pages.

Although some designers like to try out "cool" things on their sites, that tends to be the exception. Look at some of the large Web sites like amazon.com or cnn.com. There are tens of thousands of pages, all with the same look and feel. No matter how deep you have clicked or how long you have spent on each site, you know you are still on the same site.

c) How can a Web page designer help prevent "information overload"?

Answer: The simplest way is to break the material into fragments that address as few topics as possible. Unlike a book, which requires the material to be physically connected, Web documents can contain information spread across multiple pages. As we mentioned previously, this is one of the key benefits of any hypertext system.

Another way is to limit how "cool" your site is. Fancy fonts and spinning graphics might be fine for the MTV Web site, but not for most. A large number of different fonts and "loud" graphics detract from the content.

d) Like printed media, a Web page design is concerned with how the material looks on the page. How might a Web page designer determine how big a page should be?

Answer: Some of the commonly used methods for establishing the size of Web pages are:
1) *The amount of information on a "paper" page*
2) *The size of a hypertext "fragment"*
3) *The amount of information that can "fit" into a particular browser/client window on a certain size terminal screen (e.g., 640 x 480 pixels)*
4) *The amount of information that be downloaded from a server within a specific time period at a particular bandwidth*

LAB 1.6 SELF-REVIEW QUESTIONS

In order to test your progress, you should be able to answer the following questions.

1) Although a Web page is typically not going to cause your browser to crash, Web page designers are just as concerned with "reliability" as software developers.

   a) _____ True
   b) _____ False

2) For Web page designed "modifiability" simply means being able to replace or update single pages or even groups of pages.

   a) _____ True
   b) _____ False

3) Web browsers take care of the "human-computer interaction" aspects of Web pages and, therefore, this is not a concern for Web page designers.

   a) _____ True
   b) _____ False

4) Which of the following is NOT a similiarity between HDE and SDE?

   a) _____ Both disciplines are likely to involve the coordination and interoperation of multiple parts that may or may not have been developed by the same person or team.
   b) _____ Critical to both efforts is the development of interfaces between component parts and users.
   c) _____ Both disciplines are concerned with design which must be able to provide nonlinear access to each component.
   d) _____ HDE and SDE are both interested in issues such as version control and maintenance.

Quiz answers appear in the Appendix, Section 1.6.

**LAB
1.6**

L A B   1 . 7

HYPERTEXT DESIGN METHODOLOGIES

LAB OBJECTIVES

After this lab, you will be able to:

✔ Analyze and Define Structural Design Issues
✔ Redefine a Structure

In this lab, we briefly examine three hypertext design methodologies that can contribute to Hypertext Document Engineering. Each of these methodologies emphasizes the importance of Web/hypertext document usability. In each, document navigation plays a key role since one of the most important factors in the success of a document is the ease with which a reader/user is able to navigate within it, following links between the pages that compose it. Each methodology also pays attention to a user's perception of how the information within the document is organized. No one of these methodologies should be interpreted as being preferable to another. It is the decision of you as the Web author and designer to decide which is the most appropriate for your application.

Each of the three hypertext design methodologies discussed has a different focus:

- The *structure-based* methodology places emphasis on the overall structure of a hypertext document and the implied relationships between nodes/pages presented by that structure.

- The *relationship-based* methodology analyzes the logical relationships between the nodes/pages of a hypertext document and suggests the document design accordingly.

- The *information-based* methodology concentrates on the content fragmenting and organization of a hypertext document. The node/page relationships are a function of the anticipated use of the document.

One thing that you will quickly realize as we discuss these methodologies is that the popular "free-form" architecture of the Web goes away. We no longer feel free to put arbitrary links between any two pages. All Webs, no matter how complex they may appear on the surface, in fact have a well-designed structure underneath.

Each of the methodologies discussed assumes a Web/hypertext document development cycle such as the following Figure 1.2 (adapted from Isakowitz, Stohr, & Balasubramanian).

The *Feasibility* step in this development cycle would likely result in the generation of a feasibility document (probably not a hypertext document). In this document, issues such as user needs and objectives would need to be addressed. The

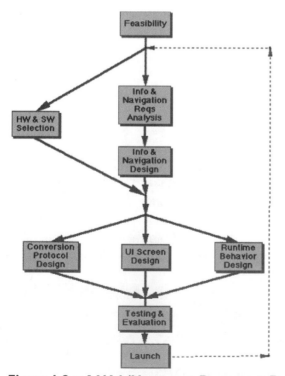

Figure 1.2 ■ A Web/Hypertext Document Development Cycle

**LAB
1.7**

Feasibility step would be followed by an *Information/Navigation Requirements Analysis* leading to the development of a requirements document. It is from the requirements document that the document designer/author works.

Each of the methodologies (or perhaps some combination) described in this lab are applicable in the *Information/Navigation Design* phase. It is in this phase that the actual structure of and relationships within the Web/hypertext document begin to take shape. It can generally be assumed that page/document content development occurs independently of this procedure. While one of the methodologies described is information-based, it does not address issues of content quality and quantity.

In the *Conversion Protocol Design* step, each element resulting from the Information/Navigation Design step is coded into the relevant format. For Web documents, this would usually indicate expressing the relationship with HTML.

User Interface Design involves the design of the "look and feel" of each element appearing in the Information/Navigation Design model. User interface design would likely include the descriptions of buttons, content layout, indices, and the page location of navigational tools (e.g., menubars and the like). Topics on User Interface Design are discussed in Chapters 2 through 6, the human-computer interface chapters of this book.

Decisions about how linking and navigational mechanisms are to be implemented are made in the *Runtime Behavior Design* step. It is also at this time when the page author considers the runtime impact of static versus dynamic pages.

THE INFORMATION-STRUCTURE APPROACH

**LAB
1.7**

Successful hypertext, just as any successful writing project, depends on good design of the contents. The hypertext author who creates a new work or the hypertext editor who takes existing materials and puts them into hypertext form must take great care to produce excellence. The designer who assumes that it is safe to throw everything into the hypertext network and let the reader sort it out will be surprised by the negative reactions.

—Schneiderman & Kearsley, 1989

One thing that does bother me, however, is the belief that hypertext will save the author from having to put material in linear order. Wrong. To think this is to allow for sloppiness in writing and presentation. It is hard

work to organize material, but that effort on the part of the writer is essential for the ease of the reader. Take away the need for this discipline and I fear that you may pass the burden on to the reader, who may not be able to cope, and may not care to try. The advent of hypertext is apt to make writing much more difficult, not easier—good writing, that is.

—Norman, 1988

Even if the decision to author a document in hypertext is a good one, poor design of the document can easily present major problems. Just because document content has been defined in terms of pages and links does not guarantee that the document will be effective or attractive. The potential positive and negative impact of creating a hypertext document is realized when you attempt to specify the relationships between the pages of that document.

The *information-structure approach* assumes that there are four common information organization structures. All other more complex information structures/ Webs that we design and use should actually be composed of these four structures. This might also be thought of as a building block approach where all of our beautiful structures and creations are composed of a few fundamental blocks.

The four fundamental information structures are:

1. Sequence
2. Grid
3. Hierarchy
4. Web

These four fundamental structures are distinguished by how difficult they are to understand by a user/reader and how difficult they are to use by an information/content author.

Figure 1.3 is an adaptation from Brockmann, Horton, and Brock (1989). It examines the powers and risks associated with these four structures. The rectangles in this figure represent elements/pages within the structure of a document. In general, these structures represent an information space, a generalization of the hypertext document concept. An information space resembles an information database structured according to content and anticipated use. The *y*-axis represents a relative measure of complexity from the perspective of the user/reader. The *x*-axis represents a relative measure of authoring complexity. Note that this figure is dated 1989, which means that its use of the term "Web" to describe a complex, hypertexted information structure actually predates the World Wide Web.

**LAB
1.7**

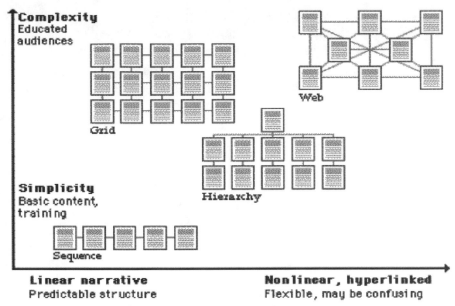

Figure 1.3 ■ Complexity and Predictability of the Four Fundamental Information Structures

Figure 1.3 therefore suggests that the *sequence* structure is the least complex from both the user/reader's and the author's perspective. It also indicates that the content in the sequence structure is more linear (rather than hypertextual) in nature. This figure also suggests that the *web* structure is the more potentially complex to both the user/reader and the author. In terms of the expressive power available to an author, the web structure offers far more than the sequence structure.

We will now discuss each of these structures in detail.

THE SEQUENCE STRUCTURE

The simplest of these information structures to design and navigate through is the sequence, because it most closely resembles a conventional paper document. The sequence structure is shown in Figure 1.4. One of the positives ("pros") of this structure is that it is predictable. Users/readers of a document structured in this manner are presented with a familiar and comfortable model.

It is characteristic of the sequence that navigation between nodes can be unidirectional or bidirectional and only to specific (adjacent) nodes. The structure assumes a maximum of two links per node (only one at the ends of the sequence) and allows for simple navigation such as "next," "previous," "forward," and

Figure 1.4 ■ The Sequence Information Structure

"back." In this way its navigational functionality is comparable to that of a browser. The structure can only be "entered" at the ends. Therefore, it is unlikely (if not impossible) for a user/reader to become "lost" while reading a document of this form.

Documents structured in this manner are the least likely candidates for hypertext. There is typically not a "rich" relationship between the content of the pages. Except for the navigational links, each of the pages would actually be a "dead end" (i.e., containing no links) page. The sequence structure would best be used for content that is linear in nature, therefore requiring that pages/nodes be read in a very strict sequence. Content that might be suitably organized as a sequence would include online books, online tutorials and courses, or tours. Also, linear documents "converted" to hypertext (modified by the addition of page navigation links—previous page, next page, and so forth) are examples of a use of the sequence structure.

THE GRID STRUCTURE

The *grid structure* is the first of the information structures that can be thought of as multidimensional. The grid structure is shown in Figure 1.5. Therefore, it can be used to define significantly richer relationships between nodes/pages than is possible with the sequence structure. In general, the grid contains pages whose relationships are best described in a tabular fashion.

**LAB
1.7**

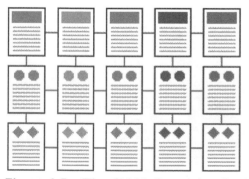

Figure 1.5 ■ The Grid Information Structure

Navigation through a grid structure can be unidirectional or bidirectional and only to specific pages/nodes. Pages/nodes can have two, three, or four links depending upon their location in the grid.

THE HIERARCHICAL STRUCTURE

Use of a *hierarchical* (or tree) structure in a hypertext document allows nodes/pages to be thought of in a hierarchical fashion. The hierarchical structure is shown in Figure 1.6. Like the grid structure, navigation between the pages is best defined multidimensionally.

The hierarchy is perhaps the most common structure for documents that are written modularly. A frequently used example of a document with a hierarchy structure is one that is navigated according to its table of contents. "Home pages" are often designed hierarchically with a tree structure. The document in Figure 1.7 is designed as a tree with a "home page" as the root node, the first level nodes as "submenus," and all remaining nodes consisting of individual pages or documents.

Along with the sequence structure, the *hierarchical structure* is probably the most generally familiar. Its use ranges from general taxonomies, genealogical charts, and organizational charts to computer file systems. The allowable navigational paths are very well defined within this structure. Navigation can be unidirectional or bidirectional and only to specific nodes/pages.

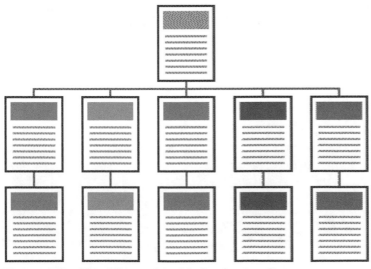

Figure 1.6 ■ The Hierarchical Information Structure

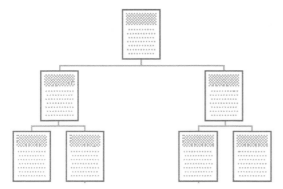

Figure 1.7 ■ A Hierarchical Web Document

The hierarchical structure is more expressive than the grid structure due to the permissible number of links per node/page. Based upon the complexity of the structure and how many nodes, subnodes, and so on the hierarchy contains, the number of links per node is basically unlimited.

There are numerous examples of defining a hierarchical information structure. In the chapter entitled "Supporting Web Servers" of Volume 2 of this series, mapping a file system taxonomy to a hierarchical information structure is described.

PROBLEMS WITH THE HIERARCHICAL STRUCTURE   There are well-known problems associated with hierarchical information structures that can lead to navigation and/or information overloading issues.

One of these problems is a hierarchy that is too deep. This means that a reader/user has to follow too long a path in order to get to the desired information. This condition is sometimes described by saying that a user must "drill too deep" or that the desired information requires "too many clicks." The fear to an author should be that a reader/user gets tired and/or frustrated and just quits. Figure 1.8 illustrates a hierarchical structure that is too deep (e.g., five clicks from the root to some pages).

Similarly, hierarchical structures can be described as "too shallow." In Figure 1.9, too many nodes/pages have been "pushed" to the top of the hierarchy. As a result, a user/reader is faced with too many choices when entering the structure (in this case, 9). Later is this lab we will propose that nine items is just too many for most people to remember.

THE WEB STRUCTURE

The *web* is, of course, the most expressive structure from a hypertextual perspective. It may also be the most misunderstood among Web authors. The web structure is shown in Figure 1.10.

LAB
1.7

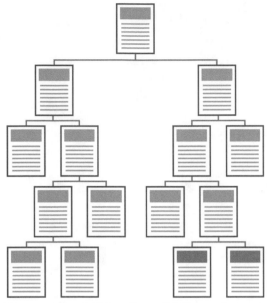

Figure 1.8 ■ A "Too-Deep" Hierarchy

Random links in webs are comparable to GOTOs in programs.
— Tomas Isakowitz

Structured programming techniques condemn the use of transfer statements (GOTO statements) in computer programs. Programs containing excessive GOTOs are often referred to as "spaghetti code." Programming languages such as Pascal were designed to support Structured Programming—software development using well-defined control structures logically eliminating the need for GOTOs. Random links in webs lead to "spaghetti webs."

Figure 1.9 ■ A "Too-Shallow" Hierarchy

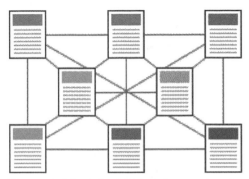

Figure 1.10 ■ The Web Information Structure

By definition the web structure supports unidirectional or bidirectional navigation between nodes/pages connected with links. It also allows pages/nodes to have any number of nodes.

THE RELATIONSHIP MANAGEMENT METHODOLOGY APPROACH

The Relationship Management Methodology (RMM) approach is an example of a relationship-based design methodology. It was invented by Isakowitz, Stohr, and Balasubramanian. It is based upon an *entity-relationship* paradigm.

The definitive description of RMM can be found in "RMM: A Methodology for Structured Hypermedia Design." Communications of the ACM 38 *(August 1995).*

Entity–relationship (ER) modeling is an analysis technique usually associated with database design and object-oriented programming (OOP). Systems are described in terms of the entities that compose them (nodes in a hypertext system) and the relationships between these entities (links or logical groups of nodes in a hypertext system). More specifically, *entities* are system object/components defined in terms of the roles they play in a specific system. *Relationships* are named associations between two or more entities.

ER diagrams are a stylized technique for specifying entities and relationships in a specific system. Entities are represented by rectangles, relationships by diamonds. The following ER diagram, Figure 1.11, describes the entities and relationships in a typical organizational structure.

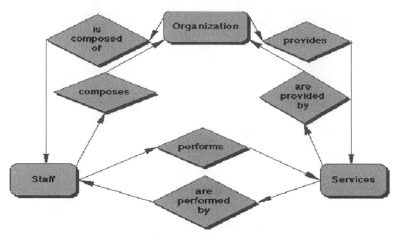

Figure 1.11 ■ An Organization/Staff/Services Entity–Relationship Diagram

If we assume that the entities in this diagram (Organization, Staff, and Services) are hypertext pages or documents, then it is only necessary to define how we express the defined relationships between them. This description of an organization is far richer and more descriptive than one that might be described hierarchically (as is often the case in an organization chart).

RMM defines three fundamental structures for describing relationships between entities/nodes. They are:

- Index—a table of contents to a list of entity instances, providing direct access to each listed item.
- Guided Tour—a linear path through a collection of entities/ nodes that permits forward and backward motion along the path.
- Indexed Guided Tour—a combination of the features of an index and a guided tour.

Let's describe these structures by example. Suppose that the "Organization" that we are describing is a part of the portion of the White House personnel of the U.S. government. The relevant "Personnel" is the President, the Vice President, and the First Lady (Bill Clinton, Al Gore, and Hillary Clinton at the time this chapter was written).

Use of an *Index* to describe the Organization-Staff relationship might look like Figure 1.12.

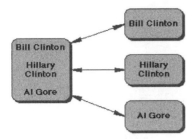

Figure 1.12 ■ Organization/Personnel Relationships Expressed as an Index

The "Organization" node (the leftmost entity) controls as a menu all access to the "Personnel" nodes. It is impossible to go from one "Personnel" node (e.g., Bill Clinton) to another (e.g., Al Gore) without going through the menu. Defining this structure in terms of HTML markup is a trivial exercise.

If the Web site designer chose to use the *Guided Tour* structure to describe this relationship, it might look like Figure 1.13.

Choice of this structure means that users/readers can learn about the "Personnel" only in a specific order. The tour begins with Bill Clinton and ends with Al Gore. However, once within the tour, the user/reader may be able to move (in this case) forward and backward. Once again, defining this structure in HTML is quite easy.

A discussion of the Indexed Guided Tour is left as an exercise.

In summary, using the RMM approach to design a hypertext system/Web site requires:

1. Determination of the core concepts/entities that make up the system; these entities can be simple pages/nodes or more complex structures.
2. Use of an entity-relationship diagram (ERD) to define the relationships between these entities/nodes.
3. Determination of the most appropriate structures (Index, Guided Tour, or Indexed Guided Tour) to express the relationships within the ERD.
4. Implementation.

As is often the case in many design disciplines, Steps 1, 2, and 3 are the most difficult and challenging. Since the relationship structures can be essentially thought of as templates, careful design makes Step 4 quite straightforward.

**LAB
1.7**

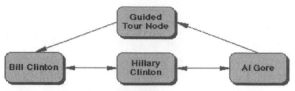

Figure 1.13 ■ Organization/Personnel Relationships Expressed as a Guided Tour

THE INFORMATION-MAPPING APPROACH

In our earlier discussion of "The Golden Rules of Hypertext," we stressed the importance of breaking information up into independent, usable fragments. It was asserted that bodies of information that could be "broken up" in this way were good candidates for hypertext systems (i.e., the Web). A larger question then becomes, how big should these information fragments be?

One issue that web designers/authors have struggled with since the beginning is "How big should a page be?" It's clear that users/readers have difficulty with long pages through which they are forced to scroll. It's also clear that small, short pages can create a maintenance nightmare for authors/designers. The *information-mapping approach* seeks to provide a logical answer to these and other questions.

The information-mapping approach was invented by Robert Horn. In the early days (pre-Web) of online documentation systems, Horn realized that use of a "paper metaphor" on computer systems was not effective.

In paper systems, information is defined in terms of sentences, paragraphs, pages, and so on. While this structure has been very effective for paper-based media (e.g, books, newspapers, and such), Horn believed that it is not necessarily the best model for information on computers. His approach was largely substantiated by the psychology of how humans obtain and retain information.

Paper documents are defined by physical size. Pages typically have a fixed size based upon the type of document of which they are a part (e.g., the page size in a legal document is different than that of a paperback book). Unlike their paper counterparts, hypertext pages have no inherently defined limitations on their size. Page size may be considered an unfortunate consequence of hypertext pages adopted by the author.

There are two strategies that can be adopted by a hypertext author and page designer in making decisions related to page sizing. These strategies address the issues of quantity of page content and factors affecting page viewing by a reader. More specifically, these strategies dictate page sizing based on human short-term memory considerations and viewing area limitations.

Viewing area limitations cannot be immediately addressed by most authors in that they are unlikely to know the wide variety of computer screens, terminals, and other hardware that reader/users are using. This is becoming more of an issue with alternative web agents such as WebTV™ and access via Personal Digital Assistants (PDAs).

SHORT-TERM MEMORY

Short-term memory refers to the facts, concepts, or ideas of which individuals are conscious or that they can recall to consciousness quickly. Short-term memory is sometimes referred to as post-distractional memory, since people can become distracted and forget if their attention is not focused on the contents of that memory.

Pioneering psychological research by Miller and Simon indicated that the capacity of short-term memory is **7 ± 2** chunks of information. "Chunks" of information imply that the information is in some way related, such as in type and form. Miller and Simon's research is consistent with our ability to remember telephone numbers (in the United States, 7 digits) and zip codes (5 digits), but also explains our fears when the telephone company and post office threaten to increase the number of digits in both.

INFORMATION BLOCKS AND INFORMATION MAPS

It was in this short-term memory research that Robert Horn found the method for making the paper to online information transition. He realized that for users reading information online, the major problem was one of retention, not unit size. (For example, after scrolling through a long Web page, can you easily remember content at the top?). The information-mapping approach is the result. In this approach, the paper paragraph is replaced by an *information block,* the paper page is replaced by an *information map.*

An information block is the basic unit of online content. Like the paper paragraph it replaces, it is the smallest unit into which similar related units of information are collected. As might be expected, an information block contains 7 ± 2 chunks of related information, where a chunk might be a sentence, an image, or a table. The relationships between the chunks within the information block are what helps the user/reader to remember them.

An information map contains 7 ± 2 information blocks about a specific topic. Therefore, the information map replaces the paper page as being the basic unit of online content to be provided to a reader/user. According to this design methodology, each Web page/hypertext node should be an information map about a particular subject or concept. If this information map/Web page is correctly constructed, then it optimizes a user/reader's ability to retain the information within it due to short-term memory considerations.

INFORMATION-MAPPING PRINCIPLES

The information-mapping approach also includes four principles to aid authors/designers in determining how to define "chunks" of information.

- The *chunking principle* requires that all information be grouped into manageable, independent units or "chunks."
- The *relevance principle* directs that each of these chunked units should contain only information that relates to one main point.
- The *consistency principle* states that an author should, for similar subject matters, use consistent vocabulary, labels, formats, and sequences.
- The *labeling principle* specifies that every unit of information and/or groups of information should be labeled according to specific criteria.

HYPERTRAILS

To this point, the information-mapping approach has focused on the definition and construction of hypertext nodes/Web pages. Nothing has been said about how information maps are organized into a hypertext system/Web site.

Robert Horn refers to an organized hypertext system/Web site as a *hypertrail*. In particular, a hypertrail is defined as a set of links between chunks of information (information blocks or information maps) that organize and sequence information about a particular function characteristic of the subject matter.

As with the other design methodologies we have discussed in this chapter, the information-mapping approach defines a limited number of hypertrail types. These types are indicative of how the hypertrail/Web site is to be used/read/navigated by a user/reader. Some of the fundamental types of hypertrails are:

- Prerequisite
- Classification
- Project
- Structure
- Decision
- Example

A number of these types directly correspond to applications we have seen with other methodologies earlier in this chapter. For a complete description of the hypertrail types, you should refer to *Mapping Hypertext,* by Robert Horn.

Figure 1.14 illustrates the use of a prerequisite hypertrail. As the name suggests, such a hypertrail requires that nodes may have prerequisite requirements associated with them. This hypertrail describes an educational curriculum leading to a Web Document Engineering course.

This hypertrail defines the courses and the order in which they may be taken prior to the Web Document Engineering course. It is interpreted as follows:

- Writing Online Documentation, Human-Computer Interaction, and Concepts of Hypertext are all prerequisites for Introduction to HTML, but have no prerequisites themselves and may be taken in parallel.
- Multimedia Design, Introduction to HTML, and Perl Programming can all be taken in parallel.
- Multimedia Design, Introduction to HTML, and CGI Scripting are prerequisites for Advanced HTML.
- Perl Programming is a prerequisite for CGI Scripting.
- Advanced HTML is a prerequisite for Web Document Engineering.

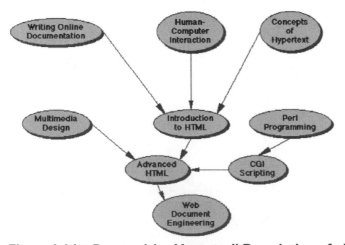

LAB 1.7

Figure 1.14 ■ Prerequisite Hypertrail Description of a Web Document Engineering Course

The contents of the nodes in this hypertrail are independent of its definition. The nodes could contain descriptions of the courses (as in a course catalog) or could even contain course content (as in an online learning system). The most important characteristic of the hypertrail is the relationships expressed between the nodes and the paths that can be used to navigate the system.

LAB 1.7 EXERCISES

1.7.1 ANALYZE AND DEFINE STRUCTURAL DESIGN ISSUES

Information structures are often combinations of the four fundamental structures. For example, a node within a hierarchical structure might actually be an embedded Web structure.

a) Define a circumstance where this might be the most appropriate structural design.

_____

_____

"Information overload" is human-computer interface (HCI) issue of concern to hypertext document designers. An example of information overload previously given dealt with hierarchical structures that are "too shallow."

b) What is the potential impact of short-term memory on information overload?

_____

_____

c) Discuss the advantages and disadvantages of a hierarchical structure versus a Web structure. (*Note:* Consider the problem of porting existing documents to Web pages.)

_____

_____

LAB
1.7

d) The size of a "chunk" of information is important to retaining it. Compare the amount of information in each article on the CNN Web site (www.cnn.com) and Time Magazine Web site (http://www.time.com/time/magazine/toc/).

_____

_____

1.7.2 REDEFINE A STRUCTURE

Figure 1.15 is a three-row, two-column grid structure. If the designer of this structure wanted to add an additional column, then navigation from the row-1, column-1 node to the row-1, column-3 node would have to go through the row-1, column-2 node.

a) How could the third column be added such that the row-1, column-3 node was directly accessible from the row-1, column-1, and the row-1, column-2 nodes? *Hint: The rows in this structure are sequence structures. Must rows in a grid structure always be sequence structures?*

_____

_____

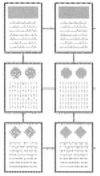

Figure 1.15 ■ A 3 × 2 Grid Structure

     b) The Indexed Guided Tour combines the best features of the Index and the Guided Tour structures. What might this structure look like?

_____

_____

Consider the Web page in Figure 1.16 as an example "information map." In this example, it really doesn't matter whether you can read the text, the number of organizational units is the most important feature.

     c) Does the Web page in Figure 1.16 meet the conditions of being a good information-mapping approach?

_____

_____

     d) What could be some other common hypertrails?

_____

_____

LAB 1.7 EXERCISE ANSWERS

1.7.1 ANSWERS

a) Define a circumstance where this might be the most appropriate structural design.

Answer: It is quite common for a hierarchically designed Web site to have links on the "root page" that extend to the Internet "in general." In such a case, the "Internet/Web" is logically one of the nodes of the hierarchical structure. For example, in the following diagram, Figure 1.17, the "cyberspace" node is the entire World Wide Web.

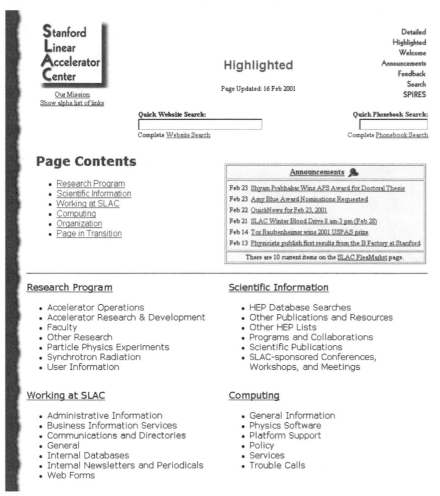

Figure 1.16 ■ A Home Page as an Information Map

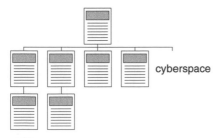

Figure 1.17 ■ A "Composite" Information Structure

b) What is the potential impact of short-term memory on information overload?

Answer: Short-term memory considerations would suggest that hierarchical structures have a maximum of 9 (i.e., 7 + 2) nodes at the first level (that level immediately below the root node). If the number of nodes at that level is greater than 9, a user would have difficulty retaining them in short-term memory (information overload) and the hierarchy would be considered "too shallow."

c) Discuss the advantages and disadvantages of a hierarchical structure versus a Web structure. (Note: Consider the problem of porting existing documents to Web pages.)

Answer: If sets of pages can be easily grouped into their own Web "documents" with little or no relationship to other groups, there is little need to have many links between them. This tends to lead away from a Web structure. In addition, the more the topics themselves are hierarchical (e.g., a company organization), the more you should tend toward a hierarchical structure.

Web-based structures are more suited to information fragments with a lot of interrelationships. On the other hand, if not properly managed, Web structures can get out of hand and may be difficult to navigate.

When porting from paper-based documents to a Web document, a hierarchical structure is quicker to implement as the document is probably already in some kind of hierarchy (chapters, sections, and so forth).

d) The size of a "chunk" of information is important to retaining it. Compare the amount of information in each article on the CNN Web site (www.cnn.com) and Time Magazine Web site (http://www.time.com/time/magazine/toc/).

Answer: Basically all of the articles on the CNN Web site are single pages that provide you with just the basic details of a particular story. There are links to other stories (others about a single incident or about related topics), but each article is short and can be typically read in a few minutes. It is therefore easier to remember most of the article.

On the other hand, the Time Magazine has magazine-length articles (what else?). These are spread across multiple pages and each page usually has more text than a page on the CNN site. Because more information is presented, a smaller percentage of that information is retained.

**LAB
1.7**

1.7.2 ANSWERS

a) How could the third column be added such that the row-1, column-3 node was directly accessible from the row-1, column-1, and the row-1, column-2 nodes? *Hint:* The rows in this structure are sequence structures. Must rows in a grid structure always be sequence structures?

Answer: Replace each row (currently a two-node sequence) with a web structure consisting of three nodes in a "ring." The nodes in the ring are aligned appropriately in order to maintain the required column/vertical relationship that exists in the original grid. The two-dimensional grid then becomes a structure more closely resembling a cylinder.

b) The Indexed Guided Tour combines the best features of the Index and the Guided Tour structures. What might this structure look like?

Answer: Using this structure, the Executive Branch "Organization" might look like Figure 1.18.

While the index node/entity on the left provides an entrance to the "Personnel" nodes, a reader/user is free to move about those nodes without always returning to a menu. The relationships between these nodes/pages can be readily expressed using HTML markup, such as creating a set of links at the top or bottom of each page. Although not shown in this graphic, links could be provided between any node (such as between the President and Vice President).

c) Does the Web page in Figure 1.16 meet the conditions of being a good information mapping approach?

Answer: Consider the components of this Web page. As an information map, it consists of seven information blocks:
   1. The logo, title, and date
   2. The menu bar (containing six buttons)
   3. A paragraph of text
   4. Some text within horizontal rules

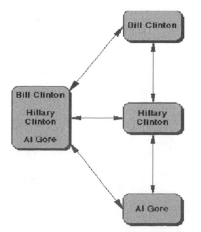

Figure 1.18 ■ Example of Indexed Guided Tour

**LAB
1.7**

5. *A bulleted list (containing a sublist); the number of bullets within each list is well within short term memory limitations*
6. *Additional text within horizontal rules*
7. *A bottom menu bar (containing four buttons)*

Even without being able to read the text, we can see that access to the information on the page would be fairly straightforward.

d) What could be some other common hypertrails?

Answer: Other common hypertrails may be as follows:

- *Definition—Links move from one definition to another. An online dictionary would be one example.*

- *Chronological—Links move along a time line. A Web site detailing a historical event would be one example.*

- *Geographic—Links move from one location to another. A company's Web site describing sales areas would be on example.*

In fact, any time you have a list of information that moves somewhat sequentially from one to the other, you have a hypertrail.

LAB 1.7 SELF-REVIEW QUESTIONS

In order to test your progress, you should be able to answer the following questions.

1) Hypertrails are what some browsers call the "History," which is a list of previously visited sites.

    a) _____ True
    b) _____ False

2) Entity–relationship (ER) modeling only applies to topics where physical objects are involved and therefore does not apply to every Web site.

    a) _____ True
    b) _____ False

3) A common problem with a hierarchical structure is that they can grow "too deep" and are therefore difficult to navigate.

    a) _____ True
    b) _____ False

4) A common problem with a hierarchical structure is that they can be "too shallow" and therefore the reader is presented with too many choices.

   a) _____ True
   b) _____ False

5) Decisions about how linking and navigational mechanisms are part of the User Interface Design phase.

   a) _____ True
   b) _____ False

6) Which of the following is not a hypertext design methodology?

   a) _____ structure-based
   b) _____ reference-based
   c) _____ relationship-based
   d) _____ information-based

7) What is the normally considered the maximum number of objects one can be expected to retain in short-term memory (± 2)?

   a) _____ 5
   b) _____ 7
   c) _____ 9
   d) _____ 11

8) The four fundamental information structures are:

   a) _____ Structured, Grid, Hierarchy, Web
   b) _____ Sequence, Grid, Hierarchy, Web
   c) _____ Sequence, Graph, Hierarchy, Web
   d) _____ Sequence, Grid, Organization, Web

9) Which are the four information-mapping principles?

   a) _____ Chunking, Relationship, Consistency, Labeling
   b) _____ Chunking, Relevance, Consistency, Labeling
   c) _____ Chunking, Relevance, Consistency, Linking
   d) _____ Clarity, Relevance, Consistency, Labeling

Quiz answers appear in the Appendix, Section 1.7.

LAB
1.7

CHAPTER 1

TEST YOUR THINKING

The projects in this section are meant to allow you to utilize all of the skills that you have acquired throughout this chapter. The answers to these projects can be found at the companion Web site to this book: http://www.phptr.com/phptrinteractive.

Visit the Web site periodically to share and discuss your answers.

1) Expand the Organization/Staff/Services example given in the discussion of the RMM approach into a well-defined hypertext information structure. Justify the use of the relationship structures that you choose.

2) Compare your result in Project 1 with a comparable organizational structure defined hierarchically.

3) The "project" hypertrail is defined as the hypertextual equivalent of the commonly used PERT chart. Create an example of a project hypertrail. (You may have to find out what a PERT chart is.)

C H A P T E R   2

INTRODUCTION TO HUMAN-COMPUTER INTERACTION

 Except for special things like computer games, people don't use computers because they want to use computers. They use computers because they want to write papers; they want to communicate with people; they want to design bridges and so on. Whatever they're doing, the computer is an enabling device that can help them do it.

—Terry Winograd, Stanford University

CHAPTER OBJECTIVES

In this chapter, you will learn about:

The first international conference on human-computer interaction (HCI) was held in 1982. This is when we began to regard HCI as a separate discipline in its own right. Even so, we recognize that HCI combines concepts from several other disciplines and applies them in a focused way to the interactions between humans and computers.

In this unit, we look at the basic concepts of human-computer interaction and how these concepts define the boundaries of the discipline. We look at how HCI relates to other disciplines and their relative importance.

L A B   2 . 1

HUMAN-COMPUTER
INTERACTION FOUNDATIONS

LAB OBJECTIVES

After this lab, you will be able to:

✔ Identify the Main Components of Human-Computer
Interaction
✔ Identify and Understand the Goals of Human-Computer
Interaction
✔ Discuss Historical and Future Issues of Human-Computer
Interaction

Today, almost twenty years from its inception, we say that human-computer interaction (HCI) concerns the design of interactive computing systems for human
use and the study of the contexts in which those systems are used. Note that HCI
is a wider area of interest than most people imagine. We must take into account
not just the actual interactions between people and computers, but the reasons
those interactions were necessary and the human consequences of the interactions after they have occurred.

USER INTERFACES

Humans interact with a computing system via a human-computer interface, usually shortened to user interface (in certain contexts this is abbreviated to UI). Naturally, when studying a user interface, the focus falls upon the three main
components:

1.   The human
2.   The computing system (machine)
3.   The interaction

While it is quite possible to consider these three components individually, we must be aware that all three are of equal importance when designing, implementing, and evaluating user interfaces. Never forget that the human requirements are considered paramount, though.

HCI GOALS

Advertisements for software usually concentrate on the features or functions that the application can perform. There is an implication that the more features, the more powerful the software package. While features are important, it is now recognized that programs must be usable and safe as well. Unusable software, no matter how many features it contains, will be installed, used a few times, then discarded. Software that crashes your computer system or destroys other data will be avoided like the plague.

HCI is also concerned with the whole system—the computer hardware, software, user, and the environment of use. The environment can be a large organization or just a single human user playing a computer game at home. Other goals include effectiveness and efficiency. A piece of software that carries out only part of a task may actually increase the workload for the user. Similarly, carrying out a task completely but taking excessive time or too many interactions with the user may be counterproductive. In both these latter cases, the frustration of the user will certainly rise leading to further negative effects on productivity.

To improve the usability of a software package, HCI specialists endeavor to:

- Understand psychological, organizational, and social factors of the combined human and computer system.
- Develop methodologies to aid appropriate HCI design.
- Realize efficient and effective interactions for single users and groups.

All of these efforts are directed at putting the user's requirements ahead of the technology as stated above. The system should be tailored for people, not the other way round.

HCI SCOPE

Teams that work to produce software to meet the goals of HCI must possess a wide range of knowledge about humans and technology. We can further break down the HCI discipline into smaller areas of concern:

- The capability of the human brain and the senses used in HCI
- The human ability to learn to use computing systems
- The context of the joint performance of tasks by humans and computing systems, called ethnography
- Structures of communication between human and machine
- Human task analysis and how the computer contributes to successful task completion
- Design of user interfaces
- Implementation of user interfaces
- Evaluation of user interfaces and design tradeoffs

You can see that this list is quite long, showing that HCI practitioners need to study in several disciplines to bring in-depth knowledge to a complex area.

HISTORICAL ROOTS

Looking back in time before the emergence of HCI in the 1980s, we can trace the areas that were influential in shaping the HCI of today. The major examples are listed in Table 2.1.

Table 2.1 ■ Historical Influences on Human-Computer Interaction

Discipline	Contribution
Computer graphics	Cathode ray tubes and pen devices
Computer science	Mouse input device, bitmapped graphics, desktop metaphor
Operating systems	Input/output device drivers, window managers, animation
Human factors	Flight instrument displays, particularly during WWII
Ergonomics	Work, stress, physiology, environmental conditions
Industrial engineering	Efficiency, production, human–machine fit
Cognitive psychology	Human performance, learnability, and usability
Information systems	Decision support systems, executive information systems, and computer-supported group work (CSCW or groupware)

Figure 2.1 structures these disciplines to show how they relate to the core of HCI. We also see how computer science and psychology play central roles surrounding HCI.

HCI INTO THE FUTURE

In the last decade, HCI has become a crucial ingredient in all large software development projects. Various estimates have been made of the proportion of code in a particular application that is devoted to the user interface. A survey by Myers and Rosson (1992) sets the figure at 48%, depending on the type of software package. "The average time [developers] spent on the user interface portion is 45% during the design phase, 50% during the implementation phase, and 37% during the maintenance phase." This firmly cements the user interface designers and implementers as major players in a software development team. Will this place of importance continue into the future?

The answer is a definite yes. We are entering an era of ubiquitous communication, where many computing devices connected by a variety of linked networks will surround us. Each device will be devoted to simple tasks, which help humans in their work in the real world. The user interfaces to these devices will vary considerably and likely will depend on the task they perform. Ensuring these disparate devices interwork between humans and between themselves will stretch

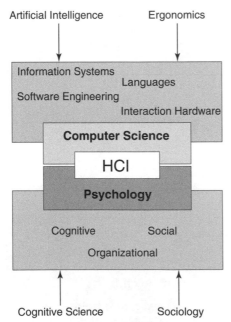

Figure 2.1 ■ Disciplines Related to HCI

the capabilities of HCI specialists. Notice the task is more likely to involve producing enhanced reality user interfaces than the much-publicized virtual reality style beloved in the movies.

Many of these new devices that will surround us in our daily lives will be small and portable. They will typically have restricted bitmapped graphics capabilities but will utilize other media such as audio in new and novel ways. To be effective, the devices will need to be customized for individual users. Being networked, these devices will provide us with excellent communication facilities with other users and devices—group communication and teamwork at distances will be possible.

The interface between human users and the Web already faces such a set of requirements. Most electrical equipment will incorporate such devices and become more responsive to the needs of their human users. To be effective, the user interface designs face enormous challenges.

LAB 2.1 EXERCISES

2.1.1 IDENTIFY THE MAIN COMPONENTS OF HUMAN-COMPUTER INTERACTION

a) Name the three main concepts of human-computer interaction and discuss their relevance to HCI.

_____

_____

b) Which of the three components of HCI is the most important and why?

_____

_____

2.1.2 IDENTIFY AND UNDERSTAND THE GOALS OF HUMAN-COMPUTER INTERACTION

a) HCI is concerned with the whole system of how humans and computers interact with each other. Consider the components mentioned in the text and discuss how they affect the behavior of the whole system.

_____

_____

b) Describe one of the major roles carried out by HCI specialists.

_____

_____

c) Considering the historical influences, why do you think HCI specialists need to study from several other disciplines?

_____

_____

d) Visit the sites www.startrek.com, home.netscape.com, and www.irs.com. Discuss how each is designed (does it remind you of anything?) and how well the information is presented (can you find what you are looking for?).

_____

_____

2.1.3 DISCUSS HISTORICAL AND FUTURE ISSUES OF HUMAN-COMPUTER INTERACTION

a) What discipline, developed during World War II to study flight instruments, is important for HCI today? Why is this important?

_____

_____

b) Computer science and psychology are the central HCI disciplines. Name one computer science specialization and one

psychology specialization that are particularly relevant to the
HCI discipline.

_____

_____

c) Consider the noncomputer devices you use that have an "interface." Analyze them from an HCI point of view in terms of
placement of controls, access to the functions you need, personal preference, and so forth.

_____

_____

LAB 2.1 EXERCISE ANSWERS

2.1.1 ANSWERS

a) Name the three main concepts of human-computer interaction and discuss their
relevance to HCI.

*Answer: The human, the computer, and the interaction between them are the three
main components. It is the human that is inputting the data. Humans are intrinsically
different from computers as well as from other humans. Therefore, how they affect and
relate to the system determines how efficient and useful it is. The computer or hardware
needs to be able to process the input that the user wants. If a user wants to input
speech, but does not have sound card, the desired interaction is not possible.*

b) Which of the three components of HCI is the most important and why?

*Answer: The human. Humans only use computers as enabling devices that help them
carry out necessary tasks.*

2.1.2 ANSWERS

a) HCI is concerned with the whole system of how humans and computers interact
with each other. Consider the components mentioned in the lab and discuss how
they affect the behavior of the whole system.

*Answer: The computer hardware and software, the user, and the environment in which
the HCI takes place are the four main components of HCI. How each component of
this (or any) system interact are key aspects of how the system behaves as a whole.*

The type of hardware you have, and how well the software processes input through the hardware are important aspects of HCI. The first character-based terminals that provided direct interaction to the operating system were a lifesaver for programmers and operators. Having the hardware to input the data and the software (a command shell) to interpret the input and react accordingly increased efficiency dramatically. Although the first GUI was seen as nothing more than an interesting curiosity, today we cannot image a computer without a windowing system (GUI).

Since it is the user that is interacting with the system, he or she is a vital part of the system. The psychology of seeing, cognitive abilities of the user, as well as physical limitations are important parts of the human side of the interaction. Even personal preferences play a role.

Ergonomics has grown from a buzzword to a key component of HCI. Products are being marketing based on their ergonomic characteristics and I have worked in companies where a pamphlet on ergonomics was part of the welcome packet.

Consider the myriad of devices available that support HCI. Depending on the system you work with most, the first thing that comes to mind is either the keyboard or the mouse (perhaps the monitor). The keyboard must be able to input the characters you need into the software. People in different countries require different characters to do their work. Even between countries with the same language there are differences. For example, the U.S. keyboard does not have a key for the British pound (£). Imagine the impact on efficiency if a person in a bank in Britain had to work on a U.S. keyboard!

However, the symbols written on the keys are just half of it. The signal that a particular key sends is dependent on its position on the keyboard and not what is printed on it. Most modern operating systems have software (keyboard drivers) that you can change to behave differently. Therefore, when you press a particular key in the U.S., a different character appears on the screen than would appear in Britain or Germany. Without this particular software, what is printed on the keys can be different from how the software interprets the key being pressed. Imagine pressing the "y" to answer "yes" to a question and have a "z" appear.

Also, so-called "natural" keyboards are sold whereby the keyboard is split in half and the halves are turned slightly so you can place your hands in a more natural position, so ergonomics plays a role here.

The introduction of the mouse increased our efficiency by allowing use to send information to the computer system without have to remember (let alone input) long commands. Technological changes in mouse design have also increased efficiency, such as the introduction of multiple buttons (the first only had one button). Trackballs can also increase efficiency because you don't have to deal with space issues on your desk, cleaning out lint from the mouse ball, and so forth. Even the physical shape of the mouse has been changed to fit more comfortably into your hand and make it easier to use.

Other technologies, such as voice recognition and text-to-speech as a combination of both hardware and software, have increased the efficiency of computers. How well the software can process the input (i.e., accurately recognize the words or produce understandable speech) greatly effects the system as a whole.

Not only can interaction be provided in situations where you need your hands for other work, such components that allow people to interact with the computer who could not before (for example, quadriplegics and the blind). Even the shape and position of these input devices has become an important aspect of them (ergonomics once again).

b) Describe one of the major roles carried out by HCI specialists.

Answer: Any one of the following:

- *Understanding psychological, organizational, and social factors of the combined human and computer system*

- *Developing methodologies to aid appropriate HCI design*

- *Realizing efficient and effective interactions for single users and groups*

c) Considering the historical influences, why do you think HCI specialists need to study from several other disciplines?

Answer: HCI specialists need knowledge about the human brain and other senses, how humans behave, the ability to communicate and perform, how to design user interfaces for these human characteristics, and how to evaluate those user interfaces to determine whether the criteria have been met.

From Table 2.1, you can see that many areas have contributed to the skill set required of HCI practitioners. Note that while the mainstream computing areas like computer science, information systems, and operating systems play a significant role, other, quite distinct disciplines like ergonomics and psychology play major roles, too. An HCI specialist is therefore quite a unique person with a carefully designed set of skills.

d) Visit the sites www.startrek.com, home.netscape.com, and www.irs.com. Discuss how each is designed (does it remind you of anything?) and how well the information is presented (can you find what you are looking for?).

Answer: Both the Star Trek and IRS sites have user interfaces that are very typical for Web sites and that adhere to the issues we discussed in Exercise 1.7.2. There is a head, a single menu that links to other areas, a central block with the important information, and a footer area with links to more "administrative" areas of the site. Both sites fit a specific paradigm. In the case of the Star Trek site, it is designed to look like a control panel from one of the series, using the same styles and fonts. The IRS site is designed to look like a newspaper, including the headlines. On the Star Trek site you can quickly tell that it is a site about Star Trek. However, it is a lot harder to figure out that the IRS site is about the U.S. Internal Revenue Service and not some company coincidentally named IRS. Even so, in both cases you can easily find the information you are looking for.

On the other hand, except for the logo, it is hard to tell that the Netscape site has anything to do with the company. In fact, this is really not the best place to look for information about the company Netscape. Instead, the page provides you information about everything else on the Internet except for Netscape. Part of the psychology of the Internet is that when you want to find out information about a company, you input www.companyname.com and there you are. With the Netscape site, you actually have to look hard to find information about Netscape (such as product information or technical support). In addition, there is simply too much information on the page (at least for someone new to the site). It is difficult to figure out all of that information. In essence, it does not adhere to what we discussed in Exercise 1.7.2.

2.1.3 ANSWERS

a) What discipline, developed during World War II to study flight instruments, is important for HCI today? Why is this important?

Answer: Human factors, such as the psychology of seeing as well as cognitive ability. Aspects such as where particular displays are placed can be a life-and-death decision for the designers. For example, if a fighter pilot in the middle of a battle spends too much time looking for a particular display, he may lose track of his opponent. Today, if fonts are too small, the user has trouble reading them or if the function buttons are spread out over the window it will take longer to find them.

Consider products like those from Adobe Systems (Photoshop, Illustrator, PageMaker, and so forth) that have an extremely consistent interface. Functions that are common to all of the products are in menus with the same names and in the same position on the screen. This allows you to seamlessly move between the various applications. In addition, many of the functions are on "floating" toolbars, which you can move to the area of the screen where you are working. This increases the efficiency of the HCI dramatically. By creating controls that are easy to find and easy to use, Adobe has increased the efficiency and usefulness of its products.

b) Computer science and psychology are the central HCI disciplines. Name one computer science specialization and one psychology specialization that are particularly relevant to the HCI discipline.

Answer: Computer science: one of Information Systems, Software Engineering, Linguistics, or Interactive Hardware. Psychology: one of Cognitive, Social, and Organizational Psychology.

c) Consider the noncomputer devices you use that have an "interface." Analyze them from an HCI point of view in terms of placement of controls, access to the functions you need, personal preference, and so forth.

Answer: What you find will depend on the kinds of devices you have and what interfaces you find.

Ever have a TV remote control with more buttons for more features than on a space shuttle? Like the Netscape Web site, you suffer from information overload. That is, there is just too much information to take in and you end up getting little, if anything at all. In the case of my TV remote control, I often have to hunt for the button I am looking for. A new TV took an interesting approach by having one side of the remote control filled with all of the buttons you could possibly imagine. You could slide it out of its case, flip it over, and then have just a handful of buttons for those few functions you use regularly.

Another example might be your microwave oven. Some are filled with buttons that are used for specific features such as "jet defrost," which is different from "thaw," which is different again from "preheat." Although there may be few enough controls to figure out which button server what function, it is difficult to understand what that function really is. In contrast, my current microwave has a dial for the time, one for the power (watts), and a button to open the door. (Closing the door turns it on if the timer is not set to zero.)

I had a car radio once that I couldn't stand. The volume control was a dial and pressing the dial turned on the scan feature. I can't count all of the times that I wanted to turn up the volume for a song I like and ended up activating the scan. Since this radio did not provide any way to save particular stations, by the time I scanned back around to the station, the song was over. This saved the manufacturer money by limiting the features, but provided (in my opinion) an extremely poor interface.

LAB 2.1 SELF-REVIEW QUESTIONS

In order to test your progress, you should be able to answer the following questions.

1) Color schemes, fonts, and other appearances related aspects of the system are not an important part of the study of HCI.

   a) _____ True
   b) _____ False

2) The shape of the keyboard, position of the screen, cushioning on your chair are all things which could be considered when designing your HCI.

   a) _____ True
   b) _____ False

3) Having a recognizable or easily identifiable interface is an important part of HCI.

   a) _____ True
   b) _____ False

4) Which of the following is not normally considered one of the main components of a user interface?

   a) _____ A human
   b) _____ A computing system/machine
   c) _____ Interaction
   d) _____ Multimedia

5) On average, what proportion of the code in each interactive application is devoted to the user interface?

   a) _____ less than 25%
   b) _____ ca. 50%
   c) _____ ca. 80%
   d) _____ over 90%

6) All but which of the following has had an influence on HCI?

   a) _____ Cognitive psychology—Human performance, learnability, and usability
   b) _____ Operating systems—Input/output device drivers, window managers, animation
   c) _____ Computer science—Mouse input device, bitmapped graphics, desktop metaphor
   d) _____ Ergonomics—Work, stress, physiology, environmental conditions
   e) _____ All of these have influenced HCI.

Quiz answers appear in the Appendix, Section 2.1.

LAB 2.2

THE NATURE OF HUMAN-COMPUTER INTERACTION

LAB OBJECTIVES

After this lab, you will be able to:

✔ Understand the Place of HCI and Its Effect on Computer Use and Development
✔ Identify Productivity Improvements

Most software construction relies heavily on HCI as a central consideration. Therefore, it is not surprising to find that HCI affects many aspects of software deployment and uses outside of the software implementation itself. We must appreciate those aspects of HCI that make it so important and the other disciplines to which it relates.

HCI: THE WHOLE PICTURE

A diagram that captures the extent of this influence is shown in Figure 2.2 drawn from the ACM Curriculum for Human-Computer Interaction (Hewett, Baecker, Card, Carey, Gasen, Mantei, Perlman, Strong, and Verplank, 1996). This diagram has become one of the most famous in the HCI literature and tries to encapsulate the breadth of the aspects of HCI, its influence on users, and the whole of software development.

The various components of Figure 2.2 are encoded in four main areas as described in Table 2.2. The two main aspects of HCI, humans and computers (H and C), are shown in the center of Figure 2.2. The significance of the figure, though, appears at the top and bottom. At the top, we see that all computer

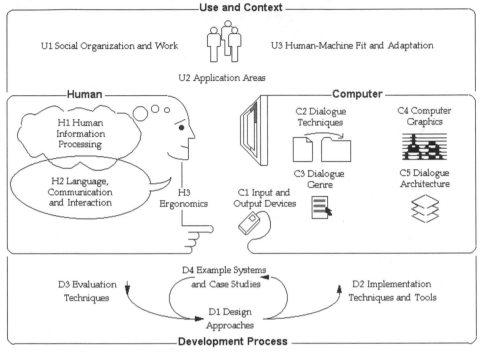

Figure 2.2 ■ Overview of the ACM Curriculum for HCI

systems used by humans (U) are affected by the H and C portions. This covers both individual use of a computer system as well as humans and computers within whole organizations. Similarly, at the bottom of Figure 2.2 we see the whole software development process relying on the H and C portions, at least for software that possesses a user interface.

Table 2.2 ■ Main Areas of HCI from ACM Curriculum

Code	Discipline Area
H	Human characteristics
C	Computer system and UI architecture
U	Use and context of computing systems
D	Software development process

From these considerations, we note that HCI stretches its tentacles into most areas of computing and its deployment for human use. All of software development must encompass the discipline of HCI, and this has led to changes in the development process and the set of skills taught to software engineers.

Similar large effects are felt when information technology equipment is planned and deployed in businesses of all sizes. The capabilities of hardware and software must be matched with the tasks carried out by the staff of the business. Long lists of powerful hardware and software features are no longer sufficient as the drivers of the selection process. Of equal importance is the matching of features with human tasks and how groups of staff collaborate to carry out those tasks with the equipment being selected. We need to understand the business processes of an organization, the capabilities of the staff, and their ability to work in teams in order to select suitable computing tools. Such knowledge of user interface design to meet these organizational goals must be integrated with traditional software engineering skills. Where Web pages form the user interface for the software used within a business, then the user interface design features must be present within the pages. To summarize, the core HCI areas of the human and the computer must be considered when undertaking software development on the one hand, and the tasks that people carry out within organizations on the other.

LAB 2.2

PRODUCTIVITY IMPROVEMENTS

The primary way of showing the benefits of HCI is by calculating tangible savings in case studies. The most important savings are likely to be in costs, work levels, and numbers of workers employed. Finding such clear-cut case studies has been difficult because many of the HCI benefits such as user satisfaction and lack of frustration are intangible. Examples of bad situations are much easier to find. System failures are common where the human operators select inappropriate software features via a badly designed user interface. Custom-made software systems written for large organizations suffer from gross underutilization with associated equipment lying idle. Many studies show that only about 20% of new software systems achieved their intended benefits, while about 40% fail to achieve any benefits or are rejected.

One of the classic case studies to show the improvement in productivity for a redesigned user interface is the study by Wixon and Jones (1996) of the DEC Rally application generator. In the second version of the Rally product, the development team worked hard to improve the usability of the user interface. The measured tangible benefits were:

- Revenue increased by about 80% compared to release 1
- Revenues exceeded an optimistic projection by 30 to 60%
- Improved usability was the second most cited reason why customers approved of release 2

The company was pleased with the return on investment that user interface usability afforded.

Another celebrated example of productivity gains is carefully documented in Gould, Ukelson, and Boies (1996). The ITS application generator separates user interface design from the application logic and content. ITS allows the user interface design team to construct reusable user interface styles that can be applied to any number of applications. Within IBM, ITS was deployed in six major projects covering a wide range of application types. Gould and colleagues (1996) describe how four productivity measures were chosen:

- Time to complete an application in person-weeks
- Developers' comments
- Quality of the end product (from informal judgments of the developers)
- Quality of application maintenance (from informal judgments of maintenance personnel)

Impressive productivity gains were achieved in all six case studies, which included a very large multimedia kiosk application used at the Seville World Fair Expo '92.

LAB 2.2 EXERCISES

2.2.1 UNDERSTAND THE PLACE OF HCI AND ITS EFFECT ON COMPUTER USE AND DEVELOPMENT

a) We have already talked about the two primary aspects of HCI (the human and the computer). What are the other two important areas and what roles do they play?

_____

_____

2.2.2 IDENTIFY PRODUCTIVITY IMPROVEMENTS

a) How can we show the benefits of good HCI?

_____

_____

LAB 2.2 EXERCISE ANSWERS

2.2.1 ANSWER

a) We have already talked about the two primary aspects of HCI (the human and the computer). What are the other two important areas and what roles do they play?

Answer: Use and context of computing systems and software development are the other two important aspects. Although it may seem an almost trivial point, knowing where software will be implemented (the context) is an important aspect of the interface. However, sometimes the details of that context are not fully understood. For example, imagine a software product designed to manage operations within a law firm. It can handle cases, references, court schedules, and even billing. What if the interface does not allow you to bill in anything less than full hours? It is common (if not the rule) that lawyers bill customers in quarter-hour increments. The interface might be efficiently designed and easy to use, but the design does not consider the context.

Although much computer software does not require human interaction (operating system functions, automation, and so forth), the development process must take the issue of HCI into consideration. Therefore, there are a great many development tools on the market that are either specifically intended to develop the user interface or have modules that ease its development.

2.2.2 ANSWER

a) How can we show the benefits of good HCI?

Answer: By calculating tangible savings in case studies.

One important aspect to remember is that not all of the benefits are "tangible." Because different environments affect people differently, one group of people might work better with one software product than another group would or with another product. Neither product is intrinsically better than the other, just as neither group is intrinsically more adept at using the software. It is simply a matter of personal preference. This might be as mundane as having the toolbar on the side as compared to the top or bottom.

It is basically the rule today that the software be configurable. The software developers have realized that customers want this configurability and have included it. For them, there is the tangible benefit of more sales. However, the purchasers of the software (or, maybe their accounting departments) may not be able to identify any tangible benefits.

LAB 2.2 SELF-REVIEW QUESTIONS

In order to test your progress, you should be able to answer the following questions.

1) With modern research and analysis techniques it is easy to identify all of the benefits, as well as cost factors of any HCI project.

    a) _____ True
    b) _____ False

2) Although once on the top of the list, fast and powerful hardware is no longer the sole driving factor for selecting computer systems.

    a) _____ True
    b) _____ False

3) On average, what percentage of new software systems achieve their intended benefit?

    a) _____ ca. 20%
    b) _____ ca. 50%
    c) _____ ca. 75%
    d) _____ over 90%

4) On average, what percentage of new software systems fail to deliver any benefit or are rejected?

    a) _____ less than 25%
    b) _____ ca. 40%
    c) _____ ca. 75%
    d) _____ over 90%

5) Which of the of the following is not a main area of HCI?

    a) _____ Human characteristics
    b) _____ Computer system and UI architecture
    c) _____ Hardware device drivers
    d) _____ Use and context of computing systems
    e) _____ Software development process

Quiz answers appear in the Appendix, Section 2.2.

L A B   2 . 3

USER INTERFACE SOFTWARE

LAB OBJECTIVES

After this lab, you will be able to:

✔ Identify Layers of User Interface Software
✔ Identify Graphical User Interface Hardware

User interfaces have become all-pervasive. The program code to support user interface technology has to be placed in an appropriate context so that all applications can have efficient access to the technology. We will see that even the base operating system has now to take account of this new body of software that is needed to support user interfaces.

USER INTERFACE SOFTWARE TECHNOLOGY

We can think of the user interface software as being sandwiched between two layers of hardware: the base computer hardware and the user interaction device hardware (interface hardware, such as a mouse, keyboard, and so forth). These latter hardware devices are specifically designed to allow a human user to interact with the computer and will be discussed in a little more detail in a later unit.

Early computers had little in the way of interaction devices, and user interfaces were extremely simple. All the software needed was built into the operating system, which controlled the execution of a variety of software applications. As more sophisticated interaction devices appeared and user interfaces became more complex, additional substantial layers of software were needed. These extra layers are shown in Figure 2.3.

From the user's point of view, the interaction hardware and the user interface code together form the user interface. Although Figure 2.3 shows logical compo-

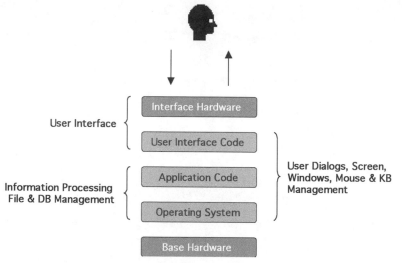

Figure 2.3 ■ Layers of User Interface Software

nents, we should note that the amount of user interface code is not small in relation to the operating system as a whole.

If we consider some of the typical types of software, we see that all of the main categories exhibit sophisticated user interfaces:

- Document preparation: Word processing, publishing, computer-aided design, software engineering
- Communications: Email, bulletin boards, conferencing
- Information repositories like the Web
- Data analysis: Spreadsheets, accounting, scientific
- Electronic commerce and finance
- Databases
- Life-critical process control: Industrial plant, medical instruments, transport
- Art, multimedia, gaming, and entertainment

That most of these applications can run successfully on a general-purpose personal computer with a single set of hardware components is impressive. The features present in the user interface must support all the different tasks that are to be carried out in these software packages. From this we understand that there must be a high degree of flexibility in the user interface. Such is the role of the graphical user interface.

GRAPHICAL USER INTERFACE

The graphical user interface, or GUI for short, is a combination of a set of interaction hardware and the software modules to support those devices. The original set of interaction hardware developed in the early 1980s was simply:

- Pixel-based display screen
- Keyboard
- Mouse (or other) pointing device

While the manufacture of high-resolution screens was not straightforward in the early years, the hardware was easy to supply. The hard work was needed for the supporting software. We see from the previous section that substantial components of the operating systems are affected, particularly to support the mouse, in all applications. In turn, the actual visual components used to construct the user interface took many design iterations. Even today, each major platform adopts a different set of visual components, more usually referred to as widgets.

LAB 2.3

Originally developed from pioneering work at the Palo Alto Research Center of Xerox, the first true GUI system appeared in 1981 on the Xerox Star machine designed for office tasks. Commercial success had to wait until the Apple Lisa and Macintosh, the latter appearing in 1984. Subsequently, the GUI became dominant on the PC via Microsoft Windows and on Unix platforms with the X-Windowing System from MIT.

For a dozen years after its introduction, the GUI remained fairly static, although the sophistication of the widgets steadily increased as new GUI designs were tried and judged to be effective. The immense speed-up of the processor chips meant it was possible to offer support of multimedia technologies, particularly audio input and output, graphics, and video. At the time of writing, the GUI interaction device list now almost always includes and audio card supporting loudspeakers and microphone. Video playback under software control is common, and small cameras for video input with supporting interface cards are becoming widely available. User interface designs incorporating audio and video are still in their infancy, and much experience will need to be gained to match the polish of GUI designs for the original set of interaction devices.

LAB 2.3 EXERCISES

2.3.1 IDENTIFY LAYERS OF USER INTERFACE SOFTWARE

Implementing the user interface adds additional software layers to an interactive application.

**LAB
2.3**

a) Name the two layers that constitute the user interface. Discuss their significance and how they relate with other aspects of the system.

_____

_____

b) How does the user interface code layer relate to the operating system?

_____

_____

c) What kinds of software do not require much (if any) user interface?

_____

_____

2.3.2 IDENTIFY GRAPHICAL USER INTERFACE HARDWARE

a) What interaction hardware devices form part of the standard graphical user interface (GUI)?

_____

_____

b) What additional interaction devices form the enhanced GUI on recent personal computers?

_____

_____

LAB 2.3 EXERCISE ANSWERS

a) Name the two layers that constitute the user interface. Discuss their significance and how they relate with other aspects of the system.

Answer: User interface hardware and the user interface code. The hardware device provides the "interface" between human understandable components (pressing a key with a particular symbol, clicking a mouse button, images on the screen) and the computer system. When inputting information, the user performs certain actions with the interface devices and electric signals are generated, which are then passed to the user interface code. This code then translates the electric signals into so-called "events" to which the computer system can react. When sending information to the user, the software identifies certain events (e.g., the image on the screen has changed), the event is translated to electric impulses and then sent to the user.

b) How does the user interface code layer relate to the operating system?

Answer: Usually the user interface code calls upon the code from the rest of the application, which in turn makes use of operating system services.

In essence, the operating system serves as the "middle man" between the different components. For example, you press a key on the keyboard, which sends information to the keyboard device driver, which may then be sent to the application or acted upon by the operating system. If intended for the application, the action may be something a simple as displaying the key on the screen (as in the case of pressing a letter in a word processing program). What the application needs to display on the screen is passed to the video driver, which sends the appropriate signals to the monitor. However, pressing a key may be something more complex like causing the application to print or saving the current document.

c) What kinds of software do not require much (if any) user interface?

Answer: Software modules that drive network protocols, provide automation or control, and monitor access to databases, for example, do not interact with users directly and have little or no user interface code.

Although there are programs the utilize these other software modules, they are typically command-line oriented and therefore do not require much in the way of a user interface (other than meaningful and useful options). Granted, there are graphical tools to administer databases or configure your network. Once the installation and configuration are done, most of the work is done without user interference. Automation tools may also provide a graphical interface, but once they are set in motion, the work is done without the user's awareness.

2.3.2 ANSWERS

LAB 2.3

a) What interaction hardware devices form part of the standard graphical user interface (GUI)?

Answer: High-resolution pixel-based display screen, keyboard, mouse (or other) pointing device.

b) What additional interaction devices form the enhanced GUI on recent personal computers?

Answer: Loudspeakers for audio information and text to speech, microphones for voice recognition, as well as video cameras for video conferences.

LAB 2.3 SELF-REVIEW QUESTIONS

In order to test your progress, you should be able to answer the following questions.

1) The first true GUI system was developed by whom?

    a) _____ Microsoft
    b) _____ Apple
    c) _____ MIT
    d) _____ Xerox
    e) _____ Digital Research

2) Which of the following types of software exhibit little, if any, user interface?

    a) _____ Conferencing
    b) _____ Spreadsheets
    c) _____ Software engineering
    d) _____ Database
    e) _____ All of these types of software have a user interface.

3) Which of the following was not part of the original set of interaction hardware developed in the early 1980s?

a) _____ Pixel-based display screen
b) _____ Speakers
c) _____ Mouse (or other) pointing device
d) _____ Keyboard
e) _____ These were all components of the original interaction hardware.

4) The program code to support user interface technology has to be placed in an appropriate context so that all applications can have efficient access to the technology.

a) _____ True
b) _____ False

Quiz answers appear in the Appendix, Section 2.3.

LAB 2.4

SOFTWARE DEVELOPMENT

LAB OBJECTIVES

After this lab, you will be able to:

✔ Compare Traditional and Modern Software Development Life Cycle Methodologies

---

The software development life cycle (SDLC) has traditionally been concerned with the functionality of software and how it can be implemented. The end users of the software were typically involved at the start of the cycle when their requirements are determined. Using methodologies that depend on process or data flows or both, the design and implementation steps are undertaken by software developers. Only during the final testing phases do end users become involved once again. When it is apparent that the software functionally does not match the work tasks of the user, or that the user interface is inadequate in some way, the whole cycle must be repeated.

With the birth of HCI, the traditional approaches to developing software have undergone change. In particular, the end users must now be involved in all stages of the software development. New methodologies are being introduced that have a major impact on the SDLC.

THE TRADITIONAL SOFTWARE DEVELOPMENT LIFE CYCLE

Quite naturally, software developers are concerned with the functionality, data flows, and correctness of the program code that they write. Traditionally, the software design process starts with increasingly detailed statements of the functions or processes that the programs will carry out. These stages are called the *requirements analysis* and *specification*. Some SDLC design methodologies begin with a description of the data and its transformation. In both cases, the end users cooperate with the software developers to produce a detailed requirements specification.

Using methodologies specifically aimed at software design, the developers alone progress to generate a design document from which the program is implemented. Only then do the end users become involved once more to help during the testing phase. The SDLC described so far is referred to as the *waterfall model* and is shown in Figure 2.4.

We should recognize that many more than five stages are involved in the waterfall model. Much iteration occurs between the main stages. Problems with the specification are found in the course of the design phase and during coding, faults are found with the design, and so on.

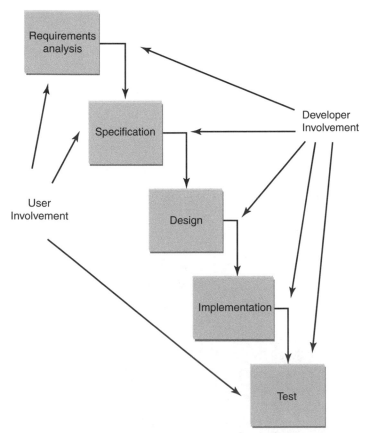

Figure 2.4 ■ Waterfall Software Development Model

THE NEW SOFTWARE DEVELOPMENT LIFE CYCLE

An obvious extension to the waterfall model is to involve the users in all stages of the development. Unfortunately, it is not sensible to assume that users will understand the notations and methodologies employed during the design and coding stages. Users do, however, understand cut-down or prototype systems with which they can interact and offer feedback to the developers. To be successful, the developers must partition the design and implementation phases into distinct subphases, each with a prototype system to present to the users.

Managing the production of prototypes is difficult. Too many prototypes will lengthen the development cycle; too few will give little improvement on the waterfall model. In addition, prototyping requires specialist software support, so that partial systems can be implemented quickly and cheaply.

LAB 2.4

We call this new approach to software development *user-centered* or occasionally, *participatory design*. The key aspects of this approach are:

- Involving users at all stages of the development; observing working environment, using models of users, and including some users on the design team.
- Applying knowledge from all HCI-related disciplines integrated with the software development; employing design guidelines and principles.
- Using highly iterative testing with user feedback after each iteration.

The new user-centered SDLC is shown in Figure 2.5, a diagram adapted from Hix and Hartson (1993). We refer to this more appropriate SDLC as the star life cycle.

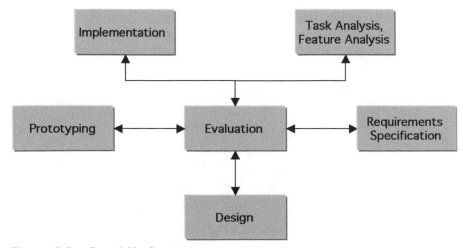

Figure 2.5 ■ Star Life Cycle.

At the center of the star cycle in Figure 2.5 is the very important evaluation stage. After every iteration, there is an evaluation process to determine the outcome of the last stage. Progress can be measured throughout the process. Of course, a range of evaluation strategies is needed to support this model, and these are discussed in a later unit.

We note as well that the star life cycle has no one particular starting stage. This allows for both top-down and bottom-up development, or a combination, to suit the type of software being developed. It may be that an initial prototype is needed to gain user support for a broad idea. On the other hand, a feature analysis might be the ideal starting point where the users' needs are better known. The star cycle even allows for the case where an existing implementation is available (already owned software) and needs to be matched with a requirements specification.

You will notice another new term in Figure 2.5. This is *task analysis,* which relates the task being undertaken by the user with the working environment. Task analysis plays a very important role in the new SDLC methodologies. Indeed, many HCI specialists would claim it is the crucial first piece of work that must be undertaken when constructing any piece of software.

**LAB
2.4**

LAB 2.4 EXERCISES

2.4.1 COMPARE TRADITIONAL AND MODERN SOFTWARE DEVELOPMENT LIFE CYCLE METHODOLOGIES

a) Discuss the major flaw in the traditional waterfall model for the software development life cycle (SDLC).

_____

_____

b) Discuss the key aspects of the participatory design method of software development.

_____

_____

c) Why is it important to include iteration in the SDLC?

_____

_____

d) How does prototyping help produce a better user interface?

_____

_____

e) Distinguish between feature analysis and task analysis.

_____

_____

f) How does RAD support the software development process?

_____

_____

**LAB
2.4**

g) Discuss the star life cycle.

_____

_____

LAB 2.4 EXERCISE ANSWERS

2.4.1 ANSWERS

a) What is the major flaw in the traditional waterfall model for the software development life cycle (SDLC)?

Answer: The major flaw in the traditional waterfall model is its lack of user involvement in the design and implementation stages of the software development life cycle.

These stages of the waterfall model make up the bulk of the SDLC and are usually the most costly. Developers are always faced with many choices when deciding on the detailed implementation, particularly when faced with the fine details of the user interface layout and the ordering of interactions with the users.

Finding a problem with the user interface during testing normally requires the developers to backtrack to the specification stage with redesign and a new implementation to follow. Thus, backtracking is a time-consuming and costly exercise.

b) Discuss the key aspects of the participatory or user-centered design method of software development.

Answer: Users (or their representatives) are involved in all stages of the SDLC. Developers observe users' working environments, use models of users, and typically include some users on the design team. Knowledge from all HCI-related disciplines is applied and integrated with the software development. Highly iterative testing is done with user feedback after each iteration.

c) Why is it important to include iteration in the SDLC?

Answer: Each stage introduces errors into the SDLC. It is important to proceed in small stages followed by evaluation. This process is iterated many times to determine progress toward the ultimate goal.

One aspect I see that a lot of developers miss is that corrections sometimes introduce new errors that are not related to the original problem. This even happens to major software developers like Microsoft, where one Service Pack broke the keyboard hardware driver for several non-English keyboards. By doing the development iteratively, you repeat all of the same steps (and therefore the same tests). This helps catch any new bugs introduced to the code by the "fixes."

d) How does prototyping help produce a better user interface?

Answer: Prototypes allow the user to visualize the user interface and comment upon the layout and interaction sequences. This feedback forms valuable input into the design and implementation stages.

One thing you need to watch is exactly what you are prototyping. As we mentioned in the lab, users will not likely understand the notations and methodologies employed during the design and coding stages. In addition, they are not likely to understand the technical aspects of the code. Therefore, it is not generally necessary to involve them in the development stages of the functional aspects of the application (such as database access, network connectivity, and so forth). On the other hand, since it is the interface that the user will be in contact with, they obviously need to be involved in its development.

Note also that a prototype for the functional aspects of the application does not necessarily need a user interface—the user interface prototype needs some functionality. Simply having the input screen to look at is not enough; the user must be able to have the system react to input and have the user react to output provided by the application.

e) Distinguish between feature analysis and task analysis.

Answer: Task analysis records the actual sequence of work undertaken by users and the data involved. From this task record, a list of features to enable the work to be carried out can be drawn up. The tasks should dictate which software features to include in the final product. Feature analysis involves turning a list of features into related groups, in order to aid the layout design of user interfaces.

f) How does RAD support the software development process?

Answer: Rapid application development (RAD) provides not only for rapid prototyping development but also rapid development of the actual code.

Such products are based upon palette-driven front-end tools, which allow user interface designs to be built rapidly. Behind the user interface, interpretive code or scripts are generated to introduce standard responses to user actions. This gives the users the impression of a working interactive system on which to base their feedback.

Indeed, the provision of rapid prototyping development software has become a lucrative niche market for software development tools. More and more products are available that are based on palette-driven front-end tools, which allow user interface designs to be built rapidly.

g) Discuss the star life cycle.

Answer: The star life cycle has no one particular starting stage. This allows for both top-down and bottom-up development, or a combination, to suit the type of software being developed. It may be that an initial prototype is needed to gain user support for a broad idea. On the other hand, a feature analysis might be the ideal starting point where the users' needs are better known. The star cycle even allows for the case where an existing implementation is available (already owned software) and needs to be matched with a requirements specification.

LAB 2.4 SELF-REVIEW QUESTIONS

In order to test your progress, you should be able to answer the following questions.

1) A key feature of the star cycle is the ability to work on all phases of development simultaneously, thereby saving time.

a) _____ True
b) _____ False

2) Task analysis is the phase of development where each development task (interface, functionality, and so forth) is analyzed in the context of managing these various tasks.

a) _____ True
b) _____ False

3) The number of prototypes to provide is based on the speed at which the application must be developed and the requirement to provide bug-free code.

   a) _____ True
   b) _____ False

4) The three stages of the traditional software development life cycle are called:

   a) _____ requirements, analysis, and specification.
   b) _____ research, analysis, and specification.
   c) _____ requirements, analysis, and development.
   d) _____ research, iteration, and specification.

5) What are the five stages in the waterfall model of software development?

   a) _____ research and planning, specification, design, implementation, test
   b) _____ requirements analysis, specification, development, implementation, integration
   c) _____ requirements analysis, specification, development, implementation, test
   d) _____ requirements analysis, specification, design, implementation, test

Quiz answers appear in the Appendix, Section 2.4.

LAB
2.4

C H A P T E R   2

TEST YOUR THINKING

The diagram shown in Figure 2.2 was drawn from the *ACM Curriculum for Human-Computer Interaction* and has become one of the most famous in the HCI literature. It tries to encapsulate the breadth of the aspects of HCI, its influence on users, and the whole of software development.

1) Expand your understanding of the basic HCI principles by reading the document located at: http://www.acm.org/sigs/sigchi/cdg/cdg2.html. Of course, there will be no right or wrong answers to this, but this project will give you more in-depth insight into the field and enrich your HCI research.

2) Visit two or three of your favorite Web sites and evaluate them using the HCI criteria you've gathered in this chapter. Post your thoughts, along with the URLs for the sites you choose, to this book's companion Web site for your fellow readers to consider.

C H A P T E R 3

HUMAN-COMPUTER INTERACTION PRINCIPLES

 Human-computer interaction (HCI) is about designing computer systems that support people so that they can carry out their activities productively and safely.

—Preece et al. (1994)

To design user interfaces, we must have grounding in several disciplines. We must understand the characteristics of the human user that touch upon HCI. Knowing these characteristics, we can develop models of the user to guide the user interface design and make some predictions about rate of learning and working in groups.

We have little choice in the selection of the actual hardware interaction devices for general-purpose personal computers. Nevertheless, we must know the limitations of the screen, keyboard, and pointing devices when carrying out different types of tasks.

Graphical user interfaces are constructed from a range of user interface components or widgets. When entering a dialog with the user, we must know which widget to use at different stages in the dialog. Furthermore, dialog structures depend upon the fundamental communication being attempted between human and computer, so communication theory can be useful here.

We have already noted the importance of user-centered design from the previous unit. Here we look at applying this concept in association with task analysis. When the user interface design is complete, the actual software must be implemented. We will look at some of the tools that can be used to generate the final application and its user interface.

L A B   3 . 1

THE HUMAN PERSPECTIVE

LAB OBJECTIVES

After this lab, you will be able to:

✔ Understand the Model Information Processor

Of the two primary concerns of HCI, the human should come first. Computer systems are designed to aid people in their daily tasks, be it at work, home, or play. We can see at a glance that humans and computers vary greatly in their ability to carry out their work. If they are to operate successfully together, we must be aware of their different capabilities.

This lab discusses the basic capabilities of the human being that are relevant to the use of computers. Much of this knowledge has been gleaned over the past century or so as part of the study of human psychology. Of the various divisions, we need only consider cognitive and social psychology. As we will see, not all the human senses are currently employed in HCI, so we need only be concerned with a small part of cognitive psychology.

HUMAN INFORMATION PROCESSOR

For our purposes, we regard a human being as being part of an information-processing system consisting of groups of other humans and computers. Bear in mind that this general model can be reduced to just a single human and a computer. We can represent a person as a collection of subsystems:

- Memory
- Perceptual (sensing)
- Motor (response)
- Cognitive (processing)

Memory, of course, is a storage facility, while the last three in the list are processing subsystems. For successful design of user interfaces, we need to understand the basic characteristics, strengths, and weaknesses of these subsystems. This treatment of humans as information processors is due to pioneering work at Xerox PARC by Card, Moran, and Newell (1983). They constructed the model human processor, which consists of three subsystems:

- Perceptual system consisting of sensors and associated buffer memories

    Visual image store

    Auditory image store

- Cognitive system

    Working memory

    Long-term memory

- Motor system, which carries out responses formulated by the cognitive system

The model of the human processor is shown in Figure 3.1. Note that the human senses of vision and hearing are connected to the sensory stores. Card, Moran, and Newell did experiments with human memory and the three processing subsystems. For comparison, they used simple model parameters. For memories and processors they used the following parameters:

- s, storage capacity in items
- d, decay time of an item
- k, main code type (physical, acoustic, visual, or semantic)

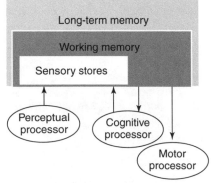

Figure 3.1 ■ Model Human Processor by Card, Moran, and Newell

For processors, they used parameter *t,* the cycle time, which also incorporates the time to access the processor.

The first aspect we must always remember is that human beings vary a lot. In other words, not only is every person different, but each one can also be very different indeed. Further, each of us varies in concentration, mood, motivation, prejudice, and judgment on a minute-to-minute basis. Despite this, the human information processor can be very powerful in our short reaction times, ability to solve complex problems, ability to be highly creative, and ability to operate complicated equipment. All of these abilities require training and experience. It is not surprising that when faced with a totally new user interface, we can be ineffective and very frustrated given no training or experience whatever.

We will consider each of the human information processor subsystems in turn, and we will extract the major characteristics that must be taken into account when designing user interfaces.

MEMORY AND PROCESSORS

Human memory can be treated as a set of storage and processing systems. Such a memory model consists of three types of memory:

- *Short-term sensory stores.* These stores hold the data received from the external world. The stores are split into visual, auditory, and tactile material.
- *Short-term (working) memory.* This is where information is processed, or "chunked," into small pieces of useful information.
- *Long-term memory.* This memory is assumed to hold information indefinitely, although not all information can be retrieved evenly.

Access to the human memory can be likened to a computer's input/output channels. The human channels are listed in Table 3.1.

Note that the channels of Table 3.1 are relative to the human being. Human input channels can be exploited by a computer's output channels, and vice versa. The original GUI made use of only a small subset of the human channels. Human motor control output is used to drive the keyboard and mouse. On the input side, human vision, and to a limited extent audition, can respond to the screen and the small loudspeaker in the computer.

From their experiments, Card and colleagues derived parameter values for the different types of memory. These values are shown in Table 3.2. Although these experimental values have been further refined by others in the intervening

**LAB
3.1**

Table 3.1 ■ Human Input/Output Channels

Input	Output
Vision	Speech
Audition	Motor control
Gestation	Biometrics
Olfaction	
Touch	
Balance	

decade and a half, the values are still indicative and can still be used for user interface design.

From their experiments, Card and colleagues also arrived at values for the processor parameters. A summary of some of the important values is shown in Table 3.3.

Table 3.2 ■ Model Human Processor Parameters for Memory

Visual Image Store	Auditory Image Store
s = 17 letters	s = 5 letters
d = 200 msec	d = 1500 msec
k = physical	k = physical

Working Memory	Long-Term Memory
s = 7 chunks	s = infinite
d = 7 sec	d = infinite
k = acoustic/visual	k = semantic

Table 3.3 ■ Model Human Processor Parameters for Processors

Perceptual Processor	Cognitive Processor	Motor Processor
$t = 100$ msec	$t = 70$ msec	$t = 70$ msec
(eye movement = 230 msec)		

Again, some of these parameter values have been revised in more recent times, but their magnitudes have stayed intact. The times can be used to set upper limits on that rate of change of visual user interface components and the number of interactions that can be expected from users in a given time. These values fit well with observed maximum typing speeds, for example, and the movements of the mouse.

Although useful, the model human processor oversimplifies the behavior of human users. Subsequent research has concentrated upon mental models, human learning, and gathering of experience. These are discussed later in this chapter.

LAB 3.1 EXERCISES

3.1.1 UNDERSTAND THE HUMAN INFORMATION PROCESSOR

Using the analogy with a computer, Card and colleagues proposed the model human processor.

a) User interface designs can employ the parameter values of Table 3.2 when deciding on physical aspects of the interface design. Discuss how designers might use this information.

_____

_____

b) One subsystem of the model human processor is memory. Describe the three processing subsystems and discuss how they are modeled in computer systems.

_____

_____

c) Discuss the three types of memory.

_____

_____

d) Name the human input/output channels that are used for the user interface of a general-purpose personal computer and discuss how this input is provided.

_____

_____

e) Looking at the response time of the human motor processor, what is the theoretical maximum upper limit to typing speed in words per minute? Assume the average word is five characters. Could a human input information faster?

_____

_____

LAB 3.1 EXERCISE ANSWERS

3.1.1 ANSWERS

a) User interface designers can employ the parameter values of Table 3.2 when deciding on physical aspects of the interface design. Discuss how designers might use this information.

Answer: This information can be used when determining such things as font and image size, frequency of change, and the type and duration of sounds. Human touch is utilized in the latest force-feedback joysticks and steering wheels used for computer games. Balance, too, is being exploited in some sophisticated simulation rides in theme parks.

One concrete example would be the storage capacity in items. Interface designers could use this parameter as the number of items stored in working memory. This could be quickly retrieved and displayed before another group of characters is retrieved.

In general, these parameters can guide user interface designers in the volume of visual and auditory information to present to the user at each stage in the interaction. In the most recent computer hardware with the extended GUI interaction devices, human speech and full audition are exploited to the fullest. Human speech input is becoming commonplace, and the personal computer now threatens the traditional stand-alone audio systems with sophisticated 3D sound output.

From the processing point of view, the actions and performance of humans during inter-action with computers are regarded as a series of processing stages. Each stage in-volves a different processor or processors, which will transfer information to and from a variety of memories. For example, when typing a key on the keyboard, the visual proces-sor will start with the transfer of the current state of the screen near to the location where the user expects the new character to appear. Next, the cognitive processor as-sesses the state information and forms a decision to press a particular key in working memory. Finally, the motor processor enacts the decision by guiding the finger to press the required key.

b) One subsystem of the model human processor is memory. Describe the three processing subsystems and discuss how they are modeled in computer systems.

Answer: The perceptual system perceives or senses the world around you. The computer perceives you through tactical inputs (keyboard, mouse), auditory inputs (microphone), and even visual (cameras, scanners).

The motor subsystem is responsible for movement. Motion can be perceived by the computer through a mouse, joystick, and even a camera. Motion can also be generated by a computer by hooking it up to any number of devices. Examples of this abound in the manufacturing industry.

The cognitive subsystem is typically equated with memory. From a human perspective there is more to it than just memory. For humans it can also be knowing. A computer can take a number of inputs and compare it to its memory. If the input is close to what it has in memory, it "guesses" that the input matches what is in memory. For example, a computer can be programmed to "recognize" people either from photos or videos. How-ever, it does not know that a particular photo is a specific person. On the other hand, a human knows. In addition, humans can make this kind of identification with much less input (e.g., a fuzzy picture) and still be able to accurately identify the person.

c) Discuss the three types of memory.

*Answer: Short-term sensory stores hold data received from the external world. The stores are split into visual, auditory, and tactile material (although tactical input can also be received from **inside** the body). The lifetime of the stored material is extremely short, just a few tenths of a second. In computer terminology, sensory stores are called buffers. A very small percentage of this buffered information is passed on to the work-ing memory. That is, you only become "aware" of a very small percent of the informa-tion your sensors receive.*

As you are reading these words, you are only aware of the words you are reading (how many depends on the individual). Although the photons from other words, the margins, your hands, and many other things around you are reaching your visual receptors (your eyes). You are not aware of them.

Short-term (working) memory is where information is processed, or "chunked," into small pieces of useful information. This is where you actually become aware of the input. The number of chunks is normally limited to the 7 we discussed early (although some people can get up to 10). These chunks typically have a lifetime of up to 15 seconds. Some chunks are passed on to the long-term memory.

Long-term memory is assumed to hold information indefinitely, although not all information can be retrieved evenly. The storage capacity appears to be very large indeed, with no sensible upper limit yet discovered. Name the human input/output channels that are typically used for the user interface of a general-purpose personal computer and discuss how this input is provided?

d) Name the human input/output channels that are used for the user interface of a general-purpose personal computer and discuss how this input is provided.

Answer: The two human input channels are vision (sight) and audition (sound); these are used for the user interface of a general-purpose personal computer.

e) Looking at the response time of the human motor processor, what is the theoretical maximum upper limit to typing speed in words per minute? Assume the average word is five characters. Could a human input information faster?

Answer: According to Card, Moran, and Newell's experiments the motor processor response is 70 msec, that is, just over 14 keys per second. This gives a typing speed of 171 words per minute. Fast professional typists can sustain up to 140 words per minute.

Although this is the (theoretical) limit for tactical input, you could choose another input method such as speech. However, speaking 171 words a minute would probably be extremely difficult to maintain, if not impossible. The catch is that the human does not need to speak that fast to be able to input at a faster rate. Dragon Systems, the makers of the Naturally Speaking voice recognition software, have developed a product that you use like a tape recorder or dictation machine. It is then hooked up to the computer and is able to input the speech at a far faster rate than you could speak it.

LAB 3.1 SELF-REVIEW QUESTIONS

In order to test your progress, you should be able to answer the following questions.

1) According to Card, Moran, and Newell's experiments, how many characters is the human eye aware of?

   a) _____ ca. 7
   b) _____ ca. 10
   c) _____ ca. 17
   d) _____ ca. 25

2) The three kinds of memory are which of the following?

   a) _____ Short-term sensory stores, cognative memory, and long-term memory
   b) _____ Short-term sensory stores, working memory, and long-term memory
   c) _____ Tactical, visual, auditory
   d) _____ Perceptual, motor, cognitive

3) What are the three subsystems of the "human processor" as developed by Card, Moran, and Newell (1983)?

   a) _____ Tactical, visual, auditory
   b) _____ Short-term, long term, cognitive
   c) _____ Perceptual, cognitive, motor
   d) _____ Perceptual, cognitive, sensory

4) Which of the following is not a human input channel?

   a) _____ Vision
   b) _____ Audition
   c) _____ Temporal
   d) _____ Olfactory
   e) _____ Touch

Quiz answers appear in the Appendix, Section 3.1.

LAB 3.2

INTERACTION DEVICES

LAB OBJECTIVES

After this lab, you will be able to:

✔ Identify the Range of Input and Output Devices for Interaction
✔ Compare the Different Interaction Devices

After understanding human characteristics, we need to turn our attention to computer hardware. We assume readers are familiar with the fundamental computer components of processor, main memory, data buses, hard drive memory, and network connectors. In this lab, we concentrate on the hardware devices used by humans to interact with the computer. Such devices are called *interaction devices*. Most interaction devices split naturally into input and output peripherals (as viewed from the computer). Input devices predominate, with the occasional example of a peripheral that is both an input and an output device such as the force-feedback joystick.

Where user interface designers are part of a team responsible for constructing both the hardware and software, the information in this lab can be used to specify the most suitable collection of interaction devices. Most user interface design, however, takes place in a situation where the interaction devices are fixed, for example, the general-purpose personal computer.

INPUT AND OUTPUT

We can distinguish different types of information as being input or output, depending on the task being undertaken. Information input comes in two forms:

- Control input—user selects the action to be performed via user interface controls
- Data input—user specifies new information object(s), which may replace or add to existing objects

For the output case, we categorize two types:

- Information only—information for the user to interpret, which will not necessarily elicit a(n) (immediate) response
- Information prompt—information that requests further input from the user (and constrains other actions)

Obviously, user interface designers need to determine which type of input or output is being used at each interaction and use appropriate user interface controls so that the user is informed.

Similarly, we can categorize interaction devices to aid in selecting the appropriate device, where there is a choice. The interaction device categories are listed in Table 3.4.

Today, the list of interaction devices is long and still growing. Some examples of more recent additions are a pen with an associated pressure-sensitive screen in personal digital assistants and an infrared remote control used like a mouse for large-screen presentations. Interaction devices that are widely available are presented in Table 3.5.

Table 3.4 ■ Task Types for Interaction Devices

Type	Information Returned
Locator	Screen location corresponding to the position of a device
Valuator	The direction and speed
Button	The code of a button currently being depressed
Pick	The graphic object currently being pointed at
Keyboard	A block of concatenated characters

Table 3.5 ■ Interaction Devices

Input	Output

• Keyboard
• Pointing devices
  Mouse
  Trackball
  Joystick
  Pen
  Graphics tablet
  Finger (touch screen)
• Voice Input
  Sound Card
  Serial Port
• Video/Image Input
  Camera
  Scanner
• Exotic
  Data glove
  Foot input
  Head pointer
	• Screen
	• Printer
	• Plotter
	• Loudspeaker
	• Exotic
	  Eye phones (virtual reality)
	  Force-feedback joystick
	  Braille reader

The choice of device will have a major impact on the usability of the software. Devices must be matched to the physical characteristics of the user. Older people and people with disabilities may have limited movement, which prevents the use of some devices. The tasks to be performed also limit the choice, as Table 3.4 revealed. The environment in which the device is used also plays a major role. Limited or no desk space prevents the use of a mouse; speech input must be used where the user's hands are used for other purposes.

LAB 3.2 EXERCISES

3.2.1 IDENTIFY THE RANGE OF INPUT AND OUTPUT DEVICES FOR INTERACTION

a) Discuss the purpose of a valuator interaction device.

Consider the following two scenarios and discuss whether the output is "information only" or "information prompt."

b) You have clicked a link on a Web browser and the page is being loaded. At the bottom of the screen is a status line indicating how many objects on the pages have already been loaded.

_____

_____

c) You have clicked a link on a Web browser and before the page is loaded, a window pops up where you are to input your user name and password.

_____

_____

3.2.2 COMPARE THE DIFFERENT INTERACTIVE DEVICES

a) Table 3.6 shows a matrix of input devices where the choice is greater. Based on your own experiences (and some logical deductions), fill in the table. Use the following key:

Key: + = Very suitable, 0 = Can be used, – = Not suitable, NA = Not applicable

b) Using the table you just completed for reference, describe two tasks that are suitable for a mouse and a trackball. The first task should better suit the mouse and the second task better suit the trackball.

_____

_____

c) Table 3.5 listed a camera as a video input device type. Discuss what type of applications could use this as input.

_____

_____

Table 3.6 ■ Device Comparison by Task

Characteristic or Task	Touch Screen	Pen	Graphics Tablet	Mouse	Trackball	Joystick	Keyboard
Eye-hand coordination							
View of display							
No parallax							
Input resolution							
Ease of positioning							
Small space							
Less training							
Comfort in long use							
Absolute mode							
Relative mode							
Pointing							
Drawing							
Tracing							
Text entry							

LAB 3.2 EXERCISE ANSWERS

3.2.1 ANSWERS

a) Discuss the purpose of a valuator interaction device.

Answer: A valuator interaction device is a hardware device capable of generating a direction and a weighting. The purpose is typically to measure the change as it is taking place and not the final result.

An example of a valuator interaction device is a joystick. In a typical joystick application (a game), the fact that we are pushing the joystick in a particular direction and by a particular amount is the most significant aspect. We might have a flight simulator program where the direction and amount we push the joystick determines how steeply we climb, for example.

Contrast this to a locator device where the location is the key factor. Although you see a mouse cursor moving across the screen, what is important is the location of the mouse at any given point. You move the mouse and see the cursor move, but the application typically responds when the mouse reaches a particular location. In some applications you need to first click on that location to get the system to react. In other case, simply being over the spot causes the reaction (for example, the onmouseover() function in Javascript).

Consider the following two scenarios and discuss whether the output is "information only" or "information prompt."

b) You have clicked a link on a Web page and the page is being loaded. At the bottom of the screen is a status line indicating how many objects on the pages have already been loaded.

Answer: The information being presented is only to ensure that the Web browser is actually doing its job by loading the pages. Since you are not expected to do anything other than wait until the page has completely loaded, this is for information only.

c) You have clicked a link on a Web page and before the page is loaded, a window pops up where you are to input your user name and password.

Answer: The information being presented is telling you that you have reached a secure area. However, in order for you to proceed you have to provide the further input of your user name and password. Therefore, this is an informational prompt.

Sometimes the boundary between information only and information prompt can be pretty vague. For example, if you were to right-click a link within your browser and select "Save Link As . . . ," you get a message prompting you for the name of the file. In this case, you have an information prompt as the program cannot continue until you either select the default or provide a new name. However, when the download is completed, you may have a new window telling you that the download is complete and you are to press the "OK" button. Granted you must press the button to have the Window disappear, but typically the application will not perform any action afterwards.

The question here is whether this is really information prompt output. Although you are not prevented from doing anything else in the application (the browser in this case), the window itself will not continue (disappear) until you press the button. Since you need that "OK" button, then you probably should consider this information prompt output. That is, the controls you provide along with the information (a button) is different from the status information (no button).

**LAB
3.2**

a) We present some device comparisons by task. This table shows a matrix of input devices where the choice is greater. Based on your own experiences (and some logical deductions) fill in the table. Use the following key:

Key: + = Very suitable, 0 = Can be used, – = Not suitable, NA = Not applicable.

Answer: See the completed Table 3.6a.

When making use of this table, the user interface designer considers each task or characteristic and then looks up the device or devices with high suitability (looks for + signs).

Table 3.6a ■ Device Comparison by Task—Answers

Characteristic or Task	Touch Screen	Pen	Graphics Tablet	Mouse	Trackball	Joystick	Keyboard
Eye-hand coordination	+	+	0	0	0	0	–
View of display	–	–	+	+	+	+	+
No parallax	–	–	+	+	+	+	+
Input resolution	–	–	+	+	+	+	0
Ease of positioning	–	+	0	0	+	+	0
Small space	+	+	–	–	+	+	–
Less training	+	+	0	0	0	0	–
Comfort in long use	–	+	0	0	+	+	0
Absolute mode	+	–	+	–	–	0	NA
Relative mode	–	+	+	+	+	0	NA
Pointing	+	+	+	+	+	–	NA
Drawing	–	+	+	0	–	–	NA
Tracing	–	+	+	–	–	–	NA
Text entry	–	0	–	–	–	–	+

One major principle unites all input devices—every user action must be accompanied by feedback of some kind. The feedback can be visible or audible or both. Of course, output devices are responsible for conveying this feedback to the user.

Visible feedback can take a number of forms. It can be the appearance of a character, symbol, or icon (small image) on the screen or its disappearance. For pointer movement, there must be an equivalent cursor that moves on the screen, synchronized with the pointer device. Audible feedback can be a single beep or any appropriate sound of short duration. Even mechanical movement in the form of vibration can be used for feedback with keyboards, Braille readers, and other force feedback devices.

Not only must feedback occur every time, but it also must occur in a very short time. In other words, the feedback must be immediate. To fit in with Card, Moran, and Newell's model, immediate means about 200 ms, that is, within a fifth of a second. The user interface design must guarantee this immediacy, even to the extent of putting up temporary feedback if the action itself will not complete until a long time has elapsed.

As the resolution and refresh rates of screens and graphics cards improve, it is increasingly possible to include animation effects in the output of information and feedback. Animation can be used to convey additional information on relative movement, the severity of feedback, and the magnitude of information generally. The user's eye can be drawn to particular parts of the user interface that might be missed without animation. Three-dimensional animated user interfaces are in their infancy but are set to play a major role in the advanced user interfaces of the future. To exploit such user interface designs, the HCI specialist will have to add multimedia skills to his or her experience.

b) Using the table you just completed for reference, describe two tasks that are suitable for a mouse and a trackball. The first task should better suit the mouse and the second task better suit the trackball.

Answer: The first task might be drawing—trackball is totally unsuitable here since the human finger cannot adequately roll the ball to control both x and y directions at the same time. The second task might be use in a small space—although the mouse can be used in very limited space, the trackball is superior.

c) Table 3.5 listed a camera as a video input device type. Discuss what type of applications could use this as input.

Answer: The most straightforward example is video processing. Many vendors provide expansion cards that allow you to hook up a video source, some of which are on the same card as that to which you connect your monitor. The video source is read in and can then be manipulated using some product like Adobe's Premiere. Since the connection is bidirectional, you can output the video either to the screen or onto tape.

Another example would be in security systems. Using the technique of biometrics (body measurement), certain characteristics of your body can be recorded and the compared later when you wish to gain access to a secure area, for example. Common implementations include finger and palm prints, as well as facial characteristics.

Just as police use fingers to identify people, so can computers. What we remember from old movies where the police find specific curves in the fingerprints to match against the suspect's fingers has now become outdated. Instead, police look for places the fingerprints start, end, or split. It is then fairly straightforward to locate these points either by the human eye or a video camera connected to a computer.

Taking this concept one step further, similar techniques can be used to identify a person's face, for example, the ratio between the length of the nose and the width of the eyes. Although these two comparisons are the same for many people, combining it with other comparisons and other characteristics can uniquely identify a person. (For example, a mole on the right cheek, at an angle of 103° and 2 cm from the corner of the right nostril.) In fact, this technique can identify specific people in a crowded room.

LAB 3.2 SELF-REVIEW QUESTIONS

In order to test your progress, you should be able to answer the following questions.

1) Hardware devices used by humans to input information into a computer are also called "interaction devices."

   a) _____ True
   b) _____ False

2) A joystick is an interaction device that falls into the category of both input and output devices.

   a) _____ True
   b) _____ False

3) Which of these are the task types for interaction devices?

   a) _____ Movement, Momentum, Button, Pick, Keyboard
   b) _____ Movement, Locator, Button, Pick, Keyboard
   c) _____ Locator, Momentum, Button, Pick, Keyboard
   d) _____ Locator, Valuator, Button, Pick, Keyboard

4) Input comes in what two forms?

    a) _____ Information and data
    b) _____ Control and data
    c) _____ Control and tactile
    d) _____ Information and tactile

5) Output comes in what two forms?

    a) _____ Information only and information prompt
    b) _____ Information only and information presention
    c) _____ Information control and information value
    d) _____ information prompt and information control

Quiz answers appear in the Appendix, Section 3.2.

**LAB
3.2**

LAB 3.3

DIALOG STYLES

> ## LAB OBJECTIVES
>
> After this lab, you will be able to:
>
> ✔ Understand Basic Concepts of Dialogs
> ✔ Identify the Range of Dialog Styles

For the most part, we can think of HCI as being like human-to-human dialog—a process of communication between two or more intelligent beings. We won't speculate here as to whether the intelligence is equal on both sides! Nevertheless, we can be guided to some extent by the dialogs between humans.

Human-to-human communication includes spoken words and signals, written words and images, and gestures and touch. This dialog involves two main concepts:

- Exchange of symbols between parties
- Meanings assigned by the various participants to these symbols

There are a number of concepts we need to bear in mind when discussing dialogs. To start with, the fundamental semantics of symbols are not sufficient—different people apply sometimes quite different meanings to the same symbol. These differences result from a number of factors including culture, social contexts, and education. In the context of the communication, the users' knowledge structures and the context of communication are as equally important as the symbols themselves. A study of this aspect of communication is called pragmatics.

When designing the human-computer dialog, we must be aware of components of the information exchange:

- Style: The character and control of the information interchange
- Structure: The parts and ordering of the dialog elements
- Content: The user's understanding of the information exchanged

Control of the dialog plays the principal role in the design of the user interface.

TYPES OF DIALOG

Put simply, an interaction dialog type (or style) is a method for prompting and getting control input from users. Different dialog types for the sequence control of tasks and subtasks should be chosen based on the level of user training required and a tolerable system response speed. For a system to remain acceptable to users, the interaction style dictated by the dialog type must adapt to different classes of users (often the same users gaining experience) and to different devices.

There are a number of ways to divide up the spectrum of dialog types. We have chosen to split the spectrum into five categories:

1. Structured command language
2. Question and answer
3. Form filling
4. Menu selection
5. Direct manipulation

It is usual to implement more than one dialog type, one for experts and one for novices. Each of the standard dialog types allows variations of input conventions and appearances. The variations may be parameterized, but the essential structure of each dialog type remains the same.

LAB 3.3 EXERCISES

3.3.1 UNDERSTAND BASIC CONCEPTS OF DIALOGS

a) Communication can only occur when all of the parties involved have common "language" in which they can apply the information being transmitted. Discuss the main concepts that are involved in communication and what problems need to be considered.

_____

_____

b) In a human-computer dialog, explain the roles of style, structure, and content.

_____

_____

3.3.2 IDENTIFY THE RANGE OF DIALOG STYLES

**LAB
3.3**

a) Command language is the oldest and still the most commonly used dialog style. Such languages originated with the need to command operating systems to carry out sequences of tasks or jobs. What features do structured command languages provide and what advantages/disadvantages do they have?

_____

_____

b) Many programs provide the user with a series of questions and await answers in order to perform their required function. Discuss the kinds of applications where this method is used and discuss the advantages and disadvantages.

_____

_____

c) Form-filling dialogs are considered a more "modern" approach, allowing several varied inputs per interaction. Discuss the kinds of applications where this method is used and discuss the advantages and disadvantages.

_____

_____

d) Menu selection allows users to select from a list of alternatives. Discuss the kinds of applications where this method is used and discuss the advantages and disadvantages.

_____

_____

e) Menus in graphic applications present a unique set of problems. Discuss these problems and how a developer would address them.

_____

_____

f) Although menus are very useful, having to take your hands from the keyboard to operate the mouse can become a burden. Discuss how menu acceleration addresses this problem.

_____

_____

g) Direct manipulation is where the data or object is manipulated directly. Discuss how this could be accomplished and what the advantages and disadvantages are.

_____

_____

LAB 3.3 EXERCISE ANSWERS

3.3.1 ANSWERS

a) Communication can only occur when all of the parties involved have common "language" in which they can apply the information being transmitted. Discuss the main concepts that are involved in communication and what problems need to be considered.

Answer: Communication involves the exchange of symbols. For humans, these symbols can be things we normally consider as symbols, such as words that represent certain ideas or even the color red to represent danger or a warning. Although transmitting the symbols between the participants, no communication takes place unless the meaning assigned to the symbols are agreed upon by all parties. If not, either no communication takes place or, at worst, the communication is actually misunderstood.

One of my favorite examples of misunderstanding symbols involves a statement by Nikita Khrushchev, who was premier of the Soviet Union when John F. Kennedy was

President. He said, "We will bury you." This was taken as a very hostile, aggressive comment. People assumed that Khrushchev and the USSR would overrun us, beat us in a war, or any number of things that meant something aggressive. Instead, it comes from an old Russian saying, whereby Khrushchev was simply implying that the USSR would outlive (not attack) the US. We understood the words (symbols) of what Khrushchev was saying, but without the correct context we did not have true understanding.

Another of my favorite examples comes directly from software. I have received messages from programs that ask "Are you sure you really want to exit?" I am then presented with the choices "Continue" and "Quit." What does this mean? Does "Continue" mean to continue the program or continue exiting? Does "Quit" mean quitting the process of exiting or really quitting the program? Here again, the symbols (words) are known but what is really meant is unclear.

b) In a human-computer dialog, explain the roles of style, structure, and content.

Answer: Style defines one of the five possible dialog styles. Structure refers to the parts and ordering of elements of the dialog. The two parties must both understand the content of the dialog elements.

3.3.2 ANSWERS

a) Command language is the oldest and still the most commonly used dialog style. Such languages originated with the need to command operating systems to carry out sequences of tasks or jobs. What features do structured command languages provide and what advantages do they have?

Answer. Structured command languages are essentially program executions with parameters specifying data inputs and outputs. Commands in the language are designed to provide a close link between the user's work context and the notation. Command language also emulates familiar human-human communication. The sequence is first to issue the command, then observe the outcome, and then respond according to the perceived success or failure of the command.

Perhaps the most significant advantage with a structured command languages is that they provide more direct, specific control over a program or system. This can be something as mundane as changing the permission on a file, but can be more complicated such as removing all temporary files older than 30 days or starting a full backup of your system. Another advantage is the ability to integrate structured command languages into your own automation or repeated tasks more easily than with other methods.

The most significant disadvantage is that there are often a large number of options, which can be overwhelming for the beginner. The options and the command names can be cryptic, making them hard to remember.

Structured command languages are not going to go away in the foreseeable future. They are an integral part of many systems such as operating systems, computer-aided manufacturing, and so forth. Plus the advantages they currently provide over other input methods far outweigh the disadvantages. Other advantages include:

- *The ability to perform tasks relevant to the user's tasks*

- *Flexibility for novice and expert users*

- *Compatibility with existing language notations*

Like any language, a command language must be learned so that a user can instruct the machine to carry out tasks. In some cases, this allows only skilled users to compose commands. However, many systems, such as the Linux operating system, have programs that specifically address this issue. Instead of just single character options, which are available on most other systems, Linux commands provide for longer options, which are more easily remembered and understood.

Command languages are designed to emulate human-human conversation. The usage sequence is:

1. *Command issued*
2. *Observe the outcome*
3. *If outcome expected, issue next command*
4. *If outcome unexpected, adopt new strategy depending on outcome*

To be successful in this dialog, the user must recall the correct notation and be capable of initiating creative action, that is, composing the command. Both of these tasks are difficult and prone to inaccuracy. In addition, the user must also be able to understand any messages, whether they indicate problems or successful completion of the program. This means the programmers need to ensure the program produces intelligible output. I am constantly annoyed by messages I have seen in the system logs of Microsoft Windows NT where they say something along the lines of "The command could not be executed due to an unexpected condition: The command completed successfully." Is it really unexpected that the command completes successfully? This is a case where the programmer did not interpret the result of an error message correctly and thereby produced a message that was confusing to the user.

Obviously, command language design is a skill in its own right. Commenting on the unsuitability of natural language, Charles Babbage says:

> *I soon felt that the forms of ordinary language were far too diffuse ... I was not long in deciding that the most favourable path ... [was] to contrive a notation which ought, if possible, to be at once simple and expressive, easily understood at the*

**LAB
3.3**

commencement, and capable of being readily retained in the memory. (Schneiderman, 1992)

The typical command language notation is the verb—noun phrase, possibly augmented with arguments for the verb (action) or noun (object). At every stage in the command language design, there are a number of important features to be taken into account:

- *Model of objects and actions*

- *Macros/procedures*

- *Prompting*

- *Error messages*

- *Command structures*

- *Naming and abbreviation*

We find command languages at almost every turn in most major operating systems and software suites. There are the multitude of command languages in Unix (shells), the batch commands of MS DOS, and even the command level in Microsoft Windows NT. Office suites and graphical design packages have their macro languages, which come close to programming languages. On the Web, we see pages containing scripts expressed in extensions of command languages.

Database management has its own special command language. A special case of command language allows users to request information from databases using the Structure Query Language, SQL. Such is the complexity of SQL that users struggle with the correct syntax. It is not surprising that visual SQL query design tools now proliferate to aid users to construct correct SQL.

User queries in help systems and online search engines attempt to use another special variant of command language, natural language itself. Ostensibly, a user's natural language allows untrained users to speak or type inputs. However, after decades of effort we know that natural language is very difficult to implement. Usually this enormous task of translating natural language limits its use to very simplified forms. Remember that when humans converse they speak in half sentences, skip words, interrupt one another once the message is understood, and utter single words that have special meaning in a particular context. Reproducing such behavior in a natural language interpreter has so far proved elusive.

b) Many programs provide the user with a series of questions and await answers in order to perform their required function. Discuss the kinds of applications where this method is required and discuss the advantages and disadvantages.

Answer: This dialog style is very common in character-based applications and installation programs. Character-based programs do not have the luxury of a graphical input, so this is the only method available to them. The dialog style is also suited to simple interactions with untrained users or elucidating input from a single important question as part of another dialog type.

The key advantage is that the programmer can guide the user along, following the necessary steps in the right order and thereby avoiding mistakes. In addition, this method is obviously a requirement on systems that do not have a graphical interface. Installation programs use this method as the questions often need to be asked in particular order or the program needs to ensure that all of the questions are answered.

One major problem is that a great many programs of this type do not allow the user any chance of backing up, depending on the environment where they are used. This usually means that if the user makes a mistake, he or she must start over from the beginning. A solution would be to temporarily store the answers for later retrieval. Often, there is no easy solution to this problem without using other dialog styles.

When using this simple dialog style, the most important rule to remember is always give the user a terminate option. This allows a possibly long sequence of questions and answers to be cancelled by the user at any time. I also believe that as much of the actual work needs to wait until all of the questions are answered just in case the user decides to quit. This helps avoid conflicts should the user restart the program later.

In addition, since it emulates a common form of human-to-human dialog, this is regarded as a "natural" interaction. Consider an exchange with your doctor, "Where does it hurt?" then "What kind of pain is it?" then "Does it hurt when you do this?"

c) Form-filling dialogs are considered more "modern" approach, allowing several, varied inputs per interaction. Discuss the kinds of applications where this method is used and discuss the advantages and disadvantages.

Answer: Form filling is well-suited to tasks where many values must be seen at one time or when the input of the information does not need to be in any specific order. For example, a registration form where you fill in all of your personal information. Humans are used to filling in paper forms. Emulating the paper form for a user interface makes it instantly recognizable.

One major advantage is the simple input method for the user. Users are already familiar with forms and do not always fill them out in a particular order. This makes it a "natural" interaction for literate users. Other benefits are that all prompts (field names) are visible and help is available on the same screen.

This input method requires a lot more work on the part of the developer. Some conventions are needed for interfield navigation that must be learned by users. From the user interface implementers' standpoint, interfield validation is necessary for each value entered into a field. Most importantly, checks for noncompletion must be included and a suitable mechanism put in place for informing users of input inconsistencies.

A full-fledged form consists of a unique identity, a title, some help text, and a series of fields. A field consists of an identifier, a prompt, some help text with information about the value to be entered into the field, such as the data type, the range, a default value, display attributes, and the entry and exit conditions (validation). You will see quickly that designing form user interfaces is a complex task.

We should also mention here the great success of the spreadsheet user interface, which is a cousin of form filling. Spreadsheets, too, mimic the accountant's ledger in a natural way. In a spreadsheet user interface, the form field names are derived from the row and column names of a regular grid. This leaves more screen space for the data values. Spreadsheets have a dual nature in that the cell values are used for both input and display. The spreadsheet user interface is regarded as one of the most valuable gems in all of user interface design.

Filling in forms is such a natural interface that it is not surprising to find it was the first interactive user interface to be implemented in Web pages. Coupled with a small set of powerful form user interface components, Web forms are flexible and powerful. Their use has always suffered from the complexities of writing CGI scripts to support their use at the Web server.

d) Menu selection allows users to select from a list of alternatives. Discuss the kinds of applications where this method is used and discuss the advantages and disadvantages.

Answer: Menu selections are useful in applications where you have a number of different possible inputs, but the inputs are limited in number. For example, a company's Web site might have a menu of the various departments. You have a choice of which department you want, but the choice is limited.

The benefits of using menus are many, and it is not surprising that this dialog category has become the interaction style of choice. Because of this universal adoption, users need little training and may easily use the system infrequently without loss of productivity. By scanning the menus, the user can receive help with the terminology of a particular application. Since the menus correspond directly with the tasks and subtasks that an application supports, users are aided in structuring their decision-making process.

Menus are also of great benefit to novice users. The menus are shown on the screen and do not require memorization by users.

There are few problems with menus. The major problem is designing the structure of complex menus, which have many options, in a manner that is intelligible to the user.

A menu is similar to a form and consists of an identity, a title, help text, and a series of options or menu items. Each item might have a title, a selector string or method, and an action to be taken if that item is selected. Menu selection is well suited to interac-

tions with untrained or occasional users as it avoids extensive learning and memorization of complex command sequences.

Menu structure plays a major role in aiding user understanding. Lessons can be learned from printed "menu" styles such as restaurant menus. However, screen space has traditionally been limited, leading to a need to structure menus into submenus in a tree structure. Effective menu selection requires careful user interface design. The important issues are:

- *Semantic organization and grouping*

- *Menu system structure*

- *Number of menu items*

- *Menu sequencing and shortcuts*

- *Selection mechanism*

- *Layout, phrasing, format, and graphics*

- *Online help*

Early visual display devices were only capable of displaying lines of characters. Menus in this environment consist of numbered lines, each containing a menu item. To select an item, the user types the corresponding number. With a GUI, we have a choice of several menu types:

- *Pull-down menus reveal a vertical list of menu items when the user clicks on the menu title. Clicking on a menu item selects it.*

- *Pop-up menus reveal a vertical list of menu items when the user employs a special click sequence (right mouse button or hold down single mouse button) anywhere on the screen (or major portion of it).*

- *Pull-aside menus result in an additional vertical list of menu items when the user clicks on a specially marked menu item from a pull-down or pop-up menu item list.*

- *Toolbar menus are arrays of icons or tools, each representing a menu item. When the cursor moves over a tool, a tool tip box containing a text menu item is revealed.*

Modern GUI applications will typically use all of these menu types in combination.

Menu organization and grouping involve the clustering of features around tasks and subtasks that the users undertake. A task analysis, discussed in Lab 3.5, will provide the grouping of the top-level menu items. The user interface designer then must decide upon the ordering and structure of the lower level menu items.

Experimental parameters from the model human information processor and experience over a number of years have resulted in some simple rules for menu design. The question of structure reduces to how many items should appear in each menu and how many menus must be traversed to reach a particular menu item—i.e., menu breadth versus depth. Early research indicated that you should restrict menu item choice at any stage to a small subset of items using the rule of 7±2. More recent research indicates that broad, shallow menus are what most users prefer.

Modern thinking guides us to design menus so that:

- *At each level the number of items is large enough for the user to scan but not so large that the screen is cluttered or confusing.*

- *The menu has sufficient levels to split the task into manageable subtasks but avoid long, boring submenu sequences.*

- *Order each list by meaningful category names into a logical sequence perceived by most users.*

Other rules relate to the expected frequency of use of menu items. Frequently used items should be placed near the top of the hierarchy. Infrequently used items, or those items intended for expert users, should be relegated to lower menu levels.

e) Menus in graphic applications present a unique set of problems. Discuss these problems and how a developer would address them.

Answer: The biggest problem is the level of complexity that menus in a graphical application have. Typically, you are presented with all of the menus at once. However, depending on the state of the application at any given time, many of the menu items may not make sense. The developer needs to address this problem.

One way is to eliminate menu entries not appropriate to the current state. This has the problem of causing the position of the menu entries to change, which cause the user to search for the appropriate entry, thereby wasting time. Alternatively, the menu entry could be "grayed out." The position of the menu entry remains the same, but may cause confusion as the user asks why he or she cannot use that entry.

With limited space, we present two examples of menus from the Microsoft Word 2000 application. This very recent application shows the trends in GUI menu design at a high level of sophistication. Several other software packages could have been selected. When we come to consider Web page user interfaces, we will see the lack of menus as a major omission.

Menu design for GUI applications has become very sophisticated. Figure 3.2 shows part of a screen dump from Microsoft Word 2000. Note that the top-level menus, the pull-down titles File, Edit, View, and so on, are nine in number. The pulled-down Edit menu

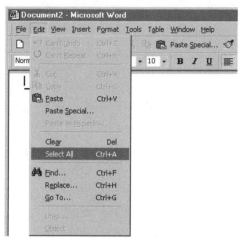

Figure 3.2 ■ Menu Screen Fragment from Microsoft Word 2000

has fourteen menu items, some of them grayed out. Note the specification of shortcut keys for some menu items. At the left of some menu items, such as **Paste,** *we see a small icon that you will see repeated on the toolbar below the pulldown menu bar. There is a growing trend to implement toolbars that repeat the capabilities of menus.*

We will see later that using an application that appears to operate in a single mode allows users to be more productive. Modeless operation dictates, however, that some menu items may not be available for selection in order to impose appropriate sequencing on tasks. It is necessary to indicate these unavailable items in some way. The method of "graying out" unavailable options has two very substantial advantages:

- *Menu lengths remain constant allowing users to learn menu item "positions" thus reducing search time*

- *Users are made aware of all the options that are available, thus becoming conversant with the full potential of the system*

We saw earlier on in our discussion the importance of feedback. This applies equally to menu selection. A feedback mechanism indicating the menu item selected is essential. Highlighting the menu item under the cursor has become the universal feedback for menus.

Another benefit of GUI menus is having the menu bar visible. This allows it to indicate the current settings where "on-off" options are involved. Tick marks or other suitable characters can be used as well as italicizing, making bold, or outlining the text. Graphic symbols or icons can also be used in menus to indicate the current status of a setting.

Other new trends in menu design are shown in Figure 3.3, another example from Microsoft Word 2000. First, it shows the pull-aside menu for **Background.** *In this case, the* *third-level menu contains much more than just text items. We see an array of buttons. In general, other user interface components controls can be present such as slider controls and the like.*

Building sophisticated menus as shown in Figure 3.3 requires considerable effort on be-half of user interface designers. Not surprisingly, specialist software tools are now available to the designers to construct the menus, visualize them, and allow for amendment and extension as the development progresses.

f) Although menus are very useful, having to take your hands from the keyboard to operate the mouse can become a burden. Discuss how menu acceleration addresses this problem.

Answer: For typical office applications, or any application that makes full use of the keyboard, moving the hand from the keyboard to the mouse is a time-consuming operation. Providing key equivalents for common menu items is essential.

We noted the use of shortcut keys to provide an alternative method of selecting menu items. This is a vital facility to keep expert users satisfied.

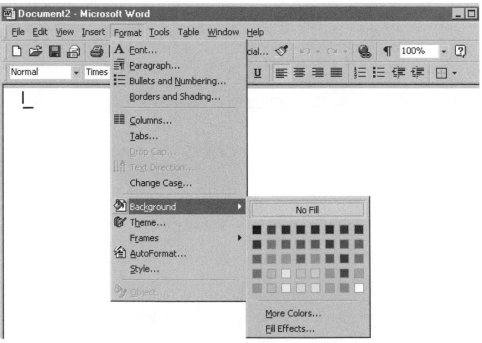

Figure 3.3 ■ Another Example Menu from Microsoft Word 2000

The key shortcut approach has a number of advantages. First, no single selection method is imposed on users, and they can switch between methods to suit themselves. Experienced users are provided with a shortcut, and the accelerator option is displayed alongside the visible option. On the other hand, it is not a completely ideal solution. Because of the limited number of keys on a keyboard, the key used often bears no memorable connection with the menu item, and not all accelerators are standard across all applications. Of course, this latter problem is similar to the diversity of commands in different command languages.

g) Direct manipulation is where the data or object is manipulated directly. Discuss how this could be accomplished and what the advantages and disadvantages are.

Answer: Direct manipulation is only possible within a GUI, and it represents the most major advance in human-computer communication using human vision and motor reflexes. Because of this, direct manipulation is often referred to as the point-and-click *or* drag-and-drop user interface.

In most situations, direct manipulation leaves the user in control of the dialog, thus giving the user a feeling of empowerment, which is one of the key advantages. For example, the user drags the file onto the email program to send it as an attachment as compared to opening up a dialog via a menu or shortcut key. Contrast this to the subservient user role with command languages—the user issues a request (command) to the operating system and waits to see if it is actioned or not.

One of the more stunning benefits of direct manipulation is the elimination of whole classes of errors. In a file storage management interface, you cannot request the deletion of a nonexistent file; this is perfectly possible in a command language dialog. You cannot select an inappropriate action since it will be grayed out. Selection of inappropriate objects is impossible since they won't respond to the selection request.

The biggest disadvantage is the limited scope of the control. You typically perform just a single action. There are no options to change the behavior.

The early GUI experiments in the 1970s aimed at a new type of user interface that would give the following benefits:

- *Novices can learn basic functionality quickly.*
- *Experts can work extremely rapidly.*
- *Intermittent users can retain operational concepts.*
- *Error messages are rarely needed.*
- *Users can immediately see if their actions are furthering their goals.*
- *Users have reduced anxiety because of reversibility.*

The direct engagement at the user interface provides the user with a feeling of confidence resulting from the perception of control. The user interface is designed to enable all commands and associated data to be represented in such a way as to be controllable with the mouse. The keyboard is only used when text must be input.

To carry out a task with direct manipulation, the basic functionality, a user performs two actions: select an object or objects and action the task to be performed.

Except in simplified browsing user interfaces, selecting an object requires a single mouse click, while dragging selects multiple objects, depending on the application. Selection feedback requires the object(s) to be highlighted in some way—usually by inverting the colors. Actioning the task either means selecting a menu item or dragging the selected object(s) over another object in the user interface. Once learned, this basic selection-with-feedback functionality applies to all similar applications using direct manipulation. Even if a long period of time elapses until next use, this functionality is so simple it is easily remembered.

With direct manipulation, the task outcomes will be visible immediately. Deleted objects disappear, amended objects remain, and newly created ones appear. Progressive feedback appears for long-running actions.

We should also mention the reversibility benefit of direct manipulation. This benefit is actually independent of the user interface to be used. It simply refers to the ability to undo any user action. We see parallels to this idea in the rollback facilities of database management systems. Reversibility can be incorporated into any software such that the current state of data structures is copied before each action. If the action must be undone, the data structures are returned to their previous state. This is a simple concept but difficult to implement efficiently without resorting to copying every data structure in the application every time an action is performed. The need for reversibility and its beneficial impact on the user interface came out of detailed studies of user behavior.

Forms were added to allow a degree of interactivity. Increasingly, Web pages are becoming the user interface for interactive Web applications. The lack of any support for GUI menus is immediately noticeable. Likewise, direct manipulation and keyboard shortcuts are also missing. These omissions punch big holes into any claim that Web page front-end user interfaces can equate to freestanding applications. It is not surprising that attempts to extend the Web page user interface with the missing features have received strong support. Plug-ins, Java applets, and ActiveX controls all fill the feature gap to a greater or lesser extent. Unfortunately, these solutions are browser or platform specific and do not offer a globally acceptable solution. However, the dynamic HTML document object model, which is available in the latest browsers, is starting to offer browser-independent solutions to this problem.

LAB 3.3 SELF-REVIEW QUESTIONS

In order to test your progress, you should be able to answer the following questions.

1) Communication occurs when the symbols are received.

    a) _____ True
    b) _____ False

2) Direct manipulation is usually composed of just two steps: select an object or objects and action the task to be performed.

    a) _____ True
    b) _____ False

3) Which dialog style was the earliest to be used when humans interacted with computers?

    a) _____ Structured command language
    b) _____ Question and answer
    c) _____ Form filling
    d) _____ Menu selection
    e) _____ Direct manipulation

4) What is another name for a menu accelerator?

    a) _____ Keyboard link
    b) _____ Menu link
    c) _____ Keyboard shortcut
    d) _____ Menu shortcut

5) Which are generally considered "natural" dialog methods?

    a) _____ Structured command and menus
    b) _____ Structured command and form filling
    c) _____ Menus and form filling
    d) _____ Structured command and direct manipulation

6) Because screen space is normally limited, which structure is used for menus?

    a) _____ Web
    b) _____ Multi-level
    c) _____ Linear list
    d) _____ Tree

Quiz answers appear in the Appendix, Section 3.3.

LAB
3.3

L A B   3 . 4

DESIGNING WITH
USER MODELS

> ## LAB OBJECTIVES
>
> After this lab, you will be able to:
>
> ✔ Understand the Different Types of Models Used in HCI

Since the user is the critical component of HCI, we must not only know the physical characteristics of humans but we must also be aware of their mental activities. Once we decide what information is to be presented in the user interface, we must have mechanisms for predicting how the users will react to the user interface design. To accomplish this, we form models of the users and use these models during the fundamental user interface design.

In turn, users form *mental pictures* or models of the system they are using. As user interface designers, we construct the user interface layout and actions to present a particular system model that we hope is the same one the users construct in their minds. To aid this process, we use examples from the real world or the users' own physical work environments.

We know there are limitations to all models of reality, so there should always be a final evaluation stage for all user interface designs. Real users participate in this evaluation and do not always agree with the predictions of the models. Evaluation is covered in a later lab in this unit.

MENTAL MODELS

Mental models are used to explain how a person acts when faced with new situations. This is exactly the context in which users new to an interactive application find themselves. When people recognize a familiar part of the context, they can call on experience to make assumptions about that context. When the context is entirely new, they look for guidance from a number of other sources.

Norman (1988) defines a mental model as "the model people have of themselves, others, the environment, and the things with which they interact. People form mental models through experience, training and instruction." Having built our mental model of a context, we can then decide what actions to take.

There are problems with mental model formation. The context may contain several familiar pieces, but these pieces may not naturally fit together. Our tendency is to hone in on a subset of the familiar pieces and form a partial mental model. Note that several partial models are now possible, none of which may be accurate. The models are often inconsistent because little time was spent in their formation. Another disturbing finding is that the mental models vary with time, mood, and previous experience.

**LAB
3.4**

Despite the drawbacks, this is how people behave. We need to take this into account when designing user interfaces. We must be aware of the conventions of our users, not the developers. If our user interface ignores these conventions, then explicit indications of this must be incorporated into our design. This will help in preventing the users from forming an incorrect mental model.

To this point we have talked of people in general. We know that people can vary significantly. We must take account of these differences, which can depend on sex, physical capabilities, age, stress, fatigue, and intellectual capacity. Our user interface design may explicitly exclude some user groupings. It is always a good idea to take into account users who are under pressure, feeling unwell, or preoccupied by other concerns.

USER MODELS

Since it is commonly used in verbal dialog, the metaphor is familiar to most users. We can exploit this fact when designing user interfaces by employing metaphors from the real world. This will help in deciding on a range of terminology that must be exposed in the user interface in menus, labels, titles, and named objects.

CONCEPTUAL MODELS

More general than mental models, the modern approach to user interface design uses conceptual models—that is, the way systems are conceptualized. Here we are concerned with how user interface designs are perceived and interpreted by different people. In particular, conceptual models are constructed for the user, the actual software, and the designers. We are very interested in comparing the user's conceptual model (user model) with the designers' conceptual model (design model). If these two models coincide, then the designers have done well.

Unfortunately, there is often a third major variable to muddy the waters. When documentation and online help are produced, the technical writers effectively produce another view of the system (system image). Bringing the user model, design model, and system image into line is extremely difficult, but must be attempted if a usable system is to be produced.

Another problem, even when there is good overlap between all the conceptual models, is that the model may not solve the user's task needs. How many times have we persisted with a software package trying to accomplish a task, only to fail at the end?

LAB 3.4 EXERCISES

3.4.1 UNDERSTAND THE DIFFERENT TYPES OF MODELS USED IN HCI

a) How do we use mental models when designing a user interface?

_____

_____

b) What metaphor does the spreadsheet employ? Why is it so effective?

_____

_____

c) Working in a familiar environment is necessary for most people. Discuss how the behavior of a word processor compares to the familiar typewriter in helping the user to work. What problems can arise?

d) Consider the metaphor of any common graphical operating environment. What metaphor is used? What familiar symbols are used to bring across this metaphor? Are there problems with this metaphor?

e) There are other metaphors that have found their way into successful user interfaces. Create a list of applications and the possible metaphors that could be used, along with the knowledge this implies.

LAB 3.4

LAB 3.4 EXERCISE ANSWERS

3.4.1 ANSWERS

a) How do we use mental models when designing a user interface?

Answer: We use mental models to explain how people react in new situations by calling upon experiences from the real world. In user interface design, we work to bring familiar situations to most aspects of the design.

b) What metaphor does the spreadsheet employ? Why is it so effective?

Answer: From Table 3.7 (see the answer to question e) we see that a spreadsheet employs the accountant's ledger sheet as its metaphor. This is a particularly simple metaphor with many direct links to the tasks being performed with a spreadsheet. This is a good example of the maxim "simple metaphors work best."

c) Working in a familiar environment is necessary for most people. Discuss how the behavior of a word processor compares to the familiar typewriter in helping the user to work. What problems can arise?

Answer: Perhaps the first obvious link is the keyboard, which appears very similar to that on a typewriter. Pressing a key in the word processor makes it appear on the screen. For conventional typing line after line, the mental model holds good, even for someone under pressure. Even pressing the backspace key keeps the mental model's accuracy. Pressing the return/enter key also has a familiar effect in that the cursor moves down a line and then back to the start of the line.

Perhaps the biggest problem is the complexity of the new environment. Although you are not likely to find someone who uses correction fluid to make corrections, how you edit the existing text is something that needs to be taught. Since the basic editing functions with cursor keys and mouse don't exist on the typewriter, new instructions on editing will have to be given to the user.

A similar problem occurs with people when working with Web-based applications. I see so many people who are used to moving with the cursor. They click on a link with the mouse, then click in the "Back" button, click on another link, and so on. In order to use the interface more efficiently they need to be taught about movement with the keyboard, for example.

d) Consider the metaphor of any common graphical operating environment. What metaphor is used? What familiar symbols are used to bring across this metaphor? Are there problems with this metaphor?

Answer: The most common metaphor used for a graphical operating environment is the desktop. You have your documents, which you place in a filing cabinet. Documents that you wish to throw away are placed in a trash can. Once the users have recognized the familiar objects from the real world, they are in a position to make decisions on how to interact with the icons.

The problem arises as to how additional features can be added to the user interface where there is no equivalent in the real-life metaphor. For example, how is searching a document for the occurrence of a word or phrase to be added to the desktop metaphor? There is no easy answer since there is no such facility on the manual desktop.

In the latter case, a user interface designer has to resort to combining two or more metaphors in the same design. Often, the designer introduces new abstract metaphors for the very new features. These, of course, must be fully tested to determine whether the users form a suitable mental model and can then deduce how to use that component of the user interface. A good example here is the hyperlink in a web page. There is no equivalent in printed materials, so the blue underlined text was introduced as an ab-

stract metaphor. When a user first uses a hyperlink, a little training is necessary. Once learned, the hyperlink metaphor can be carried into other applications like online help text and other hypertext systems.

e) There are other metaphors that have found their way into successful user inter-faces. Create a list of applications and the possible metaphors that could be used, along with the knowledge this implies.

Answer: Consider Table 3.7.

LAB 3.4 SELF-REVIEW QUESTIONS

In order to test your progress, you should be able to answer the following questions.

1) Mental models must be carefully evaluated as they are different from person to person and can even change depending on the person's mood.

    a) _____ True
    b) _____ False

**LAB
3.4**

Table 3.7 ■ Metaphors Used in Applications

Application	Metaphor	Knowledge
Operating environment	Desktop	Office tasks, file management, task launch
Spreadsheets	Accountant's ledger sheets	Columnar tables
Hypertext	Index cards	Convenient reorganization of infor-mation chunks
Learning tools	Travel	Tours, guides, and maps
File storage	Piles, filing cabinet	User-created categories and ordering
Multimedia	Rooms	Building and passageway structure
Working in groups	Intelligent agents	Travel agents, personal assistants, and other servants

2) User models are useful for building interfaces as they are consistent from person to person.

a) _____ True
b) _____ False

3) If the developer can find a good overlap between the models, designing interface is fairly straightforward.

a) _____ True
b) _____ False

4) Using a metaphor in a software product is useful for all but which of the following reasons:

a) _____ It is useful for explaining new or unfamiliar topics.
b) _____ It provides a common point of reference.
c) _____ The user can always relate the metaphor to the appropriate function.
d) _____ The concept of using metaphors is familiar to most people.

5) The three types of models are which of the following?

a) _____ mental, user, theoretical
b) _____ mental, user, conceptual
c) _____ mental, user, metaphor
d) _____ mental, metaphor, conceptual

Quiz answers appear in the Appendix, Section 3.4.

LAB 3.5

UNDERSTANDING TASK ANALYSIS

LAB OBJECTIVES

After this lab, you will be able to:

✔ Define the Task Analysis Process
✔ Carry out a Task Analysis

User-centered design starts with the premise that a software package is being written to aid users in carrying out one or more tasks. Thus, task analysis is both a starting point and a driving force for user interface development to support the tasks and therefore the user.

Over the last decade or so, many techniques and methodologies have been proposed for task analysis. We will only discuss some of the more straightforward here and describe only the basics of task derivation and simple analysis. The end result of the task analysis process is a representation of the whole system, which can be handed on to the design stage of the implementation.

We will see how naming schemes for tasks and how these tasks are decomposed have a profound influence on all aspects of the final system. This will help illustrate the important nature of task analysis.

TASK ANALYSIS BASICS

We define a task as a set of activities that change the system from an initial state to a specified goal or desired outcome state. The outcome may involve a significant change to the current state, so we split tasks into a sequence of subtasks, each more simple than the parent task. This process continues until the most primitive subtask is reached. This lowest level subtask is variously referred to as an action, simple task, or unit task. An example is pressing a single key on a keyboard.

Given these definitions, we describe task analysis as comprising a number of stages:

1. Gathering information from observation of and/or consulting with users
2. Representing tasks in a task description notation
3. Performing an analysis of the task descriptions to achieve an optimum description
4. Using the task representation to produce a new user interface design or improve an existing one

Some very complex information-gathering techniques and detailed notations have been defined. Such approaches can also be used for predicting performance, allowing the complexity of a system to be determined, and giving an estimate of how much training is required for new users.

**LAB
3.5**

Tasks are considered to be different from the functional features of a software package. Functions correspond to the actual actions or processes performed by the actual human or machine. Tasks are a human concept that includes intention and purpose. Thus tasks are goal-oriented, whereas functions are mechanical in nature in that they simply make the transformation from one state to another. Tasks are the activities that a user believes must be carried out to achieve a particular outcome.

PERFORMING TASK ANALYSIS

In Figure 3.4, we see a schematic of the various aspects involved when users actually use a computer system produced by designers. The figure focuses on how the match between the designer's knowledge and user's knowledge is achieved. The concepts are taken from Diaper (1989). Figure 3.4 superimposes the four stages of the task analysis sequence listed above.

How do we go about describing a task so that it forms useful input to the user interface design? The recommended sequence is:

1. Define objects and actions
2. Goals—identify goals and list supporting task(s)

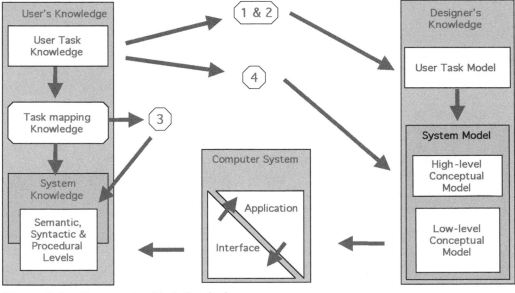

Figure 3.4 ■ Sequencing Task Analysis

3. Task description
    Action sequence on objects—user dialog(s)
    Frequency and importance
    Links with other tasks
4. User discretion: pace, priority, and procedure
5. Task demands: physical, environmental, and legal standards

Developers who work with object-oriented programming languages will recognize a similar approach to class construction. Here in task analysis, we are interested in observing existing user tasks to identify objects and primitive actions. Talking with users, we determine their goals in this context. Then the task description phase codifies the findings to this point using some useful notation, from which there are several to choose from. Stages 4 and 5 are less clear, but it is here that human aspects, workplace ergonomics, and user interface are integrated into the analysis.

Inspection of the final task analysis document allows us to start the analysis properly. Measurements of complexity and magnitude can be done. Task relationships can be noted, and simplification of these relationships can be attempted. Task duplication also shows up in these documents.

TASK MODELS

Space does not permit a discussion of the range of task models available to the software development team. Task models split into categories, depending on the prime purpose of the model. *Descriptive* task modeling systems aim to bring an element of realism to the task descriptions, even to the extent that simple user interface prototypes are generated for discussion with the users. Other task models fall into the *predictive* category. Here the aim is to be able to predict the performance of the eventual implementation.

One of the first predictive task models is worth mentioning since it has risen to a place of importance in the commercial software development market, which is another product of the highly influential Card, Moran, and Newell work. This is GOMS, which stands for Goals, Operators, Methods, and Selection rules.

The significance of these model components is:

- Goals: Symbolic structures that define states to be achieved, and determine a set of possible methods.
- Operators: Elementary motor or information processing acts, whose execution is necessary to change any aspect of the user's memory or to affect the task environment.
- Methods: Descriptions of procedures for accomplishing a goal, cast as a continual sequence of subgoals and operators, with conditional tests on the user's immediate memory and on the task state.
- Selection rules: Elements that allow a choice between two or more methods that can be used to accomplish the goal.

With GOMS, the user segments the overall task into a sequence of small, discrete subtasks or unit tasks. As an example, consider the task of deleting a word from lines of text shown in a window. The GOMS description is shown in Table 3.8.

Note from Table 3.8 that goals (tasks) and subgoals (subtasks) are described on bulleted lines, the number of bullets representing the level of subtask. In this respect, it is similar to hierarchical task description. Important additions include the selections, which recognize the fact that, at the unit task level, the user often has a choice of actions. Operators are identified in the careful description of each task, which is always in the form of operator–object with operator being chosen from a carefully selected set. Note also the verify task, which is a purely human action.

The GOMS notation goes further. Alternate breakdowns of goals can be included and weightings can be added to each selection. This allows goals and subgoals to be measured and likely user performance predicted.

**LAB
3.5**

Table 3.8 ■ A GOMS Task Description

- Goal: Edit-text
- Goal: Edit-unit-task
- Goal: Acquire-unit-task
- • Decide-unit-task (delete particular word)
- Goal: Execute-unit-task
- • Goal: Locate-text-window
- • • [select: Use-thumb-screw-method
                  Use-up/down-page-method
                  Use-up/down-line-method]
- • Goal: Locate-text (word)
- • • [select: Use-mouse-drag-method
                  Use-double-click-method]
- • Goal: Modify-text (delete-word)
- • • Use-delete-key-method
- • • Verify-edit

Task analysis today has taken on great importance. Even a decade ago: ". . . task analysis is potentially the most powerful method available to those working in HCI and has applications for system development, from early requirements specification through to final system evaluation" (Diaper, 1989).

It is vital to remember that system developers and user interface designers alone should not attempt the task analysis. Users must always be equal partners in the analysis.

LAB 3.5 EXERCISES

3.5.1 DEFINE THE TASK ANALYSIS PROCESS

    a) What is the difference between a task and a function provided by a software package? Why is the difference important?

3.5.2 CARRY OUT A TASK ANALYSIS

a) What is the output of a hierarchical task analysis?

_____

_____

b) How do actions and objects help us to perform a task analysis?

_____

_____

c) Take communication as an element of a task you need to analyze. Come up with a list of actions to take and objects which need to be accessed or manipulated. Discuss the steps necessary to analyze this task.

_____

_____

LAB 3.5 EXERCISE ANSWERS

3.5.1 ANSWERS

a) What is the difference between a task and a function provided by a software package? Why is the difference important?

Answer: Tasks include the goal of the human users and criteria for success, whereas functions relate simply to the features built in to software to carry out the specific actions of the task.

Perhaps the more important reason to understand the difference is that each is dealing with a different level of the software. The task is typically what the user sees, such as wanting to send an email message to someone else. How that task is carried out is not important.

On the other hand, developers are concerned with the specific actions. In the case of sending an email message, they not only need to provide functions for composing the message, but also interacting with the network and dozens of other functions.

a) What is the output of a hierarchical task analysis?

Answer: A hierarchy of subtasks. This hierarchy helps designers visualize the whole task and allows optimizations to be identified such as common subtasks, inconsistent ordering of tasks, and a measure of complexity to be calculated.

This aspect should not be underestimated. By breaking down the "big task" into smaller ones, you gain yourself a great number of advantages. First, design is generally easier. You need simply address the issue involving that one task, its interaction with the user, interaction with other tasks, and so forth.

For example, considering sending an email message. If you provide the functionality to save a draft copy of the message to come back to later, you need some mechanism to store in on the hard disk. If you consider this task along with the others, such as saving email that you have received, you may assume that you need an interface to save the draft message. However, considering this task separately, you might see that there is no need for an interface (other then perhaps a button "Save draft"). Like Netscape Communicator, drafts of messages are stored in the same manner as incoming and sent messages so an extra interface is not needed.

Another aspect involves testing. You can test the individual components to ensure that they would as an entity. Once you have verified this, it is easier to ensure the individual components work together.

b) How do actions and objects help us to perform a task analysis?

Answer: They help in the first level of decomposition of tasks, and help establish a terminology for communication between users and designers

c) Take communication as an element of a task you need to analyze. Come up with a list of actions to take and objects which need to be accessed or manipulated. Discuss the steps necessary to analyze this task.

Answer: You may end up with something like Table 3.9.

Having identified actions and objects, we can proceed to combine them in meaningful ways to define tasks. One example might be:

Task: Create/message/on a medium/with a text header/with a text body/to a receiver/at an address/with a device

Once you have identified the specific task, you need to describe the task in as much detail as possible and identify dependencies this task has with other tasks. Along with this you need to identify problems the users have with the current conditions (in order to

**LAB
3.5**

Table 3.9 ■ Actions and Objects

Actions	Objects
send (forward, post, mail, notify, reply)	sender (person id, group id)
create (write, draw, speak)	receiver (mailbox, board, pigeonhole)
perceive (read, notice, identify)	address (postcode, login, room)
	media (notepad, memo)
	header (title, sender, address)
	device (pen, typewriter)
	body (text, graphics)

identify specific areas to address) as well as how the solution to the task is expected to perform. The performance criteria can be anything from specific behavior the software must exhibit to speed or efficiency issues.

From such a brief description, you can flesh out the task description using a template such as:

1. *Task Intrinsics*
   - *Identify task uniquely*
   - *Inputs and outputs*
   - *Transformational process*
   - *Terminology*
   - *Equipment*
2. *Task Dependency*
   - *Dependency on other tasks*
   - *Critical effects*
3. *Current User Problems*
   - *Performance problems*
4. *Performance Criteria (if any)*

Once the full list of tasks is obtained, the next two substages can be actioned. Relationships between tasks can be identified. Users can be asked to rank the tasks in order of importance and frequency. Such a ranking is useful in the later analysis stages when simplification and complexity are being considered. More analysis effort can be placed on the tasks at the head of the rankings.

Arranging tasks and subtasks in hierarchies is a very old technique but still effective as a visualization tool for the designer. The apparently simple task of making tea is shown in Figure 3.5. The hierarchy shows ten subtasks and shows some complexity with scope for a large number of different orderings. Some readers will use quite a different sequence for their tea making. Nevertheless, this technique provides a useful visualization that allows users and designers to converse in a common way about the nature of a task.

To perform the task analysis we examine the task descriptions for certain characteristics and patterns:

- *Alternative decompositions of a single task*

- *Common tasks occurring at different points*

- *Multiple orderings of subtasks*

- *Parallel operation with multiple controls*

- *Categorization by complexity, i.e., number of levels of subtask*

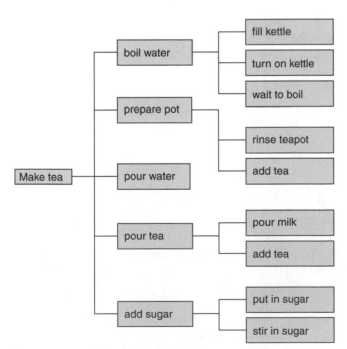

Figure 3.5 ■ Tea Making Task Hierarchy

These processes are made easier or more difficult depending on whether the task description notation is textual or graphical. Task analysis tools can help here, too.

LAB 3.5 SELF-REVIEW QUESTIONS

In order to test your progress, you should be able to answer the following questions.

1) Tasks are goal-oriented, whereas functions are mechanical in nature in that they simply make the transformation from one state to another.

    a) _____ True
    b) _____ False

2) Tasks should be arranged hierarchically for clarity as compared to chronologically.

    a) _____ True
    b) _____ False

3) GOMS stands for which of the following?

    a) _____ Goals, Operators, Models, and Selection rules
    b) _____ Goals, Overview, Methods, and Selection rules
    c) _____ Goals, Overview, Models, and Selection rules
    d) _____ Goals, Operators, Methods, and Selection rules

4) This lowest level subtask is referred to as which of the following?

    a) _____ A transaction
    b) _____ An action
    c) _____ A function
    d) _____ An operation

5) Which of the following is not a stages of task analysis?

    a) _____ Gather data from observation of users
    b) _____ Describe each task and subtask
    c) _____ Analyze and simplify the task descriptions
    d) _____ Produce a user interface design from the task analysis documents
    e) _____ Analyze implemented solution

Quiz answers appear in the Appendix, Section 3.5.

**LAB
3.5**

CHAPTER 3

TEST YOUR THINKING

Consider an interface for a Web-based version of an IRS 1040 form.

1) What mental models apply? What input controls are useful, necessary, or just nice to have? For example, like the real IRS, all you input is simple text. How could you implement a Web interface that uses discrete number or boolean values?

2) Analyze the tasks that are necessary to make this interface truly functional (i.e., automating the process, as contrasted with simply a electronic version of the form that just sits there).

3) Investigate possible input methods other than the keyboard. That is, other than typing in the information by hand, how else can you get the necessary information into this form?

CHAPTER 4

HUMAN-COMPUTER INTERACTION DESIGN

Simple things should be simple; complex things should be possible.

—Alan Kay

We now build upon the basic principles covered in Chapter 3 and apply them to the design of user interfaces. There are many approaches to user interface design, since it can be very individualistic, mainly due to the high degree of creativity that is needed when producing something new. However, it is also influenced to some extent by the relative newness of the GUI and its application. The software industry is still learning how to apply the GUI to new types of software applications that continue to appear.

At the present time, we do not have a significant body of HCI theory to call upon when designing user interfaces. We are forced to adopt other methods. Testing parts of HCI theory using basic experiments is one way and documenting previous experience is another. Currently, the favored way is to use sets of guidelines built from past experience, incorporating as much HCI theory as we have.

Acknowledgment: I would like to thank a past student and research colleague of mine, Michael Rochford, for contributing ideas to this lab on user interface design.

163

Once the design, or part of the design, is complete, we must expose the user interface to real users. That is, we must evaluate the user interface to determine its level of usability. We must observe the user reactions to determine the good and bad parts of the user interface design. By analyzing the results, we can improve aspects of the user interface design and confirm the changes by evaluating again. Windowing systems are one area where design experience is highest. In this chapter, we will look at model window managers.

L A B   4 . 1

USER INTERFACE DESIGN PRINCIPLES

LAB OBJECTIVES

After this lab, you will be able to:

✔ Apply Principles of Intuitive Design
✔ Understand the Basic Foundation for Good User Interface Design

---

Design in any area consists of a mix of rules, methodologies, and creativity. This is becoming true of human-computer interaction and the design of user interfaces. The computer industry has been undertaking GUI design for almost two decades and we can now learn from that experience.

This section outlines some of the guiding principles that have been found to be useful. These can be expressed as sets of rules and guidelines. A brief overview of some of the more important design aids is described below.

INTUITIVE DESIGN

One of the gurus of user interface design is Donald Norman, who has brought considerable insight from his original background in psychology. Norman (1988) gives us a summary of his advice and urges us to cultivate sensitivity to design. To do this, he says we should:

- Notice the everyday environment; in particular, remember the frustrations and try to avoid them in user interface designs.
- Look at the whole task, not just your piece; a single task rarely exists in isolation and will be affected by and affect other tasks.

- Use cognitive scientists, programmers, and engineers; a single set of expertise suitable for user interface design rarely exists in a person from just one discipline.

Furthermore, he urges us to interact with the task, not the computer. He goes on:

- Consider people, tasks, and the appropriate tools; it is surprising how big an impact an inappropriate tool can exert. Be sensitive to the effects of a tool upon a task.
- Cooperative work is rarely cooperative; people have their own agendas and biases even though they work as part of a team.

Norman was one of the first to urge that we take people and tasks into account as the first priority. User interfaces, he says, come a distant second. He was in the vanguard of the enhanced reality proponents. He advocates that we start with task analysis and test with users first. He reminds us that the designer is not a typical user.

INTERFACE DESIGN PRINCIPLES

We have seen an approach to task description and analysis previously. When we come to design the user interface, we find that representing a task on a computer introduces complexity beyond the task itself. As user interface designers, we have to consider the organization of user interface components on the screen. As user actions occur, we must design the navigation between different parts of the interface. Next, we have to consider how the user will manipulate the data in the new medium when we replace manual tasks with a computer system.

To justify this increased complexity, computer applications must promise productivity benefits. They must save time, increase outcome accuracy, and smooth the flow of information. At least one of these benefits must be present in each software application; otherwise, the existing tasks can be performed adequately without the need of a new software application.

Another important point to note is that the interface design—the visualization and embodiment of the application—is all the user sees. As we have seen, the interface designer must understand the user model in order to see the task as the user does. Many past designers have commented that constructing a user interface design presents a situation similar to that facing a writer or architect—meaning and order must be conveyed through visualization.

To become a user interface design specialist, a good tip is to always keep a record of the design choices made, for later reference. Once user testing has validated a design, a note can be added as to the effectiveness of the design choices. From these recordings we can construct a set of guidelines for other designers to use.

Three simple and effective design principles are:

- Consistency
- Simplicity
- Context

CONSISTENCY

Perhaps the single most important benefit of consistent interfaces is that they are predictable from the user's perspective. To be classified as consistent, a user interface must conform to some simple principles. First, the choice of menu labels and other words used to signify actions must have single meanings with no scope for ambiguity. Never use two different words for the same task. Correctly identifying objects and actions during task analysis should ensure consistency here. Second, all user actions must be reversible; in other words, everything must have an "undo" feature. Any exceptions must be clearly marked for the user—usually a warning dialog is necessary.

SIMPLICITY

Simple user interfaces are much harder to achieve, although task analysis helps here, too. Some simple guidelines that help to achieve simplicity are:

- Show no more than is needed to achieve the desired user goal.
- Require a minimum of input from the user.
- Keep both the user and the task in focus.
- Make important concepts particularly clear.
- Use visual representations with direct manipulation (where possible).

Always ask if a new feature will make it easier for the user to achieve the primary goals, or if it is just unnecessary sophistication to show the programmer's prowess. Be rigorous in the application of Occam's Razor, "keep it simple," particularly if it is not a user-suggested new feature—every extra feature, especially if inconsistent with the task, only makes it more difficult.

For the user, the benefit of a simple interface is a clean design with visual refinement, no superfluous features, and clear, direct operations using familiar representations. Follow the rules and principles of good graphic design. This may require the services of a graphic artist. The graphic artist knows that visually pleasing displays are not vividly colorful, crowded, or heavily embellished. The maxim is bury the detail.

Clarity is important at all levels of an interface:

- Information representation
- Organization and naming of interface controls
- Flow of control (dynamic behavior)
- Screen layout

CONTEXT

It is vital at all stages of the interaction that the user be presented with contextual information as well as the prime (focused) information needed for that stage of the interaction. The interaction should appear as a sequence of easily identifiable and distinct interface views.

Contextual visibility can be incorporated into a GUI with three major tools:

1. *What-you-see-is-what-you-get (WYSIWYG).* This is technical slang for presenting information on the screen in the identical form (within display constraints) as it will appear in other media (such as paper and audio/visual). This includes both text and images—drawings, pictures, and (given the technology) moving images and sound.

2. *Properties.* Each visual object possesses a range of attributes (size, shape, color, and other parameters) that can be controlled by the user. This property information appears on the screen in property boxes.

3. *Dialogs.* Whenever small amounts of information (text, number, option, yes/no) must be solicited from the user, use a minor variation on the interface view known as a dialog box. This disappears when the input is achieved.

LAB 4.1 EXERCISES

4.1.1 APPLY PRINCIPLES OF INTUITIVE DESIGN

a) Look at the icons used in the toolbar of any business application. Using what you find as examples, discuss why the everyday environment is so important.

_____

_____

b) Why should we look outside of the immediate task for which we are designing a user interface?

_____

_____

4.1.2 UNDERSTAND THE BASIC FOUNDATION FOR GOOD USER INTERFACE DESIGN

a) Why does a new software package inevitably lead to increased task complexity? In that case, why do we use new software?

_____

_____

b) What is meant by a modeless user interface? Why is this important in designing a user interface?

_____

_____

c) Start up a few different graphical (as opposed to character-based) applications on your system. Compare and contrast where the menus are, what functions are in each menu, the appearance of buttons and their functions, as well as the overall behavior of the products. Pay particular attention to applications from the same vendor.

_____

_____

d) Look again at the applications in the previous question. Are the messages presented easy to identify and understand? Do messages appear when you think they should?

_____

_____

e) In a world where users constantly demand more features, why is simplicity important? What issues need to be addressed?

LAB 4.1 EXERCISE ANSWERS

4.1.1 ANSWERS

a) Look at the icons used in the toolbar of any business application. Using what you find as examples, discuss why the everyday environment is so important.

Answer: Regardless of the application, a great many of the icons are immediately identifiable. Pressing the button with a picture of a printer lets us print the document. Pressing the button with a picture of an opening folder lets us open a new document. Pressing the button with the scissors lets us cut out something. Other applications will have similar kinds of buttons.

We deliberately use everyday metaphors in user interface design to allow users to form predictable conceptual models. In the case of the buttons, we can make predictions about the behavior of the button by comparing the picture to its real-world equivalent.

b) Why should we look outside of the immediate task for which we are designing a user interface?

Answer: A single task rarely exists in isolation and will be affected by and affect other tasks. We need to look at the whole work context that includes the particular task in hand. What the users' work context does is to often impose certain preconceptions (as well as misconceptions) about the way an interface should behave (or the way the program itself should behave).

One specific example of how the work context can influence the user's perception involves the text-oriented e-mail programs used for many years on UNIX systems. Users who were familiar with the capabilities of the then-available word processors often ran into trouble with the e-mail program. In a word processor, you could keep typing until the memory on your machine was exhausted without ever having to press the "enter" key.

However, this is a fatal mistake on character-based e-mail programs. Such programs are line-oriented and expect a new line at the end of the screen line. Some have a little tolerance and allow you to type more than one screen line before the trouble starts. What happens is the input buffer is only a certain size. Once that limit is reached, the program starts writing again to the beginning of the input buffer. As a result, a lot of what is typed is lost.

The documentation clearly says that the e-mail program is line-oriented. However, the users' work context said that when inputting text, you can keep on typing. The result is a lot of angry people and a lot of calls to the support hotline.

4.1.2 ANSWERS

a) Why does a new software package inevitably lead to increased task complexity? In that case, why do we use new software?

Answer: All new software packages require a training period when the user's productivity will drop. To compensate, new software must bring other benefits. It must save time, increase outcome accuracy, and smooth the flow of information in some combination.

b) What is meant by a modeless user interface? Why is this important in designing a user interface?

Answer: A modeless user interface is a user interface that appears to display only one context in order to carry out all tasks. Only dialog interrupts the context from time to time, if at all. Context switches cannot confuse the user since none are present. Knowing whether an interface is modeless helps the designer in determining if any components interact and to what extent.

Our daily life is filled with modeless interfaces, such as clocks or microwaves. In these cases, you are only performing a single task. Typically, you have a modeless interface when the functions are extremely limited. Understanding the context in which the interface will be applied can help determine whether the interface should be modeless.

c) Start up a few different graphical (as opposed to character-based) applications on your system. Compare and contrast where the menus are, what functions are in each menu, the appearance of buttons and their functions, as well as the overall behavior of the products. Pay particular attention to applications from the same vendor.

Answer: What you find will depend on the applications you select. One of the most important things to note is how consistent everything is. Typically, you find menus labeled "File," "Edit," "View," and "Help" in most office products, including Web browsers. Each of these menus generally has the same functions, differing slightly for different applications. Even the buttons on the toolbar and the functions behind them are pretty consistent across applications.

We can achieve consistency in the location of objects within the user interface and in the execution of tasks. An example is the position of the controls in the motor vehicle we are driving. Always bear in mind that the computer application itself is not central to a user's goals. Take care that the application does not obstruct the user's current task.

Within many organizations, consistency has not been an important issue, as can be seen from the myriad of form designs used. However, consistency should always be a long-term goal, requiring designers to look backward (to learn from previous experience and other applications) as well as forward (for innovative interface controls).

The clashing of command names between applications is a major problem, as users typically require more than one application to achieve complex goals. We should always remember that the habits users learn in applications they frequently use are carried to other contexts, resulting in confusion if consistency is absent.

It is important to recognize and implement the standard ways of interacting with a target system and to follow local conventions when transferring applications to different environments. Screen layouts vary widely with titles, action areas, and control information in different positions, even within a single application. It is like living in a house with all the door handles at different heights! From observing many different applications, we note that the greatest divergence between designers is in assigning different keyboard shortcuts, particularly function keys.

Making all user actions reversible is an almost impossible task, but should be the ultimate goal. Ensure that simple object-action pairs can be undone—examples are deletion and movement. Allow users to experiment with a sequence of actions, recovering by reverting to the last saved state, or one of a series of snapshots.

Remember that with few exceptions, if users cannot control your software, it is your fault, not theirs. By all means forgive users for their mistakes by providing reversibility, but hope they will forgive you for yours and buy the upgrades!

For the user, the benefit of a consistent interface is a much-sought-after perceived stability. This stability gives a feeling of predictability, robustness, and forgiveness. These characteristics engender confidence to explore and learn.

d) Look again at the applications in the previous question. Are the messages presented easy to identify and understand? Do messages appear when you think they should?

Answer: What you find will depend on the applications you select and the actions you perform.

One very important aspect of context is the concept of a mode of operation. Modes are present when an interface view restricts the set of objects and actions presented to the user. It is vital that modes be made visible to the user in some way. Two conventional methods are:

1. *Constraints. Access to interface controls is artificially constrained, such as beeping on an access attempt or preventing the cursor from entering forbidden screen regions.*
2. *Indicators. Change the interface view radically, or more subtle changes such as the shape of the cursor or "graying out" menu options, and so on.*

Certain modes are near universal and should be present in the knowledge structures of most users. These are online help and the use of dialogs. Keeping modes to a minimum is one guarantee of a good user interface. There are few more frustrating aspects of the user interface than finding yourself in a new mode of which you are unaware.

At this point, there is no harm in repeating the message from the last unit on user feedback. You should acknowledge all user actions with one of the following:

1. *Immediate execution (within about one second) of the action with a visible state change*
2. *Correction message*
3. *Confirmation message*
4. *In-progress message*

It is imperative that the system responds very quickly to a user's action. This will help establish user confidence and satisfaction and assists the user to understand the dialog in progress.

In addition to a quick response, the interface designer must concentrate upon informing the user of the present context. As well, the current context should list or otherwise make visible the allowable actions from which the user can choose. More difficult is providing clues to the next interface contexts or views that can be reached from the current context and making clear the routes to those contexts.

In Figure 4.1, we attempt to summarize the steps and components of a single interaction with the user. The first point to notice is the number of different subcomponents involved in the interaction. Second, there are seven steps to be followed in order to guarantee feedback and a successful interaction from the user's point of view.

Step 5' attempts to show that the context remains the same provided there are no modes involved in the user interface design. This is the best that is attainable. A one-mode or modeless user interface is extremely simple and leads to little confusion for the user. Most modern word processor applications are close to attaining the modeless state. The user sees only the formatted document, as it will appear when printed. The only mode changes are dialogs that appear from time to time.

In summary, the three user interface design principles of consistency, simplicity, and context form a clear-cut foundation for the building of good user interfaces.

1	Objective	:= Subgoal [+ Subgoal]
2	Subgoal	:= Context + Action
3	Context	:= Knowledge + Clues + Assumptions
4	Action	:= Selection + Request (= object + method)
5	Action + Context >> Outcome + Context′	
	5′ (Context′ = Context >> no modes)	
6	Outcome	:= Result + Feedback
7	Result	:= Program Activity >> Change in Data

Feedback := Activity Indicator + Completion Indicator + Change Indicator
Success := (Outcome = Objective) & (Context′ is acceptable)

Figure 4.1 ■ Components of an Interaction

e) In a world where users constantly demand more features, why is simplicity important?

Answer: Simplicity not only allows the programmer to keep track of the application, it makes things easier for the user. One key issue is to determine whether a particular task is really necessary or just "nice to have." Adding just the things that are necessary helps keep the complexity down. In addition, breaking down the application into tasks and subtasks as we discussed in the previous chapter not only contributes to consistency, but also to simplicity.

Keep in mind that simplicity does not necessarily mean lack of features. The key issue is that you don't want your users having to jump through all sorts of hoops to perform simple tasks.

User interface designers should group interface controls logically, using short simple words or accepted icons that the user will easily recognize. Avoid crowded screens and provide a smooth flow of information with sensible defaults and distinct closure—making it obvious a particular task is complete.

User analysis reveals a hierarchy of command usage—make infrequent commands less intrusive for novice and casual users (majority). Remember Alan Kay's maxim quoted at the top of this chapter "simple things should be simple; complex things should be possible."

LAB 4.1 SELF-REVIEW QUESTIONS

In order to test your progress, you should be able to answer the following questions.

1) Online help and the use of dialogs are near universal modes of operation.

a) _____ True
b) _____ False

2) Ensuring simplicity also always means having to sacrifice functionality.

    a) _____ True
    b) _____ False

3) Two methods for indicating modes of operation to users are which of the following?

    a) _____ Constraints and modes
    b) _____ Confirmation and indicators
    c) _____ Constraints and indicators
    d) _____ Constraints and evaulation

4) Which of the following is not an effective design principle?

    a) _____ Consistency
    b) _____ Simplicity
    c) _____ Methods
    d) _____ Context

Quiz answers appear in the Appendix, Section 4.1.

LAB 4.2

USER INTERFACE DESIGN GUIDELINES

LAB OBJECTIVES

After this lab, you will be able to:

✔ Judge the Effectiveness of User Interface Guidelines
✔ Apply User Interface Guidelines to Examples

In the future, we may have the benefit of a number of well-founded scientific theories to guide the design of user interfaces. We are not there yet. In the absence of HCI theories, we are forced to use other techniques and approaches.

A very influential technique that matches to some extent the methods used to implement the software code itself is the war story. By this we mean using previous examples of user interface design that are accepted to be of high quality. A user interface designer, having performed a task analysis, will look for existing examples of similar applications and adapt these user interfaces to the new software package. Examples of very bad user interfaces are useful, too—they indicate designs to avoid at all costs.

Chapter 3 mentioned early experiments on human capabilities in the HCI context undertaken by Card, Moran, and Newell. We can use the actual results of these experiments with users. Many experiments continue to be undertaken to add to this body of knowledge. To date, however, the results have concentrated on very small parts of the user interface, being concerned with such components as buttons, menus, scroll bars, and the like. This is useful but can take us only so far in overall user interface design.

Probably most helpful at this point are the sets of principles and guidelines constructed by "experts" in the area of interface design and construction. We see there are a number of important guides available to us. Some of the most important are covered in this lab. The main sources of user interface design guidelines are the large software houses, the computer manufacturers, and respected authors in the HCI literature.

SMITH AND MOSIER GUIDELINES

LAB 4.2

One of the earliest sets of guidelines that has left a lasting impression in the area of user interface guidelines is the work of Smith and Mosier (1986). They worked for the Mitre Corporation and compiled 944 guidelines. Many of the guidelines refer to character-based screens, but include many guidelines for the GUI. The guidelines can be split into six sections that are still valid today:

1. Data entry
2. Data display
3. Sequence control
4. User guidelines
5. Data transfer
6. Data protection

APPLE USER INTERFACE GUIDELINES

The Apple Desktop interface developed for the Macintosh computer provides a consistent and familiar computer environment in which people can perform their many tasks. The design takes the view, endorsed several times above, that people are not trying to use computers, they are trying to get their jobs done.

The Apple Desktop interface is based on the assumption that people are instinctively curious: They want to learn, and they learn best by active self-directed exploration of their environment. People are also both imaginative and artistic when they are provided with a comfortable context; they are most productive and effective when the environment in which they work and play is enjoyable and challenging.

Apple produced its design guidelines in a form for all designers to use (Apple, 1987). In the abbreviated summary given in Table 4.1, you see the duplication of some of the concepts mentioned in earlier labs in this unit.

**LAB
4.2**

Table 4.1 ■ Summary of Apple User Interface Guidelines

Guideline	Comments
Metaphors from the real world	Use concrete metaphors and make them plain, so that users have a set of expectations to apply to computer environments. Whenever appropriate, use audio and visual effects that support the metaphors.
Direct manipulation	Users want to feel that they are in charge of the computer's activities.
See-and-point (not remember-and-type)	Users select actions from alternatives presented on the screen. The general form of user actions is noun-then-verb, or "Hey, you—do this." Users rely on recognition, not recall; they should not have to remember anything the computer already knows. Most programmers have no trouble working with a command-line interface that requires memorization and Boolean logic. The average user is not a programmer.
Consistency	Effective applications are both consistent within themselves and consistent with one another.
WYSIWYG	There should be no secrets from the user, no abstract commands that only promise future results. There should be no significant difference between what the user sees on the screen and what eventually gets printed.
User control	The user, not the computer, initiates and controls all actions.
Feedback and dialog	Keep the user informed. Provide immediate feedback. User activities should be simple at any moment, though they may be complex taken together.
Forgiveness	Users make mistakes; forgive them. The user's actions are generally reversible—let users know about any that are not.
Perceived stability	Users feel comfortable in a computer environment that remains understandable and familiar rather than changing randomly.
Aesthetic integrity	Visually confusing or unattractive displays detract from the effectiveness of HCI. Different "things" look different on the screen. Users should be able to control the superficial appearance of their computer workplaces—to display their own style and individuality. Messes are acceptable only if the user makes them—applications aren't allowed this freedom.

Every major software producer now has a set of user interface guidelines for its software products. Most guidelines are being rewritten for Web page design as that user interface becomes more and more prevalent. Good Web sites to search for more details of user interface guidelines are Instone (http://usableweb.com/) and Perlman (http://www.hcibib.org/).

LAB 4.2 EXERCISES

4.2.1 JUDGE THE EFFECTIVENESS OF USER INTERFACE GUIDELINES

a) Why aren't the detailed experimental results of interface experiments used more widely in user interface design?

_____

_____

b) The Apple guidelines in Table 4.1 form the heart of accepted wisdom in GUI design and can be used as a checklist against new user interface designs as they are produced. Once again, take a look at the applications you did in Exercise 4.1.2 and evaluate the applications according to the checklist.

_____

_____

4.2.2 APPLY USER GUIDELINES TO EXAMPLES

a) An example of one of Smith and Mosier's (SAM) guidelines is shown in Figure 4.2. Discuss the overall structure and how easy (or not) it is to get the necessary information from it.

_____

b) What is a major shortcoming of the SAM guidelines? Discuss what effect this has on interface design.

_____

_____

LAB 4.2

1 DATA ENTRY

1.0 General

1.0/6 - Defined Display Areas for Data Entry.

Where data entry on an electronic display is permitted only in certain areas, as in form filling, provide clear visual definition of the entry fields.

Example: Data entry fields might be underlined, or perhaps highlighted by reverse video.

Exception: For general text entry of variable (unrestricted) length, no field delimiters are needed. In effect, keyed text entries can replace nothing (null characters).

Comment: Display formats with field delimiters provide explicit user guidance as to the location and extent of data entry fields. Where delimiters extend throughout an entry field, as in underlining, then any keyed data entries should replace the delimiter characters on the display.

Reference BB 2.2.1

See also 1.4/10 - Marking Field Boundaries

Figure 4.2 ■ An Example of a Smith and Mosier Guideline

LAB 4.2 EXERCISE ANSWERS

4.2.1 ANSWERS

a) Why aren't the detailed experimental results of interface experiments used more widely in user interface design?

Answer: At a low level and for discrete user interface components the detailed usability results are useful. However, these results are not so useful for the top-level user interface design. In addition, the design needs to apply to the specific environment in which it will be applied. Without doing so, you tend to miss contextual issues that may affect how the user reacts and interacts with the interface.

b) The Apple guidelines in Table 4.1 form the heart of accepted wisdom in GUI design and can be used as a checklist against new user interface designs as they are produced. Once again, take a look at the applications you did in Exercise 4.1.2 and evaluate the applications according to the checklist.

Answer: The results of your analysis will depend on the applications you select.

As we discussed previously, most modern applications use at least some metaphors from the real-word (trash can icons, buttons with printers, and so forth). In many cases, you will find that there is not always a fitting metaphor, so the designer will have to think up one.

Can you drag and drop into the application (direct manipulation)? Does it work the way you expect? For example, if you drop a document into the application, is the document opened in that application or are you simply given a link?

Is the application intuitive? Can you figure out what each function does? In general, users rely on recognition, not recall; they should not have to remember anything the computer already knows. That is, do you need to call up special dialogs before performing the necessary functions? Do you have to hunt through many levels of unclear menus? Note that this is more than "ease of use," but also includes behaving in a way you expect from the information the application provides.

However, if you have multiple applications from a single vendor, look to see if the same vendor uses the same pictures on the buttons and that menus with the same function are in the same place with the same submenus. Also check if the application is consistent within itself. For example, if you select a menu entry, does it behave the exact same way as the corresponding keyboard shortcut?

WYSIWYG is also an important issue, although there are limits. If you are dealing with a word processor, graphics program, or something similar, you can generally expect that the appearance on the screen is what will end up on the page.

However, this does not apply to HTML applications. First, HTML does not specify how the text will appear. Instead, it leaves that up to the browser. Therefore, a designer could spend a great deal of time making the page look good in his or her browser only to find that in another browser it doesn't look right. Even with the exact same version of the browser, different settings will make the page appear differently. In addition, what you get on the printed page is not always the same as on the screen.

The issue of "user control" is a sensitive spot. I want as much control over the application as possible. Being forced to do something can often be more than just annoying. However, automatically performing some task may be useful, like automatically saving your document at regular intervals.

If you perform an action, do you get status information? Are there messages when something goes wrong? These are important aspects. Without any kind of feedback, it is not always clear if the action was completed. For example, when saving a file, some applications will write specific information in the status line at the bottom of the window.

How forgiving the application is can be difficult to quantify, but this is no less important than any other characteristic. For example, Microsoft produces an HTML editor called FrontPage that is not very forgiving. If you forget a closing angle-bracket (<) or quote("), the program changes the meaning of everything else after that point. That is, things that are part of the text are now considered parts of an HTML tag and the HTML tags are now considered text. It even goes so far as to change the brackets and quotes into their corresponding name character references. For example, " becomes &quote and < becomes &lt. To make things worse, this only happens when saving the file, which means the copy you just saved to the disk has the problem. This is not a very forgiving application, plus it takes too much control away from the user.

Perceived stability is obviously arbitrary, since we are dealing with people's perceptions. How often has Microsoft Word crashed and you have blamed it, rather than the inherent instability of Windows 95/98? Since you were working in Word and it crashed, there is the perception that Word is unstable. Another example would be an application on the Web where you do some kind of search (e.g., www.amazon.com, www.yahoo.com). If the application returns errors due to network problems, you may assume your application has problems.

An additional aspect of this is the errors that are generated. You obviously cannot do anything about problems in the connection between the user and your site. However, you can produce informative messages when the problem is your fault. The General Protect Fault that was so common in Windows 3.x has done a lot to give it the impression it was stable. Windows 95/98 is more specific about where the error came from, which helps the user see which application is at fault.

Finally, there is "aesthetic integrity." If, for whatever reason, the application is not aesthetically appealing, the user will have problems with it. The most effective solution is to allow the user to configure as much of the appearance as possible. If that is not possible, you need to consider what is appealing to the most users. Windows 3.x had a Desktop Theme that looked like something out of Blade Runner or downtown Toyko at night. I have seen applications that had similar color schemes and there was no way to change it. It was painful to work with them.

When developing your own interfaces, it is well worth doing these checks before going to the expense of testing usability with real users in a controlled laboratory environment.

4.2.2 ANSWERS

a) An example of one of Smith and Moser's (SAM) guidelines is shown in Figure 4.2. Discuss the overall structure and how easy (or not) it is to get the necessary information from it.

Answer: It is highly structured with sections showing guideline section and subsection, a description of the guideline with examples, exceptions, and comments. Very importantly, a list of literature references is shown ("see BB 2.2.1"). Last but not least are the very important links to related guidelines, which help the designer be confident that all associated guidelines have been considered.

While the SAM guidelines broke new ground, their use has been limited. Probably there were too many individual guidelines to be useful for designers. Finding a SAM guideline leads you on to several others. Doing an exhaustive search for all guidelines that apply to a particular user interface leads to a lengthy list. Knowing how to apply dozens of these guidelines is difficult. Rather, the list is often used as a checklist when the final user interface design has been completed.

b) What is a major shortcoming of the SAM guidelines? Discuss what effect this has on interface design.

Answer: There are effectively too many small guidelines. Once a long list of SAM guidelines has been picked for a particular user interface design, it is difficult to formulate a design from them. That is, in many cases, the guidelines go into too much detail. Although possibly appropriate for design and development of individual actions or even tasks, these may be too low level for an interface design.

LAB 4.2 SELF-REVIEW QUESTIONS

In order to test your progress, you should be able to answer the following questions.

1) The concept of see-and-point not remember-and-type says users prefer to select actions from a list presented to them, relying on recognition not recall.

   a) _____ True
   b) _____ False

2) The concept of WYSIWYG helps ensure that the interface matches the user's everyday work environment.

   a) _____ True
   b) _____ False

3) A war story is not useful for designing user interfaces because it tends to demotivate the designers.

    a) _____ True
    b) _____ False

4) Which is not a section of the Smith and Mosier (SAM) guidelines?

    a) _____ Data entry
    b) _____ Data display
    c) _____ Sequence control
    d) _____ User Testing
    e) _____ Data transfer

5) All but which of the following is a reason why Apple's user interface guidelines are so influential?

    a) _____ The Apple Macintosh has always been regarded as the pinnacle of GUI designs.
    b) _____ The Apple has been highly regarded for its ease of use.
    c) _____ The GUI has been standardized across many platforms.
    d) _____ The guidelines advise how to achieve these characteristics when designing user interfaces.

Quiz answers appear in the Appendix, Section 4.2.

LAB 4.3

USER INTERFACE USABILITY

LAB OBJECTIVES

After this lab, you will be able to:

✔ Understand Usability and Usability Measures
✔ Apply the Basics of User Interface Evaluation

Usability is an assessment of the impacts of specific user interface design decisions upon the ease of use of the interface. For evaluating usability, it is necessary to consider the relationships between the product and its users in the first instance. However, we must not forget the other people who interact with the users, other systems, and devices. In other words, we must take into account the complete work environment.

We need to distinguish between utility and usability. *Utility* is the set of functions or features of a software package. It is the description of the raw manipulations of data of which the software package is capable. We usually are exposed to utility via a list of features for each package. On the other hand, *usability* concerns the user's ability to access and understand the effects of each feature. Package utility will answer the question: "Will it do what I want?" Package usability answers the question: "Will users be able to access the features in a productive manner?"

Once we understand usability, we next must know how to measure it, or at least be able to compare the usability of two or more competing software packages. This takes us into the realm of user interface evaluation, which is the ability to address the usability issues.

USABILITY ISSUES

When selecting a computer system (mix of hardware and software), the accepted process is to assess:

1. Functionality: Will the system do what is needed?
2. Usability: Will the users be successful in their use of the system?
3. Likability: Will the users feel the system is suitable?

LAB 4.3

Then the various costs of deployment must be calculated. Capital and running costs come first, followed by the social and organizational costs of deployment. Only then can a decision be made about the acceptability of the computer system.

We will consider the usability issues in this lab. Commercial system producers have been concerned with usability costs for at least two decades. IBM, for example, has drawn up a long list of usability issues for each major piece of software. This list is much longer than at first might be imagined. IBM's list is:

1. System performance: Reliability and responsiveness
2. System functions: Requirements analysis (task analysis)
3. User interface: Organization, interaction devices, direct and indirect users
4. Printed materials: Manuals
5. Outreach program: End-user training, online help, customer support
6. Installation
7. Maintenance
8. Advertising
9. Support user groups

Perhaps only items 1 through 4 of this list are the concern of this text, whereas the list is much longer that that. Customers of IBM's systems will be concerned with the whole list.

USABILITY MEASURES

Now let us turn our attention to the measurement of usability. In Eason (1988), we see one of the first comprehensive descriptions of the measurement of user interface usability. The measurement scenario is shown in Figure 4.3.

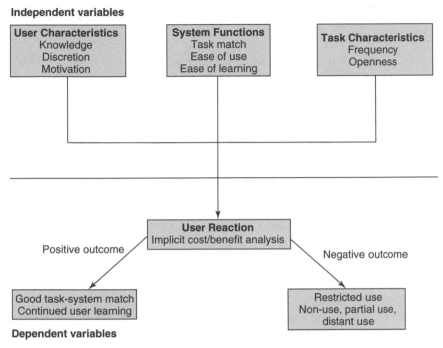

Figure 4.3 ■ **Usability Evaluation**

In Figure 4.3, Eason recognizes the importance of task analysis, which we have already discussed. The new aspects are the user characteristics and the ease of use and learning. When performing usability evaluations in controlled environments, we are then interested in measuring the user reaction and performing the cost/benefit analysis. When Figure 4.3 is applied to individual users, they implicitly perform their own cost/benefit analyses and achieve either a positive or negative outcome. If it is a negative outcome, the users restrict their use of the system possibly to total nonuse. When the outcome is positive, a user judges it beneficial to continue to invest time in further learning of the system.

Brian Shackel is one of the founding fathers of ergonomics, beginning his work in the early 1960s. By 1990, he had considerable experience in defining usability measures for user interface design. In Shackel (1990), he proposed that usability could be specified and measured by a set of operational criteria. Terms are assigned numerical values when goals are set during the "requirements specification." His measures are shown in Table 4.2.

Table 4.2 ■ Shakel Usability Measures

Measure	Comments
Effectiveness	• At better than some required level of performance (in terms of speed and errors)
	• By some required percentage of the specified target range of users
	• Within some required proportion of the range of usage environments
Learnability	• Specified time from installation and start of training
	• Based upon some specified amount of training
	• Some specified relearning time for intermittent users
Flexibility	• Allowing adaptation to some percentage variation in tasks beyond those first specified [difficult to determine in practice and can be replaced by usefulness—achievement of users' goals]
Attitude	• Within acceptable levels of human cost in terms of tiredness, discomfort, frustration, and personal effort

Note that the procedures of Table 4.2 imply some lower level measurements like the time taken for a task and the number of errors (initiation of inappropriate tasks) observed in carrying out a task. Even being able to complete tasks is a useful measure. Notice that Shackel proposed that one of the measures for effectiveness is the percentage of users tested who could complete the task.

USABILITY EVALUATION OBJECTIVES

We do not need to look far to be convinced that the evaluation of user interfaces is very necessary. There are many reasons why this is so. To begin with, user interface designers have an inadequate intuition about quality—we freely admit that user interface design is a skilled art. We must strive to be in a position to be able to measure goodness—to be able to determine the effectiveness of user interface designs.

Past experience from the days before there was a professional approach to user interface evaluation has shown us to be bad at prediction, particularly of user needs and user reactions. Without doing proper investigation with the recording of results, it is very easy to under/overestimate users' abilities in relation to their skills and their limitations. Again, we return to our admission that developers are not ordinary users and find it hard to imagine users' confusion.

Finally, if the foregoing is not sufficient, we have the evidence of too many unevaluated systems, that have performed very badly as far as the user interface is concerned.

We should first be clear about the objectives of performing user interface evaluation. The first aim is to improve system usability and utility. It often happens that when we test the usability of the system we note a lack of utility—usually omissions in functionality that make it impossible to carry out certain tasks.

Another major aim is to increase user satisfaction in early stages of implementation. It is far cheaper to evaluate the user interfaces of systems before costly implementation is embarked upon. This is where prototyping is particularly useful.

EVALUATION TECHNIQUES

Over the years, a number of different approaches to usability evaluation have been tried. Indeed, this is still an active area for HCI research. Figure 4.4 shows a breakdown of the different evaluation approaches suggested by Joëlle Coutaz. She splits the evaluation techniques into two basic categories. The one shown on the left of the figure encompasses predictive models. Here, various theories of HCI are employed to model users and the system under evaluation. Running the model results in a set of data that can be used to predict how users would react to the user interface.

The more practical category of usability evaluation techniques appears on the right of Figure 4.4. Here we carry out experiments with real users on either the actual systems themselves or a prototype system. However, the Wizard of Oz approach is a special case and can only be used in limited circumstances. In this instance, there is no actual computer system to test. Rather, other people who respond manually simulate the interactions with experimental subjects.

In all experimental techniques, sets of volunteer users are asked to complete a range of tasks while being observed. Experimental methods include direct observation of the users, video recording and analysis, protocol recording and analysis, and by system instrumentation and logging. Various measures are possible and are described in the next section.

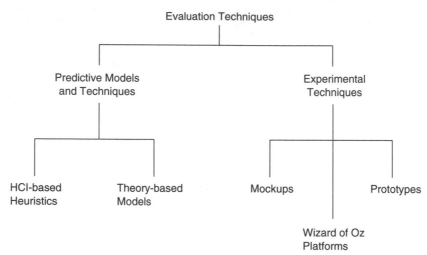

Figure 4.4 ■ Taxonomy of Evaluation Techniques (Joëlle Coutaz)

LAB 4.3 EXERCISES

4.3.1 UNDERSTAND USABILITY AND USABILITY MEASURES

a) Discuss what factors are used when performing a user analysis.

_____

_____

b) Discuss how usability differs from utility.

_____

_____

c) Discuss likability and why it is important.

_____

_____

d) Discuss the relationship of usability and effectiveness.

_____

_____

4.3.2 APPLY THE BASICS OF USER INTERFACE EVALUATION

a) Discuss why usability evaluation is important.

_____

_____

b) Discuss which of the two main types of evaluation testing is more practical.

_____

_____

LAB 4.3 EXERCISE ANSWERS

4.3.1 ANSWERS

a) Discuss what factors are used when performing a user analysis.

Answer: The data gathered about a user includes the target user group and its gender, age, and cultural characteristics. Also take into account the job characteristics such as job description, the main activities and responsibilities, the management reporting structure, and any system of rewards. We also need to take into account a user's background such as education, experience, knowledge, skills, and training. The work environment may also introduce usage constraints such as a factory floor, mobile position, and other nonoffice locations. Finally, any user preferences should be collected.

b) Discuss how usability differs from utility.

Answer: Utility is represented by the feature list of a software package—data manipulation functions. Usability is the measure of how well human users understand the user interface and how effective they are at using the features.

For many people this difference is not intuitive. The utility of a jumbo jet is pretty straightforward: moving a large number of people from place to place through the air. The same jet could be converted to cargo to transport goods or converted to a spy plane for military purposes. In every case, the utility of the plane (what functions it provides) is fairly simple. However, for the vast majority of the people the plane is too complex for us to use. Although we may eventually be able to learn how to fly it, a jumbo jet has limited usability for us.

Let's take two software products as another example: MS-Word and Wordpad, which is provided as a free editor with recent versions of MS-Windows. MS-Word has far more features than Wordpad. We could say that it has greater utility. However, the sheer number of menus and buttons can be intimidating. People will try to do fancy things and get lost because there is simply so much there. As a result, it has low usability.

Wordpad has a fewer features and therefore less utility. However, for most people, it is relatively more intuitive to learn. It is easier for most people to use, therefore it has greater usability.

c) Discuss likability and why it is important.

Answer: Likability refers to the concept of pleasurable engagements user have with a product. A system may be usable, but may leave users without a sense of achievement or pleasure in carrying out a task. For example, users who are accustomed to a GUI do not "like" the command line and get no pleasure out of using it, although it may be the only way of carrying out certain functions.

Consider Shackel's usability measure "attitude". If a person is using a product only because someone else made the decision or he or she has no other choice, that user will typically have a bad attitude about the product. If the product is difficult to use (perceived or real), users are not as effective with the product. I know people who are almost intentionally careless with the command line because they say it's hard to use, so why bother making any effort (despite the fact this attitude is counterproductive).

d) Discuss the relationship of usability and effectiveness.

Answer: Effectiveness is essentially a measure of how well the desired goals have been achieved. An application is considered effective if it reaches or exceeds a particular goal. The easier a product is to use, the greater the likelihood that the goals will be reached and the greater the effectiveness of the product.

One key aspect is that effectiveness is not absolute. First, you have the obvious factor of human preferences. You may be familiar with the expression "Close enough for government work." Some people seem to have the attitude that someone working for the government has (or needs) lower goals. Although this is meant as a jab at government employees, the implication is that the goal for government employees can be less than that for private businesses.

Consider a hotline. If you are talking about a mail-order company, then having as many us 10% of the people getting busy signals is acceptable. For a software support company, this may need to be as low as 5%. For an emergency service like the fire department or police, busy signals are not acceptable at all. Whether you need a new sweater or need to get your document to print is an emergency is a matter of opinion. Therefore, what constitutes an acceptable "drop" rate on callers differs for each situation. If the mail order only drops 7%, it is very effective, at least in the opinion of the manager who wants only a 10% drop rate. However, the software company is of the opinion that 7% is too high. Both have the same absolute value (7%), but their perception of the effectiveness is different.

As with a hotline, the effectiveness of software often depends on the user. As we discussed in Exercise 4.3.1c, how much the person likes the software helps determine the usability and therefore the effectiveness. If the interface is not usable (for whatever reason), the user cannot be effective. However, the product may still be considered effective as a whole. For example, your company with 500 employees might use MS-Word, but you prefer Corel's WordPerfect. Although there are plenty of reasons why WordPerfect is better than MS-Word, your company standardizes on MS-Word, sacrificing your effectiveness for a higher aggregate effectiveness. This is addressed in Table 4.2 in that a product is effective for "some required percentage of the specified target range of users."

Despite the features, MS-Word is not very good at drawing. Within the "range of usage environments," which includes graphics, one cannot use MS-Word very well to create graphics and it is therefore not effective.

4.3.2 ANSWERS

a) Discuss why usability evaluation is important.

Answer: One reason evaluation is important is that quality (regardless of the context) is often arbitrarily defined and there is inadequate intuition about quality. One user calls a product "good," but there needs to be some subjective measure of this goodness. In addition, people making the decisions about products often make mistakes about user needs and their reactions, particularly if they aren't the ones who are going to use the product, but are basing their choice on other sources. These same people often under/overestimate users' skills and limitations. When developing something internally, many people forget that developers are not ordinary users and cannot imagine users' confusion or lack of understanding.

We saw in Chapter 2 that evaluation lies at the heart of the modern software development life cycle, and it is involved in several iterations as implementation progresses. Therefore, it is essential that evaluation methods should be fast to apply and minimize work by evaluators. The outcomes of evaluation quite naturally should be the identification of problem areas and suggestions for possible solutions.

These objectives should be independent of the type of user interface type (character-based or GUI), the hardware and software, the design stage, the evaluation method used, and the type of data gathered.

Figure 4.5 shows some figures calculated by Hewlett-Packard for the costs of software production. The vertical axis is logarithmic and shows the cost of fixing faults at different stages in the software life cycle. Each black bar also shows the number of hours needed to perform usability evaluation at different stages of the life cycle of a software product. It is assumed that the user interface is improved after each evaluation, and the high cost during maintenance is caused by the deployment costs when a new version has to be distributed to end users.

Figure 4.5 shows that usability evaluation is a major software development cost factor. In fact, it forms 20 to 60% of the initial code development cost. Early detection of usability problems is needed as the cost during the specification and design stages is much lower. Problems found in later stages cost much more to fix. We saw in Chapter 2 that high usability measures can increase income, resulting in better reviews and more satisfied and productive users. Evaluation of usability shows tangible savings, from about 2:1 for small projects up to 100:1 for larger projects.

b) Discuss which of the two main types of evaluation testing is more practical.

Answer: The two types of evaluation technique are predictive models and experimental techniques. Predictive models rely on HCI theory, which is not perfected. In many cases, the evaluations are very subjective and many not apply in a specific circumstance. On the other hand, experimental techniques rely on controlled circumstances and so are more reliable. It is generally straightforward for you to define evaluation criteria that fit your particular situations and define specific results that you want to achieve.

By experiment, a number of useful measures have been used to determine the level of usability of systems under test. Table 4.3 shows the more important measures used.

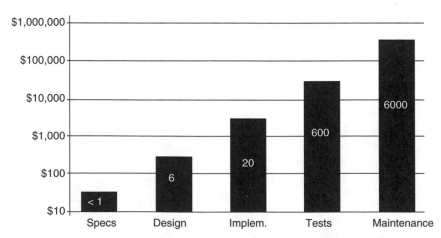

Figure 4.5 ■ Time and Costs for Evaluations in the Development Cycle (Hewlett-Packard)

Table 4.3 ■ **Usability Evaluation Measures**

Measure	Remarks
Task completion	• Number of tasks correctly completed
	• Number of tasks completed in given time
	• Time taken per task
Action usage	• Frequency of use of different commands
	• Use of command sequences
	• Use of special command (e.g., "help")
Shortcuts	• Use of keyboard equivalents
Display perusal	• Time spent looking at display
	• Comparative data for different screen designs
User errors	• Classification of error types
	• Frequency of error types
	• Time spent in error situations
	• Time taken to correct errors
Input devices	• Comparative time taken to execute tasks

LAB 4.3

Specialist tools are needed to set up, carry out, and analyze the results of usability evaluation experiments. Additional software development may be needed to instrument the systems under test so that they can record the measures in Table 4.3. Some of these measures can be extracted from direct observation or video recording. However it is done, teams of evaluators and locations in which to perform the evaluations are needed. We refer to the evaluation locations as usability laboratories.

All major software manufacturers now utilize usability laboratories in which to test prototypes of the products. The laboratories contain special observational equipment such as video cameras, hidden observation points, and specially instrumented computers and workstations.

LAB 4.3 SELF-REVIEW QUESTIONS

In order to test your progress, you should be able to answer the following questions.

1) An effective product means that all of the desired performance goals have been reached.

   a) _____ True
   b) _____ False

2) *Utility* is the set of functions or features of a software package.

    a) _____ True
    b) _____ False

3) *Effectiveness* is the user's ability to access and understand the effects of each feature.

    a) _____ True
    b) _____ False

LAB 4.3

4) Which of the following is not one of Shakel's usability measures?

    a) _____ Effectiveness
    b) _____ Learnability
    c) _____ Flexibility
    d) _____ Consistency
    e) _____ Attitude

5) All but which of the following are measures of effectiveness?

    a) _____ At better than some required level of performance (in terms of speed and errors)
    b) _____ By some required percentage of the specified target range of users
    c) _____ Learned by some required percentage of users within a predefined period
    d) _____ Within some required proportion of the range of usage environments

6) What is the ratio of cost between correcting a usability problem during the design stage compared to the testing stage?

    a) _____ 10 to 1
    b) _____ 50 to 1
    c) _____ 100 to 1
    d) _____ 200 to 1

Quiz answers appear in the Appendix, Section 4.3.

L A B   4 . 4

IMPLEMENTING USER INTERFACES

We build GUI applications from a large range of user interface controls. Modern GUI builder tools typically give developers access to thirty to forty different controls, each with a different set of features. Space does not allow us to describe all of these controls. However, the window user interface control is fundamental to all GUI applications, even those appearing on the Web. We therefore introduce the basic concepts of window creation and management in this lab. You will see that even this fundamental user interface control is far from simple and contains a long list of features. Remember that each feature requires significant application or operating system code to support it.

The user interface controls to support windows have become universal, particularly in Web browsers. As the Web page contents evolve toward an application user interface of their own, they will need to compete with the window controls of freestanding applications. This aspect is discussed in the unit following this.

WINDOWING SYSTEMS

Of all the GUI components that the users see on the display screen, the windows are the most crucial. A window is the foundation component of the GUI concept. It is not surprising that some of the most comprehensive code libraries for building GUIs are named after windows. The two prime examples are Microsoft Windows and MIT's X Window System (often referred to as X Windows or simply X).

A *window* is an area on a display screen with a particular shape (usually rectangular) and a delimiting border. Within the border is a view representing the user interface of a particular software package. This simple definition of a window makes it highly flexible and allows windows to be used for a variety of purposes within a user interface. We see a whole family of windows in the more sophisticated windows implementation systems. Menus of various kinds, dialog boxes, and alerts are special window family members.

Windows were first adopted to reflect the way users normally work in mixed-task environments. Users routinely monitor and manipulate information from a wide variety of sources, then synthesize, summarize, and reorganize that information. From observations of desktops in the real world, people position paper-based information in a spatial fashion according to category. The spatial mapping helps structure the tasks.

LAB 4.4

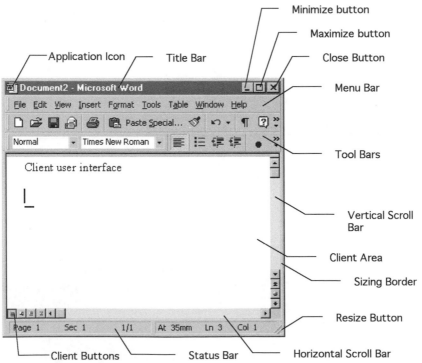

Figure 4.6 ■ A Model Window

Table 4.4 ■ Window User Interface Control Summary

Control	Window Operations
Title Bar	Window identity, move, maximize
Close, Minimize, Maximize Buttons	Terminate window, iconize window to desktop or task bar, use full screen
Application Icon	Menu access to close, minimize, and maximize buttons; also move and size
Menu Bar	GUI menus
Toolbar	Application-dependent tools; usually equivalent to menu items
Scroll Bars	Sophisticated multiuse controls for changing the view of the application client information in the client user interface displayed in the client area
Sizing Border	Resize window horizontally or vertically
Resize Button	Resize window both horizontally and vertically
Status Bar	Read-only display of application client data
Client Buttons	Application-dependent buttons that normally make significant changes to the client area

**LAB
4.4**

A MODEL WINDOW

Figure 4.6 shows a typical window. It is a screen dump of the application used to prepare this text, Microsoft Word 2000 running under Microsoft Windows 98. This windowing system is probably the most widely used and has reached a high level of sophistication over approximately fifteen years of development.

Each label in Figure 4.6 represents at least a separate window control: some labels represent several. The first point we note is the high number of window controls; there are fourteen labels. Most applications running on the Microsoft Windows platform will use all of the window controls. Table 4.4 summarizes the substantial range of window control functions that the window user interface controls provide.

The implementation of the all the window management via the controls of Table 4.4 represents a very significant development effort. In common with other window managers, Microsoft Windows offers application developers access to the basic windowing facilities without the need to write the code from scratch. At the same time, user interface designers can concentrate on the unique application display layouts and controls. Of course, the downside is that each platform adopts widely differing windows controls with quite distinct programming interfaces. Thus, porting an application to another windowing platform is an expensive operation.

WINDOWING MANAGERS

If we consider the structure of the windowing manager, we see that a number of important attributes must be handled. The first is window layout and the control of overlapping windows (nonoverlapping or tiled windows are now rare, although they still find a use in some specialist applications like software development systems). Next, the window icon design must be considered—the small images that represent minimized windows. Windows are also given the responsibility of responding to keyboard input and must arrange that only one window at a time accepts key presses, that is, holds the keyboard focus. Of course, window managers must be aware of the pointing device (cursor on the screen) and where in a window it is currently positioned. Indeed, an entire text editor is provided that is integrated with the pointing device and cursor keys.

A window manager must support an imaging model controlling output planes and image creation within windows. Since menus and dialog boxes are part of the window family, there must be full support for pull-down and popup menus together with modal and modeless dialog boxes. Closely tied to the imaging model are the scrolling facilities linked to the scroll bars.

Just to convey the complexity of modern window managers, Table 4.5 lists the window characteristics that must be controlled. A more detailed treatment of window managers is given in Helander (1988).

X WINDOWS

Worthy of mention because it attempts a vendor-independent solution is X Windows, originally developed at MIT. The X Windows system is a network-transparent, vendor-independent GUI presentation manager at a basic level. Using X Windows primitives, families of high-level user interface presentation managers may be constructed, and several manufacturers of Unix-based systems have adopted this approach. Figure 4.7 illustrates the basic X Windows architecture.

Quite unusually, X Windows is a client-server architecture with the server running on each user's workstation. Applications, run on behalf of users to carry out their tasks, run on central server machines, but act as clients to X Windows.

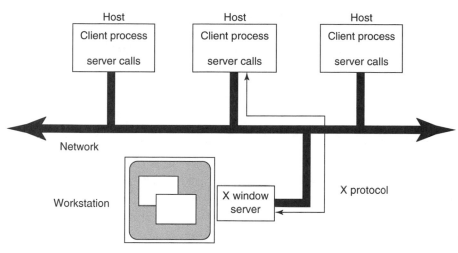

Figure 4.7 ■ X Windows Architecture

Table 4.5 ■ Window User Interface Control Summary

Presentation Aspects	Window Operations	Customization
Title bars	Create and kill (close) window	Reassign mouse buttons
Window borders	Change/set focus	Change listener
Window in focus	Back to front ordering	Mouse command feedback (outlining, rubber banding)
Window icons	Move window	Dynamic menus
Shape of windows	Resize window	Graphics in menus
Icon control	Iconize (minimize)	Macros
Window management control appearance	Size zoom	User profiles
Special control areas within windows	Undo last change	
Fonts	Abort window operation	
Colors	Application hooks	

X Windows supports graphical displays, where a display is a workstation consisting of a keyboard, a mouse (or other pointing device), and one or more screens with the cursor crossing screen boundaries. Application processes may run on the workstation or on any other remote host connected to the network.

LAB 4.4 EXERCISES

4.4.1 UNDERSTAND THE BASICS OF WINDOWING SYSTEMS

a) Discuss the advantages that a windowing environment has over command-line or character-based environments.

_____

_____

b) What is meant by window focus and why is it important in a windowing environment?

_____

_____

4.4.2 UNDERSTAND THE BASICS OF THE X WINDOWS SYSTEM

a) Explain the client/server relationship of X Windows.

_____

_____

b) Find a system running a newer version of MS-Windows (Windows 95 or later) and a system running the X Window system. Compare and contrast the behavior and appearance of the interfaces.

_____

_____

LAB 4.4 EXERCISE ANSWERS

4.4.1 ANSWERS

a) Discuss the advantages that a windowing environment has over command-line or character-based environments.

Answer:Windows were first adopted to reflect the way users normally work in mixed-task environments. Several pieces of work are visible, in part, on the screen at the same time, and the user can quickly switch between them.Windows allow many tasks to be visible, and in some windowing systems, each task is operating with the same priority. External events cause changes in focus of the various tasks (windows). Compared with single screen (task) displays, windowing offers a significant range of benefits.

A window:

- *Allows users to apply spatial ordering of documents on a desktop to display screens (particularly with overlapping windows)*

- *Allows the user to change the focus from one task to another with little effort*

- *Eliminates the need to re-establish context in task switching since the contents of a window are preserved (or can quickly be regenerated) even when the whole window is hidden by others*

- *Provides a visual memory cache that is useful for monitoring tasks peripheral to the main task or for information integration from several sources*

Windowing support is so important that it is now built into the operating system on most platforms.

b) What is meant by window focus and why is it important in a windowing environment?

Answer:The window holding the focus receives input from the keyboard. It is important to keep track of which window has the focus, because it is not always the one on top. Particularly in cases like the X Windowing System, you can have many different windows, all of which are at the same priority, all doing something constructive, so it is impossible to tell where your input is going without keeping track of which window has the focus.

There are several things to keep in mind. First, the term "window" is used very loosely. When you talk about applications on the X Windowing System, you typically talk about "clients." This is partly due to the fact that it is not X that is providing the appearance and behavior of the windows, but rather the windows manager.As its name implies, the windows manager "manages" the windows or clients.

a) Explain the client/server relationship of X Windows.

Answer: The user's workstation, where the windows are displayed, acts as the server. Applications running on the same workstation, or any other machine on the network, act as clients by sending windows requests to the server.

This is an important difference that is both confusing and extremely useful. The easier way to remember the difference is that the machine that is providing the display services is the server. This is the same in other client-server contexts. That is, the machine that provides the service is the server. The machine that uses these services is the client.

Under the X Windowing System, a machine can act as both a client and a server. In fact, the same machine can be both a client and a server at the same time. Therefore, it is best to think of the applications that are using the services as the clients and not the particular machine.

Each display is controlled by an X server process that allows access to the display from multiple clients, interprets network message from clients, passes user input to clients across the network, provides graphics drawing primitives (image model), and maintains resources (windows, cursors, fonts, pixel images) shared between clients.

The screen layout is under complete control of a window manager. Client processes are written as event loops responding to asynchronous events such as key press, mouse click, and mouse movement notified by the X server.

Client applications call upon the services of the X server by issuing a series of requests. Typical requests are to create, destroy, and reconfigure windows and to display text and graphics in a window. Client requests may prompt the server to return status information about windows or other resources. The X server and the entire set of client processes run asynchronously. Requests are queued by the server and serviced in the order of reception. No guarantee of response time is made, since the server may be servicing a large number of clients. Note the response time implications!

Client processes communicate (over the network if necessary) with the X servers using the X protocol. The X protocol is packet-based with four types of packets: requests such as specifications for drawing a line or changing the color value in a cell, replies that contain data solicited by (round-trip) requests, events that contain information about a device action, and error notifications. X protocol packets are buffered to improve the network utilization and decrease delays.

Of similar age to Microsoft Windows, X Windows is dominant on Unix platforms. We may well see the two windows managers competing on an equal footing on the same hardware platform.

b) Find a system running a newer version of MS-Windows (Windows 95 or later) and a system running the X Window System. Compare and contrast the behavior and appearance of the interfaces.

Answer: One of the most significant similarities is the range of features that each provides. If you look at the list of features in Table 4.5, you see that both MS-Windows and X Windows have the same set of features. There are buttons and menus that change the appearance of the window, you can move and resize the window, and you can change the order by which the windows are stacked. It is not until you dig deeper that you start to see differences.

Perhaps the biggest difference is that with X Windows you typically have a choice of window managers. This means that the appearance (and perhaps behavior) can be selected that best fits your needs (or even preferences). If you want, you can even choose a window manager for X that is almost identical to MS-Windows.

The designers of window managers under X have taken this to the extreme. There are complete development environments. That is, you can create applications within the window manager without the need to learn complex programming languages as is the case with MS-Windows.

Another aspect you need to dig for is configurability. Looking at what MS-Windows can configure, you are fairly limited by comparison to the X Windowing System. MS-Windows allows you to define "schemes," which define a common appearance (colors, fonts, etc.) and are then valid for every application. Although many window managers also provide these schemes, you can define your own characteristics down to the application level. That means (if you want to) each application can have a different scheme. For example, all applications that access your live database have yellow letters on a red background and those accessing the test database have the standard black on white. In fact, you can define these characteristics down to individual instance of an application.

The primary task of the window manager is to provide the interface to the graphics server, like the X Windowing System. On an MS-Windows system, the graphics server and window manager are integrated into a single unit with the operating system, which cannot be split apart. Although this can be an advantage in some cases, it is mostly a problem as a client that crashes can effectively take out the operating system with it. An X client may take out the X server, but the operating system is still intact. In addition, whereas both MS-Windows and X Windows can be classified as "good" interfaces, based on the usability and consistency, MS-Windows falls short in configurability and stability.

LAB 4.4 SELF-REVIEW QUESTIONS

In order to test your progress, you should be able to answer the following questions.

1) An X server is the software providing the graphic services and not necessarily the physical machine.

   a) _____ True
   b) _____ False

2) A machine can be simultaneously both a X Windows client and server.

   a) _____ True
   b) _____ False

3) Configurability is the one area where the MS-Windows user interface has advantages over X Windows.

   a) _____ True
   b) _____ False

4) Unlike the MS-Windows GUI, the X Server does not control the appearance of the windows.

   a) _____ True
   b) _____ False

5) Focus determines which window is accepting keyboard input.

   a) _____ True
   b) _____ False

6) How do windows convey the concept of a visual memory cache?

   a) _____ Using part of the hard disk to store the unused portions
   b) _____ By quickly scanning the partially exposed windows and window icons
   c) _____ Storing the unused portion in data structures within the X server
   d) _____ Storing the unused portion in data structures on the client machine

Quiz answers appear in the Appendix, Section 4.4.

CHAPTER 4

TEST YOUR THINKING

1) As we previously discussed, computer software is not the only thing that has a user interface. Observe the user interfaces that you come across in your daily life and consider the aspects we discussed in chapter, such as the usability, effectiveness, intuitive, and so forth.

2) Do some Web surfing and consider the sites you come across in terms of the issues we discussed in chapter, such as the usability, effectiveness, intuitive, and so forth. Post your thoughts, along with the URLs of the sites you chose, to this book's Companion Website.

3)` Consider the messages you receive in your daily life in terms of messages that might appear in a user interface. Are the messages easily understood? Do you require any previous knowledge (that may not be common to everyone) in order to understand the messages?

C H A P T E R 5

HUMAN-COMPUTER INTERACTION FOR THE WEB

Web technology and new applications for the Web have introduced an entirely new class of mistakes.

—Jakob Nielsen

The study of HCI as a separate discipline had a head start of about a dozen years before use of the Web became widespread. While the contents of a Web page present designers with a new type of user interface, many of the basic HCI principles still apply.

It took probably a decade to fully master GUI designs. We are not halfway through the similar time it will take to achieve really polished and effective Web page user interfaces. We present some of the techniques from HCI that are beneficial for Web page user interfaces.

One person has become an expert in applying HCI usability engineering to the design of Web pages. He is Jakob Nielsen and his Web site (Nielsen, 1994) has become the repository of valuable information on Web page user interface design, implementation, and testing. This information is being constantly updated and is provided free to the Web designers of the world.

L A B   5 . 1

DESIGNING WEB PAGE USER INTERFACES

LAB OBJECTIVES

After this lab, you will be able to:

✔ Understand the Characteristics of the Web as a User Interface
✔ See How Consistency, Simplicity, and Context Apply to the Web

---

When users view a Web page, they do so via another freestanding application called a *browser*. At least that is still how the majority of Web page users interact with the Web. We should note here that Web page viewers are steadily being incorporated into other applications as help pages and information pages associated with multimedia viewers and so on. Even the traditional desktops within operating systems are turning into Web pages, a quite natural progression.

Developers of freestanding browsers continue to design the user interfaces using traditional HCI techniques that we described in earlier chapters. We will refer to such a user interface as a *traditional GUI*. Thus the windows, menus, toolbars, and dialogs within browsers will look the same as they have for the last few years. The tasks of opening and managing windows, setting preferences, and interacting with the local files remain the same. Remember that each major computer platform has its own way of representing these tasks in the user interface, but we can assume users on each platform are familiar with working this way.

Of course, the differences come in the content of the Web pages themselves. We will refer to page content as the *Web page user interface*. Here we are largely in a new world of user interface design—the world of hypermedia. By this we mean rich information content containing hyperlinks. Within a Web page, we use hyperlinks to navigate to new parts of the user interface, and not a single traditional menu is in sight. Hyperlinks can also be stored locally on our workstations in a hyperlink store, usually called *bookmark*s or *favorites*. We must interact with the hyperlink store to reach certain Web pages quickly.

As user interface designers, we must learn the characteristics of the new medium and how to exploit them. We find some similarities but also some important differences that will guide our user interface designs. Much of the discussion that follows is adapted from Nielsen (1997a, b).

WEB CHARACTERISTICS

Let's start with the similarities for Web page user interfaces. After all, we are still dealing with an interactive software system when we view Web pages. It is the nature of the interaction that changes, with most traditional user interface controls absent and a few new ones taking their place.

The contents of Web pages can start with the print medium model. From this source we borrow basic typography and text layout. Static pictures and figures can be laid out using rules garnered over the centuries of printed publications. Where multimedia content appears, there are the broadcast media to fall back on for rules of presentation. The only really new type of content in a Web page is the *hyperlink*. At a stroke, this novel interaction method impacts much of traditional GUI design, as we will see.

Nonetheless, when we come to evaluate the Web page user interface for usability, the good news is that the traditional HCI evaluation techniques are still appropriate. The new Web page user interface still has to interact with the same humans after all. Scott Butler in Nielsen (1997b) puts forward a good discussion of the issues.

DEVICE DIVERSITY

Delving more deeply into the Web page user interface, we come upon some quite significant differences. The first is much greater device diversity. In the traditional GUI, we control the placement of every pixel on screen. Looking at the range of screens on high-end workstations compared to laptop screens, we see a ratio of one workstation screen to about six laptop screens. This ratio triples with hand-held portable devices that are at last becoming more common.

Looking at the Web, we see a situation where one workstation screen equals about 100 cell phone screens. Yes, the display in the most modern cell phones can be used to view Web pages. Our user interface designs for Web pages must begin to take this into account. In effect, this means that WYSIWYG has to be abandoned as a design aim for Web pages. In fact, HTML that defines Web pages has no absolute requirement to display particular fonts and font sizes. As well, the browser will render the HTML in windows of any width and depth, so there never has been the guarantee of WYSIWYG on the Web.

Furthermore, if we look at network bandwidth, which has a large impact on the responsiveness of the Web page user interface, we see that one T3 data line equals the speed of about 1000 modems. This brings us to the notion that looking different is a feature, not a bug.

In the very near future, therefore, we must design the Web page user interface to allow the presentation to be determined by the interplay of page specifications and preference settings and other characteristics of the client device.

CONTEXT

Remember that in the traditional GUI we use modal dialogs and graying out to limit the options available to the user at each stage in the interaction. Essentially, both of these options are missing for Web pages. The range of options is represented by the hyperlinks that the user can click on at any particular time. We simulate graying out by presenting the same set of hyperlinks with selected ones disabled. This method also helps the user decide upon the context, since the grayed-out hyperlink effectively defines the particular location of the page within a set of pages.

Our one big problem in a Web page user interface is the transition from one page to another. In the traditional GUI, the user interface designer has absolute control of the user interface view transition process. For the most part on the Web, the users have absolute control of each page transition. They can access the browser back/forward buttons from every page; they can jump directly to a page from a search engine; they can even arrive at any specific page using the hyperlink store. Therefore, it is better to design for this freedom of movement. As an example, put a logo (linked to the home page) on every page to provide context and navigation for users jumping straight to that page.

Another very important difference for Web page user interfaces has to do with context. Always remember that no matter how extensive your Web pages, they are still only a very small part of the whole Web. With traditional GUIs you use only one application at a time, even though you may switch between several applications. On the Web, the switch may occur on every mouse click. This rapid switch back and forth between very different user interfaces has led to a new genre of user interface design.

THE CHANGING WEB

Even your own Web pages are not static, or should not be so. In Benjamin (1996), we are reminded of this: "One of the differences in publishing on the Web is that unlike a television program, magazine, or newspaper, whatever it is you're working on is never finished." Your Web should always continue to evolve, and we don't have version numbers any more. From time to time then, it is necessary to perform evaluations afresh to check the Web page user interface and the structure of the pages to see if consistency still holds.

Not all of our traditional GUI design expertise needs to be changed. Our old standby, the metaphor, can still be employed productively for structuring Web sites. In Rosenfeld (n.d.) we see a familiar discussion of the use of real-world metaphors. Rosenfeld gives us some hints about what type of metaphors work for structuring Web sites. He indicates that organizational metaphors are generally bad. He cites an example of how he used a "new bookstore" metaphor for a bookstore Web. Good metaphors are "places, such as maps, malls, libraries, and industrial parks, and publications, such as encyclopedias, magazines, and newsletters."

LAB 5.1 EXERCISES

5.1.1 UNDERSTAND THE CHARACTERISTICS OF THE WEB AS A USER INTERFACE

a) Discuss different applications that are being converted to understand and display Web pages. Are there any applications that are using the Web technology?

_____

_____

b) When we disable a function in traditional graphical interface, the menu item is grayed out. Discuss how can this be accomplished in a Web page.

_____

_____

c) Discuss the difference between the traditional GUI and the Web page user interface.

_____

_____

5.1.2 SEE HOW CONSISTENCY, SIMPLICITY, AND CONTEXT APPLY TO THE WEB

a) Saying that WYSIWYG is dead on the Web reflects the fact that browsers have never displayed a Web page in any exact format. Load up several Web pages and make changes in your browser configuration to see how the appearance changes. Discuss how this applies to the statement that WYSIWYG is dead on the Web.

_____

_____

b) Discuss the statement that the Web page user interface is ever changing.

_____

_____

LAB 5.1 EXERCISE ANSWERS

5.1.1 ANSWERS

a) Discuss different applications that are being converted to understand and display Web pages. Are there any applications that are using the Web technology?

Answer: Most office and business products are now capable of at least displaying HTML pages. Word processors, spreadsheets, and even some databases are capable of generating Web pages. There are even file and directory managers that are not only capable of understanding and displaying HTML pages, but can do so on servers that are only accessible through Internet protocols other than HTTP (such as FTP).

As we discussed previously, many help systems are already using hypertext. However, many have taken the next step and have converted to HTML. This allows the user to access the help information with needed a separate application.

b) When we disable a function in traditional graphical interface, the menu item is grayed out. Discuss how can this be accomplished in a Web page.

Answer: Using standard HTML, you could simply not include a link to any URL behind the menu item. Therefore, that particular item would not appear as the other menu items and clicking on it would have no effect.

Because links are typically displayed as underlined text, having a line that is not under-lined in a menu would indicate to the user that there is something different about this entry. Clicking on this menu item would have no effect, since it is just like any other text. Some browsers allow the user to control the appearance of the link so this might be a problem. However, the user will still have a problem trying to figure out what text is a link.

c) Discuss the difference between the traditional GUI and the Web page user interface.

Answer: The traditional GUI is platform-dependent and is used to implement free-standing Web page browser applications. The Web page user interface refers to the con-tents of the Web page itself, viewed in the main browser window. The contents of this window should be platform-independent.

Another key difference is the range of controls that you can provide using a standard GUI. Basically anything is possible with a typical GUI, but you are extremely limited with HMTL. Most GUI development packages provide predefined controls with built-in func-tions. You might be able to create similar control in some cases, but you are still limited in scope.

Unfortunately, the platform-independence of Web pages is not guaranteed by any means. One common example is Microsoft's Jscript, which is a "dialect" of the Web standard Javascript. Web pages that are written in the non-standard Jscript tend to make non-Microsoft browsers spit out one error after the other. The result is that they cannot be effectively viewed on platforms that do not have Microsoft browsers, such as most UNIX variants. However, platform-independence is fairly certain using standard HTML (assuming it is supported by your browser version).

ActiveX provides the ability to have basically the same range of controls provided in a standard interface. However, it is only available on MS-Windows browsers and therefore not available for UNIX.

Using Java you can gain platform-independence and still have access to most control types. Once again, Microsoft has provided its own nonstandard version, which is not the same as the standard defined by the creators of Java, Sun Microsystems.

5.1.2 ANSWERS

a) Saying that WYSIWYG is dead on the Web reflects the fact that browsers have never displayed a Web page in any exact format. Load up several Web pages and make changes in your browser configuration to see how the appearance changes. Discuss how this applies to the statement that WYSIWYG is dead on the Web.

Answer: Modern browsers allow you to change how different things are displayed on the screen. Even something as basic as whether a link appears as underlined text can be controlled by some browsers. Therefore, a Web designer may think that elements on a page will be displayed in a particular way, but there is no guarantee that the user did not configure his or her browser differently. What the developer sees is not necessarily what the user gets.

b) Discuss the statement that the Web page user interface is ever changing.

Answer: There are two primary reasons that the Web interface is considered to be ever changing. The first is the media itself. Web documents consist of individual pages and text is extremely easy to update. In contrast to printed documents, making changes to Web pages takes almost no time at all with almost no effort. Quick changes can be made "on the fly" that are immediately available to visitors. This enables Web authors to provide literally up-to-the-minute information.

The other aspect is that users have come to expect that Web pages be continually up-dated with new information or that old information is kept up to date. Readers generally accept the fact that printed material is already out of date by the time it is printed. Since books have publishing cycles upwards of six months, it is no surprise that they are outdated, particularly when you consider how fast the computer industry changes. However, users know how easy it is to change Web sites and therefore it is expected that the sites are up to date.

In contrast to books, there should not be a sense of version number, rather a record of the last date of change. Most Web servers allow you to add special HTML tags to your pages that automatically display the date the page was last changed. The less frequently you change the pages, obviously the less current the information. People start visiting your site less and less often and eventually stop coming all together.

There has been more than one occasion when I was on the CNN Web site and while I was visiting the site, the home page changed with some breaking news. Even if I had simply stayed on the start page, it would have eventually refreshed itself using the HTML tag:

```
<META http-equiv="REFRESH" content="1800">
```

This means the page would reload after 1800 seconds or 30 minutes. If CNN can have up-to-the-minute news, you certainly can make changes once a day, if necessary.

LAB 5.1 SELF-REVIEW QUESTIONS

In order to test your progress, you should be able to answer the following questions.

1) According to L. Rosenfeld, using "metaphors" in Web interface design is intrinsically "bad" because they tend to confuse new Internet users.

   a) _____ True
   b) _____ False

2) Platform-independence is not guaranteed with Web pages because there are many examples where vendors create their own versions of "standard" programs, protocols, and so forth.

   a) _____ True
   b) _____ False

3) Why is device diversity more acute on the Web?

   a) _____ The resolution available for noncomputer devices is currently too low.
   b) _____ Hand-held devices can only load static pages.
   c) _____ The size of the display on cell phones and other hand-held devices plays a key role.
   d) _____ Computer monitors are limited in the video protocols they support.

4) Which of the following is a reason why the hyperlink is so special for the Web page user interface?

   a) _____ Moving between different parts of the of the web document (i.e. different functions) require special attention.
   b) _____ There is no direct equivalent to the hyperlink in the traditional GUI for navigating the user interface.
   c) _____ Programming technology has not reached the point of allowing the concept of hyperlinks in a traditional GUI.
   d) _____ With traditional programs there is no equivalent of the "Back" button as on a browser.

5) Why do Web page user interface designers lose control of interface transitions on the Web?

a) _____ The nature of the Web allows for nonlinear access of pages.

b) _____ The browser back/forward button, search engines, and bookmark lists allow the user to break an otherwise controlled transition from one Web page to another.

c) _____ Web page user interfaces consisting of sequences of pages should not assume a user would follow such a sequence.

d) _____ All of the above.

Quiz answers appear in the Appendix, Section 5.1.

LAB 5.2

WEB PAGE DESIGN PRINCIPLES

LAB OBJECTIVES

After this lab, you will be able to:

✔ Apply Web Page Usability Measurement
✔ Recognize Examples of Bad Web Page Design

Knowing the characteristics of the Web and their relationships to HCI practice, we can look for principles of Web page design. Most of the design approaches involving task analysis are relevant for Web page user interfaces. The same applies to the usability of Web pages and its measurement. Of course, the layout of static text and images is exactly the same as the GUI applications.

WEB USABILITY MEASUREMENT

The contents of a Web page and the embedded hyperlinks form another type of user interface using the same interaction devices we discussed in earlier units. Traditional evaluation methods of usability still apply. In this section, we look at where we need to place emphasis in order to account for some of the special requirements of Web users. Once again, we call upon the expertise of Jakob Nielsen to guide us in this respect (1999a,b).

During the initial design stage for a Web site, some broad guiding metaphors and top-level descriptions are needed. Nielsen assures us that only a small number of users need to be tested at this stage. Up to five users are given tasks that the new Web site will support. They will reveal a list of most of the important usability problems in the design. Only a short time is needed to conduct these tests, and the design input is very valuable. Most initial designs have so many problems that the list of changes after five users will be long.

SIZE OF WEB PAGES

New Web page designers often ask the question, What size should my Web pages be? We must strike a balance between conveying a useful amount of information in the page and keeping the download time (response time) to a sensible maximum. Because of network constraints, we know that response time after clicking a hyperlink in a Web page can be very long. Designers of Web pages cannot influence the network and the Internet but they can take sensible precautions against long response times.

One of the best discussions of this problem of response time is Nielsen (1994). Nielsen reiterates original HCI research, which has found three thresholds for response times:

1. 0.1 second: Interaction seems instantaneous; no special feedback needed except to display the result.
2. 1.0 second: The limit for the user's flow of thought to stay uninterrupted, even though the user will notice the delay. No special feedback needed.
3. 10 seconds: The limit for keeping the user's attention focused on the dialogue. Feedback needed.

Nielsen concludes that feedback is especially important if response time is likely to be highly variable as it is on the Web. Note that page designers are completely reliant on the browser to give progressive feedback when the response time exceeds 1 second. If Web page designers aim for a response time of 1 second or 10 seconds, then some page sizes to aim at are listed in Table 5.1 for the different types of Internet connection.

Table 5.1 ■ Size Limits for Web Pages

	1 Second Response Time	10 Second Response Time
Modem	2 KB	34 KB
ISDN	8 KB	150 KB
T-1	100 KB	2 MB

Web page editors, like Microsoft FrontPage, calculate the expected download time at a chosen bandwidth as the page is being edited. As you design your Web pages, you should have a maximum download time in mind for every page. Of course, your home page is crucial and will generally have a lower limit than some other pages. The only way a Web page design can attempt to meet a particular response time is to limit the size of the Web page and any components it contains.

An interesting recent study (Flanders, 1999a) looked at the download times of the top fifty Web sites. Flanders took the top ten and the bottom ten sites from the fifty and measured the sizes of the home pages. An example measurement from a site was:

Ranking	Site	Load Time	Total Objects	Total Size	Total Connects	HTML	Images	Other	Time at 28.8	Time at 56K
1	Yahoo	Excellent	5	17652	3	10334	7318	0	7.15	4.96

The average page size from Flanders' sample was 49024.7 bytes or 47.8 KB. From his study he concludes that the most visited sites have the fastest download times, that is, the smallest sizes. It is interesting to see some of the famous Web sites whose home pages exceed this size.

WEB PAGES THAT SUCK

Vince Flanders started his "Web Pages That Suck" (WPTS) Web site with tongue in cheek to calm his frustration. This site has become one of the most cited for Web page designers. WPTS exploits a well-known design tool—keep records of bad examples to avoid at all costs. So successful is this site that it is now published as a book (Flanders & Willis, 1998).

LAB 5.2 EXERCISES

5.2.1 APPLY WEB PAGE USABILITY MEASUREMENT

a) It has been said that only five users are needed to test out initial Web page designs. Discuss why you think this is valid.

_____

_____

b) What is the best usability measure for Web page designs?

_____

_____

Take a look at the Yahoo Web site at http://www.yahoo.com.

c) Discuss what aspects allow the Yahoo site to load faster than other sites (such as the CNN Web site, http://www.cnn.com).

_____

_____

5.2.2 RECOGNIZE EXAMPLES OF BAD WEB PAGE DESIGN

Visit Flander's page "Web Sites That Suck" at http://www.webpagesthatsuck.com. Additionally, visit Stevyn Pompelio's site "How to Make Annoying Web Pages" at www.users.nac.net/falken/annoying/main.html.

a) Consider what it is about the examples that Flanders (1999b) and Pompelio (1999) provide that make them poor design choices.

_____

_____

Visit Nielsen's original document outlining the top ten mistakes of Web page design at http://www.useit.com/alertbox/9605.html.

b) Discuss why some of the original Nielsen top ten mistakes of Web page design in 1996 still received a very severe rating in 1999?

_____

_____

LAB 5.2 EXERCISE ANSWERS

5.2.1 ANSWERS

a) It has been said that only five users are needed to test out initial Web page designs. Discuss why you think this is valid.

Answer: Early Web page designs are so bad when applying the standards of today that only five users are needed to discover the faults. Because so many people still use the same techniques and approaches, the statement still applies to Web pages today.

Note that these user tests can be done quickly in the space of a day or so and are relatively inexpensive tests to conduct. However, as with any test, you need to have a good cross section of people testing. For example, you will get lopsided results if the only people testing are from the same area within the company. Highly trained IT who understand the technical aspects of the software give a different result from clerical staff who use software from a user perspective, who, in turn, give different results from managers, who only use their computer once a month.

The measure we are making here is the percentage of test users capable of accomplishing the specific task they were given. Many users will give up after a certain time in tests. Bear in mind that in real life they are likely to give up much earlier. This means that the percentage derived from tests will most likely be an optimistic number.

A useful side effect of the success rate measure is that a thinking-aloud study can be carried on in parallel. Making users think aloud as they attempt the tasks results in very useful qualitative feedback for the Web page designers.

Of particular value on the Web are usability measures for novice users. Users rarely become highly experienced with a particular Web site since they visit so many. Note that this will not be true for intranet use and some external sites that undertake crucial support for a user's everyday tasks. Here it will be necessary to acquire usability measures for expert users as well.

Nielsen tells us that if you are satisfied being an average site, then you could set a goal of having a success rate of slightly less than 50% for the most common things people want to do on your site. Being average on the Web is not usually a good strategy because user choice is so vast. Nevertheless, this might be a good way to go when design funds are very limited or a Web presence is vital at all costs.

Success rates of 90% or even 95% are overly ambitious and probably not realistic on the Web today. A more realistic success rate might be 80% for a company that values its customers very highly. Achieving a success rate of 60% is a reasonable target for most other projects.

b) What is the best usability measure for Web page designs?

Answer: For Web designs the simplest usability metric is the success rate for a user performing a typical task, i.e., the percentage of test users able to complete the allotted task, the average time it takes a specific number of users to complete the task, and so forth.

Keep in mind what "usability" means. Too often usability is equated with "ease of use." Although ease of use is an important factor is usability, it is by no means the only one. For example, something that is easy to use but does not allow the user to complete the task within the required amount of time has low usability.

c) Discuss what aspects allow the Yahoo site to load faster than other sites (such as the CNN Web site, http://www.cnn.com).

Answer: The first thing that should come to mind is the almost complete lack of any graphics. Although there are a few at Yahoo, they are fairly small. This means the page is almost completely text. There is a lot of information, but it can all be quickly loaded. In contrast, the CNN Web site relies heavily on graphics. There is a least one graphic for the lead article, advertisements, and many other graphics. Granted, one picture is worth a thousand words, so it is expected that a Web site devoted to news would have pictures. The result is that takes longer to load the page.

If your visitors have wait too long for the page to load, it typically isn't usable. I know many applications written for traditional GUIs where there is an extremely long load-up time, but this decreases the access time later. For example, static information is loaded from a database, which takes a long time to transfer. However, once the data is on the local machine, reaction times are very fast. The tradeoff is slow loading times, but fast reaction later on.

The Web is different. First, you cannot expect to have all of the data on the local machine. Neither you nor your users want this, really. Therefore, you need to work on fast loading because the reaction time (i.e., database queries) is dependent on the connection (assuming that the programmers have optimized database activity).

Note that limiting the amount of graphics is not the only way to decrease the load time. Some sites (such as Yahoo) take advantages of something called "client-side image maps." Most people are familiar with clicking on an image to load a particular page. You will also find almost as many sites where clicking on different places within the image loads different pages. Until recently this was done with server-side image maps. The browser was able to identify the location on the page where the user click and send that information to the server. The server then looked in its map file to find which URL to load. It then sent the URL back to the client, which actually made the request. This back and forth communication takes time.

Recently, more and more pages are using client-side maps now that more and more browsers support them. Instead of having to send messages back and forth to figure out what URL to load, all of the work is done at the client side. Here is how a client-side map looks on the Yahoo site:

**LAB
5.2**

```
<map name=m>
<area coords="0,0,52,52" href=r/a1>
<area coords="53,0,121,52" href=r/p1>
<area coords="122,0,191,52" href=r/m1>
<area coords="441,0,510,52" href=r/wn>
<area coords="511,0,579,52" href=r/i1>
<area coords="580,0,637,52" href=r/hw>
</map>
```

When you click on the rectangle enclosed by any of the listed coordinates, the client immediately knows which page to load (the href= tag). This means there is nothing send to the server except for the page request. Since this will happen in any case, the loading time is a lot less.

Another good example of this is the SCO Web site (http://www.sco.com). Although it still uses client-side maps, it couples them with JavaScript for some interesting effects. Some sites get the same effect using Java. However, this means retrieving even more data from the server, which takes even longer to load.

Graphics and Java applets are not the only reasons why pages take long to load. It might just be that there is too much text on the page. The author goes on and on and on and on and on and there are few breaks in the page and it is extremely hard to keep track of where you are in the text.

A different method for estimating average Web page size is described in Sullivan (1999). He does random probing of the Web. His results are shown in Table 5.2. Note the size is 66% larger than the Flanders' number for very popular sites. Maybe Web page user interface designers generally should take a closer look at these popular sites. Note also that the figure for 1999 has dropped by 1.6% compared with 1998. Perhaps page designers are actually responding to good Web page design guidelines.

Table 5.2 ■ Average Page Size

	May 1999	May 1998	August 1997
Pages Sampled	200 pages	213 pages	44 pages
Avg. Page Size	60 KB	61 KB	44 KB

For an up-to-date sample, you should check out the Gif Wizard site (uswest. gifwizard.com). This site survey lists the top 100 sites using a number of different measurements, plus they have a wide range of tools to help make your own site more efficient.

5.2.2 ANSWERS

> **a)** Consider what it is about the examples that Flanders (1999b) and Pompelio (1999) provide that make them poor design choices.
>
> *Answer: It is difficult to present WPTS examples in this book because many of the faults involve the bad use of color and the overuse of animation and other dynamic effects. Both Web sites give you guidelines as what to avoid. For a short checklist, we have summarized the major faults in Table 5.3.*

Table 5.3 ■ Page Design Faults to Avoid

Fault	Comment
Pretentious Front Page	Dispense with heavy colors and long-running animations on home pages that are visited frequently.
Forcing the Browser	Don't make the browser window a certain width or change the default fonts.
High on Kai	When you get your new graphics package, don't insist on putting every effect on your Web pages.
Free Backgrounds That Suck	Fiery flames look great in some images; don't use them for backgrounds just because they're free.
Widen Your Background Images	Background images are used with tables to produce vertical color bar effect. Remember the background images repeat horizontally. On wide monitors the effect is disastrous. Note that some people have very big monitors indeed.
Too Much Text	A common fault. Keep pages short.
Bad Text	Don't use a different color for each character in text, even if it's a title.
Java Jive	Never use Java applets for graphics effects.
Needless JavaScript	Don't use JavaScript mouseover effects just because you can. When something becomes popular, it usually starts to suck.
Cascading Style Sheets	The latest and greatest way to make ugly pages.

Some of the advice in Table 5.3 is somewhat irreverent and personal, but all of it makes the Web page user interface designer think carefully about the page layout and structure. Don't forget to send your own candidate pages to WPTS.

In his Alertbox article (1996), Jakob Nielsen listed his top ten mistakes of Web page design. These have become extremely well-known design aids. The mistakes are listed in Table 5.4.

**LAB
5.2**

Table 5.4 ■ Top 10 Mistakes of Web Page Design

Mistake	Comment	Severity of Problem in 1999
1. Using Frames	Frames are very confusing for users: • Frames break the fundamental user model of the Web page. • Cannot bookmark the current page and return to it. • URLs stop working. • Difficult to print. • Who knows what information will appear where when you click on a link?	Medium
2. Bleeding-Edge Technology	Latest Web technology may attract a few nerds, but mainstream users will care more about useful content and your ability to offer good customer service. When desktop publishing was young, people put twenty fonts in their document. Avoid similar design bloat on the Web.	Very severe
3. Constantly Running Animations	Never include page elements that move incessantly. Moving images have an overpowering effect on the human peripheral vision. Give the user some peace and quiet to actually read the text! <BLINK> is simply evil.	Very severe

(continued)

Table 5.4 ■ Top 10 Mistakes of Web Page Design (continued)

Mistake	Comment	Severity of Problem in 1999
4. Complex URLs	URLs should be hidden from the user interface. However, users do see URLs in current Web browsers. A URL should contain human-readable directory and file names. Also, users need to type a URL, so use short names with all lower-case characters and no special characters.	Severe
5. Orphan Pages	All pages should include a clear indication of the Web site they belong to since users may access pages directly without coming in through your home page. Every page should have a linkup to the home page as well as some indication of where it fits within the structure of your information space.	Medium
6. Long Scrolling Pages	Only 10% of users scroll beyond the information that is visible on the screen when a page comes up. All critical content and navigation options should be on the top part of the page. Page is usually long because it is a leaf node that is only read by people with special interests—make it shorter!	Smaller problem
7. Lack of Navigation Support	Don't assume that users know as much about your site as you do—they always have difficulty finding information. Users need support in the form of a strong sense of structure and place. Provide a site map and let users know where they are and where they can go. Also, include a search feature since even the best navigation support will never be enough.	Severe

(continued)

Table 5.4 ■ Top 10 Mistakes of Web Page Design (*continued*)

Mistake	Comment	Severity of Problem in 1999
8. Non-Standard Link Colors	Don't change the standard colors. The ability to understand followed links is one of the few navigational aids that is standard in most Web browsers. Consistency is key to teaching users what the link colors mean.	Severe
9. Outdated Information	Weed out old information. Keep old pages up to date—the information is still valuable.	Very severe
10. Overly Long Download Times	Should be obvious! Traditional HCI guidelines indicate 10 seconds as the maximum response time before users lose interest. On the Web, users have been trained to endure so much suffering that it may be acceptable to increase this limit to 15 seconds for a few pages. Bandwidth is getting worse, not better.	Very severe

The third column in Table 5.4 headed "Severity of Problem in 1999" shows Nielsen's update of the severity of the mistakes three years later in 1999 (Nielsen, 1999a). Despite his well-publicized warnings, only the problem with long Web pages had improved.

Following on from his assessment on Web page design improvement, or otherwise, Nielsen has now published a second list of ten mistakes of Web page design (1999b). These new mistakes are:

1. *Breaking or Slowing Down the Back Button*
2. *Opening New Browser Windows*
3. *Nonstandard Use of GUI Widgets*
4. *Lack of Biographies*
5. *Lack of Archives*
6. *Moving Pages to New URLs*
7. *Headlines That Make No Sense Out of Context*
8. *Jumping at the Latest Internet Buzzword*
9. *Slow Server Response Times*
10. *Anything That Looks Like Advertising*

These mistakes are fairly self-explanatory. We refer the reader to Nielsen (http://www. useit.com/alertbox/990530.html) for further details.

b) Discuss why some of the original Nielsen top ten mistakes of Web page design in 1996 still received a very severe rating in 1999.

Answer: With each new generation of Web technology, there are always people who think that something is "cool" and tend to abuse it on their site. Bleeding edge technology is more irritating than ever as we receive fewer browser updates. Constantly running animations are on the increase. Web pages become more outdated as more pages are published and fewer updates are performed. Download times may actually be increasing as more pages are generated dynamically putting more load on the servers.

One of the key points to remember is that just because you can do something doesn't mean you have to. Flanders' own site fails in this area. On at least one of his pages he requires the use of Macromedia's Flash but does not warn you in advance. Even with my screen resolution at 1024×768 I don't see any reference to needing Flash when the page is first loaded. Based on Table 5.4, only 10% of users scroll beyond the information that is visible on the screen when a page comes up. Therefore, 90% of users won't immediately understand why the page is taking so long to load. So you end up waiting and waiting and waiting until you get a popup saying you need Flash. On Flanders's site it takes over a minute just for the popup to appear across my ISDN line that I need Flash, not to mention the time it takes to download Flash.

LAB 5.2 SELF-REVIEW QUESTIONS

In order to test your progress, you should be able to answer the following questions.

1) Forcing specific colors or font sizes is still one of the few ways the Web page developer can maintain control of the page's appearance.

    a) _____ True
    b) _____ False

2) Despite increased download times, it is a good idea to have home pages with fancy graphics or plug-ins like Macromedia Flash in order to attract customers.

    a) _____ True
    b) _____ False

3) From Table 5.1, what is the upper limit on Web page size for a modem link to keep the response time below 10 seconds?

    a) _____ 20 KB
    b) _____ 34 KB
    c) _____ 48 KB
    d) _____ 54 KB

4) Which of the following is not a problem when using frames?

    a) _____ Frames are very confusing for users.
    b) _____ Frames break the fundamental user model of the Web page.
    c) _____ The user cannot bookmark the current page and return to it.
    d) _____ Frames are difficult to print.
    e) _____ None. They are all problems.

5) Which of the following is not generally considered a means of reducing download times for your users?

    a) _____ Using few and small graphics
    b) _____ Using less text
    c) _____ Increasing your internet connection
    d) _____ Avoiding "bleeding edge" technology

Quiz answers appear in the Appendix, Section 5.2.

C H A P T E R   5

TEST YOUR THINKING

1) Web-based programming languages such as JavaScript enable you to use many of the same programming constructs and techniques. Using the onclick() function in JavaScript, how would you create a menu with the ability to "disable" specific menu options?

2) Investigate WAP (Wireless Application Protocol) and see how it applies to Web-based interfaces.

3) Visit the Gif Wizard Web site (http://uswest.gifwizard.com) and then test several different kinds of sites using its analysis tool. Consider why the sites have different results. Compare the results provided by Gif Wizard with your own personal experience when visiting the site. What can you say about the difference?

C H A P T E R 6

WEB PAGE NAVIGATION

Navigation. *The science or art of conducting ships or vessels from one place to another, including, more especially, the method of determining a ship's position, course, distance passed over, etc., on the surface of the globe, by the principles of geometry and astronomy.*

—Online Medical Dictionary

CHAPTER OBJECTIVES

In this chapter, you will learn about:

In this unit, we will discuss the second of the two great pillars of Web page information: content and links. We'll talk about links under the general topic of *navigation,* a term borrowed from finding your way about the earth's surface and the space above. Make mistakes with the navigational elements of your Web pages and readers' visits to your pages will soon cease. It is important that you understand the rules of creating and laying out the navigational elements and adhere to those rules closely.

L A B   6 . 1

WEB PAGE NAVIGATION

LAB OBJECTIVES

After this lab, you will be able to:

✔ Understand the Difference Between Content and Navigation
✔ Compare Web Navigation to Earth Navigation
✔ Understand the Importance of Web Navigation

The number of navigation elements within Web pages and how those elements are laid out will vary considerably depending on the purpose of the Web site. Even for the navigation elements themselves, there are often choices as to how they are presented to the page reader and their relative locality on the page. It is vital that the reader is able to recognize the navigational elements quickly after a very brief scan of the page.

In later labs, we will discuss the choices that are available to the page designer when constructing navigation elements. Then we will develop simple rules that dictate where the navigation elements should be positioned and how much of the page they should occupy. Much of this rule base relies on the development of a clear plan by the designer as to which type of navigation page is being built. An understanding of the likely user (reader) profiles is important here. To aid the thinking of the page designer, we will consider the analogy between navigation in physical space and the Web.

NAVIGATION IN WEB PAGES

If we refer back to the definition of navigation at the head of this chapter, we see quickly why this earthbound definition can be applied to the navigation of the Web. When viewing one Web page, the reader is able to navigate or move to a following Web page and, just as importantly, return to the original page, if needed. However, the Earth navigation definition is applied to two- and three-dimensional space, whereas the links in Web pages essentially apply to a multidimensional Web space with an almost infinite number of dimensions.

Note that the definition mentions position, course, and distance passed. All of these have parallels in the Web space. It is important that, as a Web page designer, you keep these aspects of navigation to the fore when constructing the navigation elements in your pages. If the page reader loses a sense of position, course, or distance between Web pages, then that reader is, literally, "lost in Web space." This is the dreaded situation that must be avoided at all costs. Unfortunately, it is a situation that occurs all too frequently, even with some pages designed by professionals.

POSITION, COURSE, AND DISTANCE

Let us elaborate on the meaning of position, course, and distance in terms of Web pages. We will see that there are some strong parallels, but also some distinct differences from Earth navigation. Web technology provides each page with a unique address, the URL. If the browser is not displaying a set of frame pages, knowing the URL of a page gives us pinpoint accuracy as to where we are in the Web space. Also, given a URL, we can navigate directly to that page.

NAVIGATING AND THE NAVIGATOR

Where the earthbound navigation analogy still holds is the position of the act of navigation itself. It is not surprising that navigation tasks are vested in a human navigator, a designated person endowed with the necessary skills and capable of guiding the ship or aircraft successfully. A navigator is respected as a person of high importance since the safety of all fellow travelers is at stake. In Web space, the navigators are the page readers themselves, and they must be given the necessary tools and techniques to navigate successfully to their destinations. The important person in Web page navigation is the page designer who must make sure that the required navigation tools and techniques are present within the page in order that the reader navigates without difficulty. *Navigation design* is thus the important skill here.

LAB 6.1 EXERCISES

6.1.1 UNDERSTAND THE DIFFERENCE BETWEEN CONTENT AND NAVIGATION

Web pages contain both information content and navigation elements.

   a) Discuss the difference between content and navigation.

_____

_____

b) Discuss the necessity of having navigation elements on every Web page.

_____

_____

c) Why are user profiles important? How can they be employed in designing navigation aides?

_____

_____

6.1.2 COMPARE WEB NAVIGATION TO EARTH NAVIGATION

Navigating across the Earth and through the Web are similar tasks.

a) Discuss how navigation is very similar in the two domains.

_____

_____

b) Discuss how navigation is very *different* in the two domains.

_____

_____

c) What navigation methods are provided in printed media? How do these compare to Web navigation?

_____

_____

d) Create a navigation system that might be found on a site discussing world geography. Draw on things from previous chapters as well and design an appropriate interface. What navigational aids could you provide?

_____

_____

6.1.3 UNDERSTAND THE IMPORTANCE OF WEB NAVIGATION

Think about the differences between a ship's navigator and a Web page navigator.

a) Discuss who the Web page navigator is.

_____

_____

b) Why is the designer of Web page navigation elements so important?

_____

_____

LAB 6.1 EXERCISE ANSWERS

6.1.1 ANSWERS

a) Discuss the difference between content and navigation.

Answer: Content is comprised of those things presented on the page that are intended to provide information. These can be text, graphics, or a combination of both. In general, the content would have the exact same significance or importance in a different media. Navigation is the process of moving through a particular Web document or moving between different Web documents.

One advantage hypertext has is that certain elements can be used both as content and for navigation. For example, a textual description of something might contain a link to something else. You are provided the information as well as a means of moving (i.e., navigating) somewhere else.

b) Discuss the necessity of having navigation elements on every Web page.

Answer: Without navigation elements on every page, the reader will quickly become "lost in Web space." Although a user might be able to backtrack using the "Back" button, he or she may have gone to so many different sites and followed so many different links that finding the original starting point may be hard. Navigation aids help the traveler reach his or her destination or, at the very least, help him or her return to a known starting point.

Think about a terminal at a large international airport. There are corridors, elevators, stairways, and many other ways of getting from place to place. Signs are helpful pointing to specific areas and the closer you get to that area the more specific the signs become. The airport in Frankfurt, Germany is one of the busiest in the world, serving as a hub between Europe, Asia, Africa, and the Americas. However, because of the navigation aides provided, it is one of the easier airports to navigate.

c) Why are user profiles important? How can they be employed in designing navigation aides?

Answer: Different users will have different navigation needs. It is important that the characteristics of expected users be known while considering the navigation needs of a Web page. In other words, no two people access the same information always in the same way, just as one person does not access all kinds of information in the same way.

There are three primary methods of navigation on the Web. The first is direct, where you know the URL you want and simply type it in the Address line. The second is also direct, but requires previous knowledge of the site. This is the navigation provided by the Web site developers. These are the links that they provide themselves. Finally, there is the search engine. This gives you the ability to jump from one place to another, without having to go through the intermediate pages.

In other context you will hear the terms "drill down" and "keyword search." Drill down is what we typically do in a file manager, where we click on one folder, then the next, then the next until we reach the directory and file that we want. On a Web site, this is equivalent to clicking on a link in a menu, clicking on the next menu, effectively going deeper into the site. Keyword search is nothing more than the search function available on so many sites.

Note that typically both of these methods are required. If you cannot find the exact information you are looking for, the search engine allows you to input words and phrases to help you find it. However, if you end up with 38,942 matches, then you have a problem. Knowing where to start looking allows you to zero in (drill down) on the information.

6.1.2 ANSWERS

Navigating across the Earth and through the Web are similar tasks.

a) Discuss how navigation is very similar in the two domains.

Answer: A map reference specifies the location on Earth exactly. Similarly, a URL locates a Web page exactly in the Web space. Both values convey a sense of place.

Movement in the direction of a specific location is accomplished through markers. In the case of the real world, moving from one room to the next is accomplished by moving through a door. We see a tree in the distance and head for that tree. In the virtual world, these markers are the links we click with our mouse that takes us to the next page.

In both worlds, we have different methods of movement depending on where we are heading. Traveling short distances in the real world, we generally rely on visual signals to navigate, such as road signs, and the method of movement is a car or our own feet. In the virtual world, short distance is generally traveled by navigation aids within the site itself.

If we are traveling a greater distance, we typically rely on others who have been there before or at least know how to get there. In the real world, this is accomplished by airports (with the airplanes being the actual medium). In the virtual world, we travel the great distances using search engines, which take us immediately deeper into specific sites.

b) Discuss how navigation is very *different* in the two domains.

Answer: At first sight, a URL and a map reference on the Earth's surface seem very similar. Both tell us the exact position in our area of discourse. Moving to the two positions from where we are at present is vastly different however. On the Earth, we can easily visualize the direction to take in order to move to the new position and our course takes shape. In the Web space, there is no course. Instead, we move instantly to the new position, just like teleporting in Star Trek. This anywhere-to-anywhere movement capability is truly one of the sources of power for Web travelers.

The direction of travel of a ship, for example, can be used to deduce future position. On the other hand, moving from one URL to any other does not constitute a course with the same meaning. The course of a vessel or craft describes a line across the Earth or through the space above it. There is no such equivalent in the Web. At best, we have a list of URLs most recently visited that may have no structure and can hardly be compared to a course or path.

As we flit effortlessly from one page (place) to another we lose orientation because there is no course or direction, to give us an impression of the relationship between source and destination points. We have take a particular path and can move forward or backward along this path, but the only real relationships are the pages that are immediately forward or backward.

As we will see later, it is necessary for the designer of Web navigation to try and impart a sense of path or direction to help the page reader decide which link to take and to convey a sense of moving toward the desired objective.

On the Earth's surface, the course and the speed that are followed help to convey the sense of location. There are various visual cues that can be presented to the page reader to show a course through Web pages. The longer or larger the course visualization, the further the reader has progressed, and hence the rate of progress can be conveyed. It important that these travel cues from the real physical world be utilized fully in the Web space.

Another very important difference between Earth position and Web URL is the distinct lack of structure in the latter case. Knowing our exact current position on the Web is rarely, if ever, enough information to help us decide on the next link to follow. We cannot deduce a course or direction in Web space without additional information being given to us about every link in the current page. A hyperlink, of course, consists of two pieces of information:

1. *Link visualization: a text phrase or image*
2. *Link destination: a URL*

The first piece of information is the more important and must carry the responsibility of conveying the course or direction mentioned above. In this respect, we should not forget about the link destination entirely. Most browsers will display the link destination in some way when the cursor moves over the link, where the URL appears as a popup or in the status line at the bottom of the window. At least part of the URL is discretionary—the file and folder names. As will be mentioned in more detail later, even file and folder names can be chosen wisely to help convey some context of the destination link.

A course on Earth follows a simple line, the most straightforward of figures. There is just no equivalent on the Web. A ship's log records position at various times so that the course line can be reconstructed. A log, or history, is kept of our travels through the Web, but when this is reconstructed in time all we have is a long list of URLs with no particular structure. With some effort, the URL history can be used to advantage, as seen later in this section, but the simplicity of a line course is not available.

c) What navigation methods are provided in printed media? How do these compare to Web navigation?

Answer: The two primary methods of navigation in printed media are the table of contents and index. A table of contents is equivalent to menus that you click on, going deeper into the document (drilling down). An index is a like a predefined keyword search. Although you are dependent on the person who decided on the specific words in the index, you typically can jump to anywhere in the text.

Take a look at the Yahoo Web site (http://www.yahoo.com). This a great example of both drill down and keyword search. If you know the general area of where you are going, you select the appropriate topics, getting closer and closer to what you are looking for. If you are not sure of the correct category, you can do a keyword search. Plus you have toolbars to jump to specific areas of the site.

Another useful feature of Yahoo is that you can start your keyword search at any level. Assume you have already drilled down five levels and still cannot find what you are looking and decide to do a keyword search. You can. However, the kicker is that you can do a search on all of Yahoo or restrict it to just that one area where you currently are. In addition, if you have done a keyword search, the search engine will tell you exactly where the particular entry is found is their hierarchy. Therefore, even if you don't find a match, you often find the appropriate area within Yahoo and can do a drill-down search from there. In essence, what Yahoo does is combine the best of both techniques.

d) Create a navigation system that might be found on a site discussing world geography. Draw on things from previous chapters as well and design an appropriate interface. What navigational aids could you provide?

Answer: One thing we talked about in Chapter 3 was the issue of user models and employing metaphors for your Web pages. The metaphor you could use in this case could be a world map. Obviously, clicking on a specific area of the map either takes you the informational page about the region or continent, or clicking on the map takes you to an even more detailed map on which you can click. The latter choice would give you the ability to drill down. Of course, if someone wanted information about a specific geographical location, but did not know exactly where it was, a search mechanism would be appropriate.

One navigation aid would be a textual interface (menu). That is, having the pictures is not enough. What if the person does not know where each continent is located? If you watch the "Jaywalking" segment of the Tonight Show, finding people who couldn't find the continents on a map is probably a pretty easy thing to do. Many of us make assumptions about what is "common knowledge" and, as a result, we might build things into user interfaces based on these assumptions.

In Lab 3.4, we talked about mental models and how people's experience affect these models. Although someone may be able to recognize that the image was a map of the world, their experiences may not give them the knowledge to label the continents let alone find smaller components like Singapore, Jamaica, or the Isle of Man. It would therefore be necessary on our geography site to provide other navigational aids like the text menu or search mechanism.

6.1.3 ANSWERS

Think about the differences between a ship's navigator and a Web page navigator.

a) Discuss who the Web page navigator is.

Answer: It is an essential concept of the Web that the reader of the Web page—any user of the Web—is the navigator. He or she decides where to go and what course to take. As with a navigator on a ship, a Web navigator must be capable of using the navigational elements contained within the page. However, unlike a navigator of a ship, the Web navigator may be completely new to the environment. In other words, the Web page navigator may have little or no experience of Web navigation. Therefore, the tools provided for navigation must be identifiable as such, as well as easy to use.

b) Why is the designer of Web page navigation elements so important?

Answer: Following on from the previous answer, the assumed lack of experience of the reader means the Web page designer must pay particular attention to the Web page navigation elements. Equal care must be lavished on navigation and the page contents.

Remember the old saying, "You can't get there from here." If the Web navigation elements are unusable, then the user will not be able to find the information you are trying to provide.

LAB 6.1 SELF-REVIEW QUESTIONS

In order to test your progress, you should be able to answer the following questions.

1) "Visual clues" are just as important in Web navigation as in earth navigation.

a) _____ True
b) _____ False

2) Unlike coordinate systems for Earth navigation, a URL provides human-understandable references to where the document is in cyberspace.

a) _____ True
b) _____ False

3) A hyperlink consists of two pieces of information:

a) _____ Link visualization and hypertext
b) _____ Hypertext and link destination
c) _____ Link visualization and link destination

4) Which of the following is not one of the three primary types of web navigation?

a) _____ Inputting the URL directly
b) _____ The browser's history
c) _____ Menus/drill down
d) _____ Search engines

5) Which of the following is not important for web navigation, although it is for Earth navigation?

a) _____ Position
b) _____ Course
c) _____ Distance
d) _____ Navigational aides

6) The best analogy for a URL would be which of the following?

a) _____ Telephone number
b) _____ Social Security number
c) _____ Longitude and latitude
d) _____ First, middle, and last names

Quiz answers appear in the Appendix, Section 6.1.

L A B   6 . 2

BASIC NAVIGATION FEATURES

LAB OBJECTIVES

After this lab, you will be able to:

✔ Understand the Main Requirements of Navigation Links
✔ Apply Solutions to Meet the Main Navigation Requirements
✔ Understand the Relationship Between Page Links and Browser Navigation Features

---

This lab introduces the key aspects of Web page navigation. These aspects must be taken into account for each Web page that is constructed. Depending on the intended use of each Web page and the expected audience, it may be necessary to vary the importance placed on each navigation feature. Some examples of this variation are presented as case studies later in this unit.

The key navigation aspects are:

- Sense of location
- Link choices from this page
- Return to previously read pages

The first navigation aspect gives the user an indication of the position within a series of Web pages or of a site within the Web generally. Link choices should convey to the user a set of alternatives or a sensible course to follow. The third aspect should offer the user a safe return to pages already viewed in a simple and consistent manner.

SENSE OF LOCATION

When viewing a Web page, it is vital that the user is aware of the current context or location of that page. In other words, the user must be presented with a sense of place. This gives the user a sense of orientation and of being in control of the access to information contained within the page. Failure to encourage this situation will lead to user disorientation and a sense of being lost or out of control. Should this occur, the user would abandon further reading of such pages.

In order to foster a sense of place, we can learn a lot from the print media that has faced this problem before. Several solutions to the problem have been developed. A simple novel consists of a linear set of pages and a single page number is sufficient to define a location. In more structured books, chapter and section numbers are used to convey where in the structure each piece of information resides. Tables of contents and indexes help overcome the otherwise daunting linear search problem when the reader is interested in going directly to a particular part of the information presented in the book.

Web pages can use all of these solutions to good effect. For the most part, we can assume that browser users will be familiar with a table of contents and book pages split into chapters with page numbers (see Figure 6.1). Use this structure model for simple Web sites, and for the top-level pages of more complicated Web sites. This basic structure for page content was discussed in the previous unit.

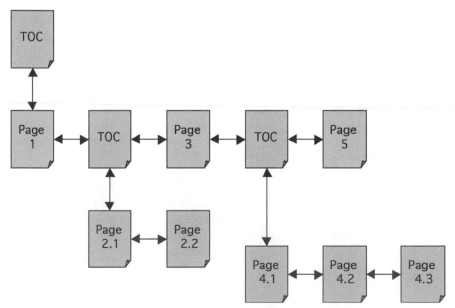

Figure 6.1 ■ Table of Contents Plus Pages Structure

Where more complex site structures are needed, the Web site designer can take each top-level page and repeat the table-of-contents-plus-pages structure at the next level.

At the very least, each page should convey the top-level Web site and an indication of the subsite in which the page belongs.

LINK CHOICES FROM EACH PAGE

To give the user a sense of direction or course, it is necessary to list all the possible alternatives in an obvious and well-structured fashion. Human users are already familiar with direction choices, depending on the mode of transport in use. A railroad offers little choice, driving on roads usually much more, and on sea and in the air complete freedom of choice is often available (weather and tides permitting). The Web transcends all these transport categories and can offer free choice in a limitless number of dimensions.

To avoid giving users too much choice, which only confuses them, we must reduce the choice of links to sensible proportions. Web portal sites that offer a single page access to a very large amount of information face such a design choice.

RETURN TO PREVIOUSLY READ PAGES

From real-life experience we learn various methods that allow us to venture into new locations and return safely to our starting point. In complex environments like a deep forest or a maze, we can use crude solutions like trailing a thread of cotton or leaving breadcrumbs. We can deliberately lay a trail by scattering pieces of paper like a paper chase. What are equivalent solutions in the Web space?

Solutions that roughly equate to the thread of cotton can be found at the useit.com and Yahoo Web sites. The marker that portrays the location with the Web site in both cases contains links that lead us back to each level in the Web site hierarchy that we have visited. In effect, this allows users to jump to any position on the thread in order to retrace their steps. Thus, we see a sense of the return path.

Such a solution works well within a single site and also between related sites, but it is not a solution at all when the user visits several sites—the normal situation. You will explore these issues and more in this lab's exercises.

LAB 6.2 EXERCISES

6.2.1 UNDERSTAND THE MAIN REQUIREMENTS OF NAVIGATION LINKS

**LAB
6.2**

a) Describe several means of showing the location of a page within a Web site.

_____

_____

b) Visit the Yahoo.com site. You will see that it uses the table-of-contents-plus-pages model of navigation. Why is it so effective?

_____

_____

6.2.2 APPLY SOLUTIONS TO MEET THE MAIN NAVIGATION REQUIREMENTS

a) An example of a site that gives a sense of location is Jakob Nielsen's useit.com site. Visit this site and discuss the technique.

_____

_____

b) Visit the Yahoo site and discuss it in terms of the link choices.

_____

_____

6.2.3 UNDERSTAND THE RELATIONSHIP BETWEEN PAGE LINKS AND BROWSER NAVIGATION FEATURES

a) Find the features that your browser has implemented to aid navigation and discuss their purpose.

_____

_____

LAB 6.2 EXERCISE ANSWERS

6.2.1 ANSWERS

a) Describe several means of showing the location of a page within a Web site.

Answer: The simplest form is on a single line, showing the names of the levels where this page is located within the current Web site. Include the name of this page at the end of the list. Alternatively, you could have a menu on each page listing all of the entries and the entry for the current page has a different appearance (color, font, is not a hyperlink, and so forth.). Using Web scripting languages like JavaScript, you can create a menu that expands as you go deeper into the hierarchary. You not only have an indication of where you are located, but you have access to the other areas as well.

One of the advantages of the first choice is that is very straightforward to develop, particularly if your directory structure matches the structure of your site (which is a good idea, anyway). When you create the pages, you just include the paths to the file (preferably in a human-readable form).

Server-side scripting languages can actually automate the process for you. Such scripts can determine the directory path on the file system (among other things) and automatically generate the menu for you, including links back up to the previous levels. Such a scheme generally requires that you have a default page (i.e., index.html), so the script simply provides a link to the directory and the server handles the issue of the default page or it tacks on the name of the default page to the end of the link in generates.

You can take this mechanism one step further by using the ability of most Web servers (e.g., Apache) to automatically include files at particular locations. The file you include can be a script that creates the line. When you want to change the layout, all you need to do is change a single file and not on every page.

Both the useit.com and Yahoo sites have navigation markers like this, where the individual entries are links back up the hierarchy.

The Web site for the Hewlett-Packard product OpenView is a great example of a menu that expands out to show you where you are located in the hierarchy. (Open-View is an outstanding system monitoring and administration tool.) In addition, the menu entry for your current location appears a different color, making it easy to zero in on where you are.

Each of these methods has its own shortcomings. On relatively small sites like useit.com, a single line list is not a problem. However, on the Yahoo site with millions of entries, you end up with some very long lines, for example:

Error! Bookmark not defined. > Error! Bookmark not defined. > Error! Bookmark not defined. > Error! Bookmark not defined. > Error! Bookmark not defined. > Error! Bookmark not defined. > Error! Bookmark not defined. >

This may become a problem on systems using a lower resolution and larger fonts. However, in the case of Yahoo, it is necessary in order to provide the level of service they want. That is, they sacrifice appearance for usability and consistency.

b) Visit the Yahoo.com site. You will see that it uses the table-of-contents-plus-pages model of navigation. Why is it so effective?

Answer: Most users are familiar with reading printed books that universally employ this model. Adopting the model for a Web site provides users with a familiar structure and gives them confidence to navigate within the site. Each general area of information available is grouped together, with just a few of the more important areas listed at the second level. As we discussed in the previous exercise, such "shortcomings" are necessary for sites with so much information. However, each time you go deeper, you still have the same table of contents (only that it applies just to the current section).

6.2.2 ANSWERS

a) An example of a site that gives a sense of location is Jakob Nielsen's useit.com site. Visit this site and discuss the technique.

Answer: The top of each page tells you in which section you are located. This gives you a sense of how deep in the hierarchy you are.

At his top-level Web site, the top of the page is as shown in Figure 6.2.

When links are followed to take the user to pages in a sub-site, the top of the page is as shown in Figure 6.3.

Note that this is a very compact method of conveying the location within a Web site.

e) Visit the Yahoo site and discuss it in terms of the link choices.

Answer: Let us consider some examples from the Yahoo site. The top portion of a page at one of the major subsites of the Yahoo portal is shown in Figure 6.4.

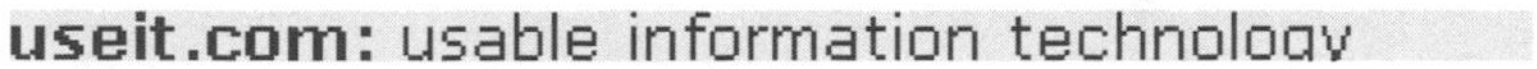

useit.com: usable information technology

Figure 6.2 ■ Top-level Location

useit.com → Alertbox → May 1999 New Top-10

Figure 6.3 ■ Location Indicator Two Levels Down

*First, notice how the sense of location, discussed under the previous heading, is used to
show we are located at Home > Computers and Internet > Internet > World Wide
Web. For the many links that necessarily must appear on this page, the designer has
used three main groupings. Along the top of this page, and on virtually every page on
the Yahoo Web site, appear the links to the main Yahoo subsites. Down the right-hand
side of the page are displayed the links to the top level of the News subsite. Note once
again how Yahoo shows the location within the directory structure by removing the link
from the words "World Wide Web."*

*Yahoo is essentially a set of directory and subdirectory pages. The main content of the
example page contains links to the next levels of subdirectories. Note that particularly
important subdirectories merit their own list of links, separated from the rest by a horizontal line.*

Finally, note the powerful search feature at the top of the page for the serious reader.

*When the user follows a link to one of the news articles and descends a level in the
subsite, a new link design problem appears (see Figure 6.5).*

*Major changes to link arrangements have been made. The presentation of the sense of
place shows all places from "Home" to "Health" and highlights the current location,*

Figure 6.4 ■ Page at Yahoo Portal Site

Home - Yahoo! - My Yahoo! - Help

Yahoo! Platinum Visa : 2.9% APR ~ Instant Credit ~ Rewards with
GiftCertificates.com ~ No Annual Fee.

Home | Top Stories | Business | **Tech** | Politics | World | Local | Entertainment | Sports | Science | Health

**LAB
6.2**

Technology Full Coverage   Last Updated Jan 17 9.14 AM EST

Full Coverage > Technology > **Domain Names and Registration**

News Sources	**News Stories**
- NewsLinx Web News	- Wrestling Group Wins Back Use of Its Name on Internet - NY Times (registration req'd) (Jan 17, 2000)
- Yahoo! Technology News	- WWF Wins First Cybersquatting Case - AP (Jan 17, 2000)
- ZDNNews	- Computer Glitch Gives Canadian Microsoft Web Site - Reuters (Jan 16, 2000)
- News.com	- Wrestlers Win Fight Over Internet Address - Reuters (Jan 15, 2000)
	- Lucasfilm fights for the rights to Tatooine.com - CNet (Jan 14, 2000)
Opinion & Editorials	- Linux Domains Up for Auction - InternetNews (Jan 14, 2000)
- How We're Losing the War Against Cybercriminals - Inter@ctive Week (Jan 14, 2000)	- Verio Opens Domain Registration Service - Inter@ctive Week (Jan 14, 2000)
- No Toying Around - Industry Standard (Dec 15, 1999)	- Generic domain names are choice Internet real estate - CBC.CA (Jan 14, 2000)

Figure 6.5 ■ Fragment of a News Item Page within Yahoo News Site

"Tech." A second level of location is required on this page, using the ">" method as already described.

The links down the left side of the page show other headings and news articles to be read. This is a clever device to save the user having to return the main list of articles before selecting another one to read.

Furthermore, this page is a collection of other articles about the topic of the headline, so a further article list of links is presented. Note that four different types of navigation links are presented in this small page fragment.

In the examples shown so far, the link text has been grouped in horizontal and vertical lists. This draws the user's attention to the link category. Links were originally designed so they could appear within the text and image content of the Web page itself. Thus, links can appear within the body of sentences and be distinguished from other words by markup in blue and underlined weight. These links are referred to as embedded links.

Again using a Yahoo news article as an example, we see the use of embedded links in Figure 6.6.

Where a whole line forms a link, such as the headlines Figure 6.6, this is not a problem and stands out well within the article text as a whole. The links for "microsoft.com" and

Tech Headlines

Saturday January 15 8:09 PM ET

Computer Glitch Gives Canadian Microsoft Web Site

TORONTO (Reuters) - A Canadian had a taste of what it meant to be a media mogul after owning two prime pieces of Internet real estate for an hour, The Globe and Mail reported on Saturday.

Chris Gronski, 31, an e-business manager, was the proud owner of microsoft.com and yahoo.com after he discovered a small computer glitch on Friday at the Web site of Network Solutions Inc., the leading U.S. company registering dot-com Web site addresses.

Figure 6.6 ■ Part of Yahoo News Item Page

"yahoo.com" are more problematic, particularly if several links are included in the same sentence. Recent research into the use of embedded links is showing that users tend to miss these links when intent on reading the words of the text.

More modern thinking dictates that the embedded links should at the least be repeated at the end of the article, so that all links that relate to the text appear in one place. A second benefit of this approach is that suitable meaningful text can be used for the links themselves, rather than twisting the words of a sentence to act as link text. Many embedded links in a sentence also detracts from reading, and in this case the embedded links should be abandoned in favor of a list of links at the end of the article.

6.2.3 ANSWERS

a) Find the features that your browser has implemented to aid navigation and discuss their purpose.

Answer: Although most of the features have become standards, where they are located depends on the browser. See the discussion for details.

Web sites with navigational aids often allow us to move to many different places on the Web site. However, users have tended to fall back upon features built in to the browser. All users are familiar with the Back button, and, provided they wish to return on the same path through which they entered, this simple feature works very well. In his Top 10 New Mistakes of Web Design at http://www.useit.com/alertbox/990530.html, Jakob Nielsen warns about problems beginning to emerge with the Back button model. He refers to the Back button as the lifeline of the user, because we can try a link, and if unhappy with the outcome, we can return to the familiar page we were viewing. Jakob points to the following problems that break this simple model:

- *If a link opens a new window, the Back button is disabled and cannot be used.*

- *Scripts in the page trap the Back button event and decide to redirect the user to a fixed page, not the one the user was expecting.*

- *Caching of the page is disabled when sent back to the browser. The Back button still works but a possibly long delay ensues because the browser has to make another trip to the server.*

All browsers by necessity treat Web pages as the single unit of navigation. There is no notion of page collections such as the closely related pages on a single Web site. However, a simple analysis of the base URL of pages visited in a sequence can be used to foster a sense of the Web site.

The modern browsers have now added extra features to the Back button using this simple URL analysis. In an equivalent to the thread solution described earlier, when the user right-clicks on the Back button, a short history of the last half dozen or so sites is listed (see Figure 6.7). A user can then simply select one of the previously visited Web sites to view next. It is vital that the user be presented with a list of sensible site labels rather than the raw URL text, although, as we will see later in this unit, it is sometimes useful to know the URL text as it can convey hints about the site.

Browsers have also improved the way they present the complete history of pages visited. In the past, the user was presented with a very long list of URLs in reverse chronological order. Now, browsers like Internet Explorer still retain the time ordering but add a sensible site hierarchy with easy navigation within sites (see Figure 6.8).

When designing the navigation link structure, we must take into account all three categories of links mentioned. Note that each category has its own set of problems and suggested solutions.

One feature that most browsers have is not often considered a navigation aid: bookmarks. Like their real-world counterpart, a Web bookmark remembers your place so you can find it again later. Some browsers, like Netscape Navigator, allow you to organize your bookmarks to make finding the bookmarks, and therefore Web navigation, easier still.

Figure 6.7 ■ Right-click Menu for Back Button in Internet Explorer

Figure 6.8 ■ Structured History List in Internet Explorer

One of the newest crazes are the "my" sites, such as my.netscape.com. These sites are offshoots of the parent site where you can design the interface to the information the way you choose. You can activate and deactivate features or display specific kinds of information (sports scores, stocks, weather in your home town, and so forth). Depending on the site, you can also define what kind of information from that site to display.

LAB 6.2 SELF-REVIEW QUESTIONS

In order to test your progress, you should be able to answer the following questions.

1) Since your site is there to provide information a key usability feature is a large number of links to other sources of information.

    a) _____ True
    b) _____ False

2) Why is there no universal rule about where to place links on a page?

    a) _____ Each type of page will have different navigation requirements.
    b) _____ Users can change the appearance of the web
    c) _____ Search engines provide better navigation to specific locations.
    d) _____ Language difference (and therefore different character sets) create placement problems.

3) Which of the following is not generally an aid to navigation in your browser?

  a) _____ The Back button
  b) _____ The History list
  c) _____ Bookmark/Favorite list
  d) _____ Address field

LAB
6.2

4) Which of the following is not reason why a sense of location is so important?

  a) _____ It gives the user the confidence to understand the context of the information presented on the page.
  b) _____ It allows the user to move more easily up and down the hierarchy.
  c) _____ It gives the feeling of being able to control the next page of information to be read.
  d) _____ It makes the site easier to administer.

5) Which of the following is not considered a key navigation element?

  a) _____ Sense of location
  b) _____ Link choices from the page
  c) _____ Search mechanisms
  d) _____ Return to previously read pages

6) Which of the following is not an issue with embedded links?

  a) _____ Too many embedded links in a sentence detract from readability.
  b) _____ Users can change the appearance of the links and tend to miss them.
  c) _____ Management of embedded links is more difficult.
  d) _____ It is preferable to put links that relate to the text content in a separate list at the end of the text.

Quiz answers appear in the Appendix, Section 6.2.

L A B 6 . 3

NAMING NAVIGATION ELEMENTS

LAB OBJECTIVES

After this lab, you will be able to:

✔ Understand the Importance of Labels
✔ Use Site Maps and Indexes
✔ Construct Meaningful URLs

We have talked about the need to incorporate links into Web pages to provide efficient navigation between pages. In this lab, we discuss not only the placement of links but also how those links are named. Usually, the Web page designer must keep the space allocated to links to a minimum to maximize the screen space for page content. Thus the amount of text dedicated to links is usually small, so it is vital to choose abbreviated but meaningful names.

Because links are so important, the browser gives us some special user interface help when we build links into a page. It is necessary for us to capitalize on all help that the browser provides.

CONSISTENT LABELS

Simple links in Web pages can be represented as link text or as link images. (Note that various interactive components such as applets and ActiveX controls can also act as links, but are not considered in this unit.) It is surprisingly easy to make mistakes when choosing simple labels. Some good advice on this matter is available from Rosenfeld and Morville (1998). Bear in mind that simple parts of the Web page like headings and subheadings can be effective labels.

Rosenfeld and Morville start by emphasizing the need to maintain consistency. For example, using "home" in one place and "main" in another place for the top-level page confuses users. Another good piece of advice is to use either nouns ("Index," "Contact Details") or verbs ("Inquire," "Send Message"); don't mix the two. Also, check out other Web sites to determine a set of terms that are in common usage; don't invent your own. For example, don't use "find" instead of "search," which has become the standard.

Avoid labels that are too vague or general, and labels used as link text that don't match the page titles to which they point. On the other hand be aware of the common pitfall of using a label that is too specific to an individual site. It is worth spending time to design a labeling scheme for the whole site.

Except where space if limited for other reasons, users will benefit from link text being as comprehensive as possible. Use extended phrases to describe accurately the type of information the user will see if that link is followed. Research into long link text has shown that users can navigate more accurately when longer texts are used.

MEANINGFUL NAMES

Let us start by looking at some of the names used in the examples of Lab 6.2. The names of the first level subsites at most portal sites have to appear in a list of links in the narrow right-hand column. It is not possible to use more than three short words here, so very great care has been taken to choose the subsite names. And of course, these names must be used in every subsite main page to maintain consistency.

The short names must attempt to convey to the user the exact nature of the page content should the link be followed. We might wonder at a link labeled "Communications." This is a very general title and does not convey meaning very clearly. Telecommunications or personal communications would be more meaningful titles.

RELATIVE NAMES

Let us assume that Web site designers have followed our guidelines and constructed a clear page hierarchy for their sites. They have the site plan before them when constructing links and are very tempted to start using relative names like "Up" and "Next" for the link text when linking to nearby pages in the hierarchy. This will be very confusing for readers if they are not aware of the hierarchy being used.

Note that "Forward" and "Back" are acceptable because of their use in browser navigation buttons. Mixing these terms with "Next" and "Previous" can cause great confusion with users. In the Yahoo examples above, you will see no use of these relative terms.

There is a cost to avoiding relative terms, however, and, again, we see this in the Yahoo examples. The full names of the top level and next level subsites must be used repeatedly in the navigation links. Notice this takes up a lot more space than using terms like "Up," "Down," and "Next," but do not fall into this trap.

SITE MAPS AND INDEXES

The easiest way to inform users of the hierarchy of the Web site is to present a graphical site map or diagram. Such a site map can make explicit:

- The number of levels
- Where the information pages are placed at each level

Having seen a site map, it makes more sense to use relative names for moving through the hierarchy. Indeed, many Web site management tools now provide the Web site designer with facilities to construct the page hierarchy as a site diagram. Then the software can generate the navigation links automatically.

LINK RECOGNITION

While the convention is that link text should be blue and underlined, the growing use of link images and other script effects for links means that users must have other user interface feedback. Fortunately, modern browsers provide us with significant feedback. When the cursor moves over a text link two pieces of feedback are given:

- The cursor changes into a hand symbol.
- The URL to be loaded if the user clicks on the link is displayed in the status line at the bottom left of the browser window.

THE URL AS AN INFORMATION OBJECT

While the link text, which is displayed at the link itself, is of prime importance, we should not forget that the URL displayed in the status line can carry a significant amount of information—provided, that is, that the page designer takes time to ensure the URL is as readable for a human user as possible. Jakob Nielsen points this out in no uncertain terms. He rightly points out that URLs will be used on the Web for many years to come.

LAB 6.3 EXERCISES

6.3.1 UNDERSTAND THE IMPORTANCE OF LABELS

Take a look at the Yahoo site at http://www.yahoo.com.

Its purpose is a huge index of links, with information on other sites.

a) How does Yahoo differ from a traditional index? What do the links at Yahoo tell you about the information behind the link?

LAB 6.3

Visit the Star Trek site at http://www.startrek.com. Also, visit the Jet Propulsion Laboratory site at http://www.jpl.nasa.gov.

b) When you move your mouse over the images at these sites, what do you see?

6.3.2 USE SITE MAPS AND INDEXES

Compare the site maps at the HP OpenView site and the White House site at the following URLs:

http://www.openview.hp.com/sitemap/

http://www.whitehouse.gov/site_map.html

a) Discuss why a site map is so useful and what makes the Open-View and White House sites different. What advantages does either have? What problems does either have?

b) Indexes are generally only useful if you have a lot of information to provide. If you have access to an MS-Windows system, start the help program in any application. What features does it provide?

6.3.3 CONSTRUCT MEANINGFUL URLs

Visit the useit.com and Yahoo Web sites at the following URLs:

http://www.useit.com

http://www.yahoo.com

Move around the site and compare the page headings to the URL.

a) How does each site (useit and Yahoo) relate its page heading to the URL? Why is it important to choose short and meaningful names for the folder and file names used within a URL?

LAB 6.3 EXERCISE ANSWERS

6.3.1 ANSWERS

a) How does Yahoo differ from a traditional index? What do the links tell you about the information behind the link?

Answer: Perhaps the biggest difference is that the information is grouped by subjects, which are sorted alphabetically. Even as you go deeper and deeper into the hierarchy, the links are organized by category. Once you get down to pages with individual links, they are still ordered alphabetically.

Another aspect of the links is that they are pretty much consistent through out the site. You don't have a mixture of verbs and nouns for the links, here they are all nouns or noun phrases.

In general, the index links are very short, and is intended to convey accurately the content of the page the user will see next when the link is clicked. However, if long horizontal or vertical lists of links must occur on, say, an index page, then a few words (around three) might be the limit.

Let's assume we were looking for a new car in the San Francisco Bay areas. The Yahoo link might look like this:

Error! Bookmark not defined. > Error! Bookmark not defined. > Error! Bookmark not defined. > Error! Bookmark not defined. > Error! Bookmark not defined. > Error! Bookmark not defined. > Automotive/Dealers.

**LAB
6.3**

That's a lot to type, but you will typically get there through the successive links or through a keyword search (i.e. "new car san francisco"). The key is that you don't have a link like this:

"Purchasing a new automobile in the San Francisco Metropolitan Area of California, USA"

This has fewer letters and is easier to type, but the usability is actually less. It is harder for the administrator to create a structure based on links like this and it is harder for the user to figure out. Looking at the first example (the real Yahoo link), at each subsequent level the next choice is pretty clear. Another advantage of indices like Yahoo, you are not restricted to one specific search path. I could have found the same information by taking a path that started like this:

Business_and_Economy/Shopping_and_Services/Automotive/Dealers/
By_Region/U_S__States/California/Cities/

At this point if I click on the link for San Francisco, I actually end up back at the exact same place as in the first example.

b) When you move your mouse over the images at these sites what do you see?

Answer: In the status bar you see the URL being linked to. In some case, there is a popup giving additional information.

In general, moving the cursor over the image link has the same effect as for a text link, except for the addition of a small popup text window showing the ALT attribute of the IMG tag (depending on the browser). If no ALT attribute is specified, then the name of the image file is used instead. The small popup window is sometimes called a tool tip or scope notes. If care is taken to provide an appropriate link description, a great deal of information can be conveyed to the user about the nature of the page referred to by the link.

Some browsers allow users to turn off images to speed up download and display of Web pages. Again, the ALT attribute text can be displayed in place of the image to give users information about the content of the missing images.

It is important to choose a sensible image when it is to be used as a link. Images or icons are often thought to be universal in nature and to transcend national languages. Research with real users soon reveals that icons very rarely mean the same to people from different cultures. We therefore recommend that an image link always contain some text, even just single words, to help convey the meaning of the page that is the destination of the link.

6.3.2 ANSWERS

a) Discuss why a site map is so useful and what makes the OpenView and White House sites different. What advantages does either have? What problems does either have?

Answer: A site map conveys the Web site structure in an easy to understand graphical form. Generally, each node in the site map can be a link to the information page(s) for that part of the Web site. Rather than overloading the user at the very beginning of his or her visit with the multitude of choices, a site map still lets the user see "everything at once," but still be prepared in advance.

The HP OpenView site provides an alphabetical listing of the site. This is a different order than the menu provided on the left-hand side of the page, which is grouped by category. Since this is a logical organization when there are a lot of entries, it makes sense.

The White House site map has the same structure as the menu on left. Although the word "President" appears alphabetically before "Vice President," the site map (and the menu) is actually grouped based on "importance" or some other arbitrary criteria. One big problem that the White House has is that you cannot tell immediately that the entries are actually links.

If you look all over the site, it is not always easy to tell by looking what are links and what are not. At least, it is not easy to tell what text is a link based on its physical appearance (i.e. the color). However, if you consider the location of the link or other clues, what is a link and what is not is pretty straightforward.

An advantage that the White House has is that you can change the number of levels that the site map displays. By default, you are only shown two levels. However, by using the menus on right side you can change this.

Keep in mind that the site map fulfills two major functions:

1. *It allows the user to visualize the Web page hierarchy.*
2. *It provides links to all pages in the hierarchy.*

Structure diagrams for books are more rare because linking from the diagram to an actual page in the book is more tedious than on the Web. Because Web site diagrams change whenever a page or index is added or removed from the hierarchy, designers must use software tools to produce such a diagram and incorporate the correct links.

b) Indexes are generally useful only if you have a lot of information to provide. If you have access to a MS-Windows system, start the help program in any application. What features does it provide?

Answer: See the discussion.

Most readers are familiar is the alphabetical index, usually placed at the end of the book. This, too, is an obvious tool to add to a Web site. In effect, an index is just another page hierarchy, this time arranged in alphabetical order. Several extra pages are needed to support and index as opposed to single page for a site map or diagram. At a minimum an index requires a top-level page plus extra pages for each letter. Depending on the number of information pages, some of the single letter index pages may be aggregated.

Microsoft provides an example of a fairly large index for its online documentation. The top-level page contains is shown in Figure 6.9.

The user is given a choice of which index entries to display and then invited to click on the chosen letter link. Assuming the "B" link was chosen, the user would see something like the example in Figure 6.10.

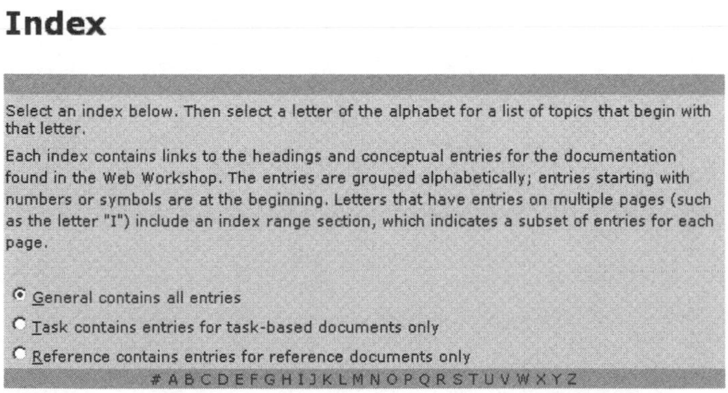

Index

Select an index below. Then select a letter of the alphabet for a list of topics that begin with that letter.

Each index contains links to the headings and conceptual entries for the documentation found in the Web Workshop. The entries are grouped alphabetically; entries starting with numbers or symbols are at the beginning. Letters that have entries on multiple pages (such as the letter "I") include an index range section, which indicates a subset of entries for each page.

⦿ General contains all entries

○ Task contains entries for task-based documents only

○ Reference contains entries for reference documents only

\# A B C D E F G H I J K L M N O P Q R S T U V W X Y Z

Figure 6.9 ■ Microsoft Online Documentation Index

Web Workshop | Index

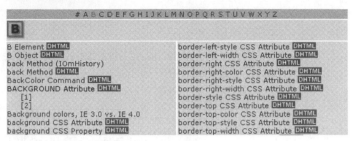

Figure 6.10 ■ The B Index Page

As with all well-designed index pages, the links provided at the "letter" level should:

- Show a link for all entries for that letter

- Allow the user to link to other letter levels

All text entries shown in the index page figure are links that highlight when the cursor moves over them.

6.3.3 ANSWER

a) How does each site (useit and Yahoo) relate its page heading to the URL? Why is it important to choose short and meaningful names for the folder and file names used within a URL?

Answer: Although the URL is intended to be used by the browser, it can also be a useful navigation tool. On the Yahoo site, the URL names correspond to the category where you are. The unfortunate result is that you can have some really long URLs. For example, consider what the URL would have to be for the page mentioned in Exercise 6.2.1b. Granted it would take a bit of typing and is prone to mistakes, but it can still be a useful navigation aid.

On the useit.com site, the home page has a link to "hotlist of links." However, the title of the page is titled "Recommended Other Websites" and the link is www.useit.com/hotlist. The name of the link fits with the home page, but not with the title of the page. The link on the home page "Portal Traffic" links to a page titled "Statistics for Traffic Referred by Search Engines and Navigation Directories to Useit" and the link is "www.useit.com/about/searchreferrals.html." Despite the fact that a search engine is not necessarily a portal, there is no consistency in the naming. It is not clear that "portal traffic" means "searchreferrals." In addition, the first link we mentioned (the hotlist) refers to a directory (/hotlist), whereas the portal traffic refers to a specific page (searchreferrals.html). This provides a relatively inconsistent interface. In general, it is difficult to guess the URL unless you know the site.

If we take a look at the HP OpenView site, the links are very straightforward. I guessed and simply input the link www.openview.hp.com/support/. Sure enough, I was brought to the support page for OpenView. As a writer, I want press information. Inputting www.openview.hp.com/press/ sends me to the press page.

Despite the occasional faux pas, Nielsen's site has some useful tips. He suggests:

- *The domain name of the Web server be chosen carefully so that it is easy to remember and easy to spell.*

- *Short URLs are used wherever possible. Achieving this will have a great impact on the file and folder names used when creating pages for the Web site. Short, meaningful names, which convey meaning to the user, must be used, rather than names that are significant to the Web site designer and page creators.*

- *Following on from the last point, URLs should be easy to type, which means not using underscores and other special characters in file and folder names.*

- *Refining the last two points further, the actual names used for folders in particular must be related to the visible link text that in turn reflects the site hierarchy.*

- *URLs should be "hackable" [Nielsen's term]. He means that judicious editing of the URL should take users easily to other parts of the site hierarchy or content pages.*

- *Finally, and most difficult to guarantee, URLs should not change over time. In other words, once a URL is chosen for important points in the site hierarchy, the URL should not alter. This can be achieved provided the domain name of the Web site does not change.*

LAB 6.3

It is pertinent to ask the question "Why should a URL, which is the machine addressable mechanism of the Web, be so important to browser users?" The answer is that in practice raw URLs are gleaned from many sources. Again, Jakob Nielsen explains:

- *After some experience with URLs, users will make a guess at a domain name when looking for a new Web site. This means that you must start with a domain name corresponding to your organization.*

- *Users are lazy about keeping bookmarks and so will often try and guess the URL of sites they have visited before.*

- *Research indicates that receiving raw URLs via an e-mail message is the second most popular method of acquiring a URL behind search engines. It is wise to keep a URL below about 70 characters in length so as to prevent line wrapping in an e-mail editor.*

- *Short URLs encourage users to type them. Using mixed case in URLs simply frustrates this.*

All this usage evidence means that Web page creators must take care in their choice of folder and file names, an area that has often been regarded as their private reserve in the past.

One important aspect, despite what Nielsen says, is that it is not always desirable or even possible to have URLs that are understood by the user, let alone "hackable." There are uncountable sites on the Internet that are almost completely dynamic. That is, there are a few static pages and the rest are created on the fly based on information in a database. Although you might be able to "force" URLs to be intelligible, it makes little sense as there is basically no way to input them by hand and they may be different the next time.

One example of this is Unix Guru's Universe (www.ugu.com). This site uses a central program that reads from a huge database of information about the various dialects of UNIX. Each link calls this program with specific parameters allowing it to call up the necessary information. This makes managing the vast amount of information easier. The site authors don't need to hunt through dozens of pages to update information. Instead, they just update the database and it is immediately available on all of the appropriate pages.

LAB 6.3 SELF-REVIEW QUESTIONS

In order to test your progress, you should be able to answer the following questions.

1) An advantage of sending a URL via email is that you can make the URL as long as you want.

   a) _____ True
   b) _____ False

2) It matters little whether nouns or verbs are used for link text. It is more important to use either consistently for labels.

   a) _____ True
   b) _____ False

3) On large sites, "relative" links like "backward," "forward," "up," and "down" should always be used extensively as navigation aids.

   a) _____ True
   b) _____ False

4) Which of the following is not a way a browser provides feedback for the user?

    a) _____ Changing the cursor to a hand

    b) _____ Displaying of the URL for the link in the status line at the bottom of the browser window.

    c) _____ Popup a tool tip box showing the ALT text for the IMG tag.

    d) _____ All of the above.

5) A labeling scheme is which of the following?

    a) _____ A means of associated the URL of a page to the page header (label).

    b) _____ A set of simple rules to decide how to compose headings and link text.

    c) _____ An HTML specification for defining page titles.

    d) _____ A scheme by which menu labels are matched with their appropriate page (URL).

LAB 6.3

6) What is a way a user receives raw URLs?

    a) _____ E-mail

    b) _____ Search engines

    c) _____ Newsgroups

    d) _____ All of the above

Quiz answers appear in the Appendix, Section 6.3.

L A B   6 . 4

TYPES OF WEB SITES

**LAB
6.4**

LAB OBJECTIVES

After this lab, you will be able to:

✔ Understand Users and Their Needs
✔ Recognize Different Navigation Needs

This lab addresses the issues that vary depending on the main type of Web site being constructed. Sites with different aims will inevitably have different sets of navigation requirements for their users. We present some examples of the main Web site categories and their different needs.

Of course, we design a Web site with a particular set of users in mind. It is important at the outset to identify the characteristics and needs of our expected users. Some hints on how to accomplish this are given.

KNOW YOUR USER

Navigation elements on a Web page are effective if they meet their users' goals. A Web page designer must be able to calculate the needs of the users. Note that pretending to be a user is rarely a good course of action. The page author always carries a bias. Instead, some careful research into user needs must be carried out.

In her excellent book *Web Navigation,* Jennifer Fleming, (1998) tells us how to predict problems with navigation elements by constructing user profiles and working with planned scenarios. Obviously, different users do not generally share the same goals. It is also important to realize that rarely do users' desires correspond to goals for a company Web site. Consumers of information, goods, and services have different needs than the producers of that information or seller of goods and services. The different Web site goals are shown in Table 6.1.

Table 6.1 ■ Company vs. User Web Site Goals

Site	User
Wants to make money on the Web	Wants to purchase securely
Wants to find information about customers	Wants to retain privacy
Wants to offload excess stock	Wants to buy a particular item

ELECTRONIC SHOPPING

A related type of site, which is becoming very popular, is a site selling mass goods in a narrow product range. The obvious example is Amazon.com. Following the user profile technique, again from Fleming's *Web Navigation,* we come to user goals and expectations as shown in Table 6.2.

This profile is obtained once again by asking people in focus groups, user tests, and other research.

INFORMATION SITE

Where the purpose of a Web site is just to convey authoritative information, the navigation layout rules are different again. Performing a user goals profile for a Web site that gives information about human health might yield Table 6.3.

Table 6.2 ■ Amazon.com User Goals and Expectations

Purpose	Product
How do I know my financial information is secure?	How can I find books by a particular author?
How can I protect my privacy?	How can I find books similar to those I like?
How can I find an item I want?	What is the reading level of the book?
How can I preview products?	Where can I get reviews?
Can I return items?	How do I find out about new releases?

Table 6.3 ■ Health Information Web Site User Goals and Expectations

Purpose	Product
How will I know the site contains the information I am looking for?	Is this accurate and current data?
How do I find the specific information I need?	Is there any bias?
What search terms should I use?	What are the search categories?
What is the authenticity of the information?	Can you search by gender, age and so on?
How can I store the information for future use?	

LAB 6.4 EXERCISES

6.4.1 UNDERSTAND USERS AND THEIR NEEDS

Taking an example from Jennifer Fleming's book listing the goals and audience groups for a company selling language-learning materials, the company goals for the Web site are:

- Sell audio and video tapes, CD-ROMs, and books for learning a language
- Support customers in using the products
- Provide information about new products
- Conduct user research

Identified audience groups are:

- Business travelers who need to learn quickly, require speedy shipping, and need portable formats
- Tourists buying online and requiring more information about culture and customs
- College students interested in cheap alternatives and ease of use

a) Given these goals and the site's audience, what might the top level links for this site be?

_____

_____

b) What other links would be necessary? Hint: Think about the things you look for from a business.

_____

_____

c) Discuss the importance of constructing a user profile. How would you go about creating one?

_____

_____

d) A college or university is not selling goods like an online store, nor is it purely informational. Create a table like Table 6.2 as precursor to a user profile for the college's Web page.

_____

_____

LAB 6.4

6.4.2 RECOGNIZE DIFFERENT NAVIGATION NEEDS

a) You want to buy a book on queueing theory for your company's help desk. You go to Amazon.Com to buy it. Find the answer to the questions posed in Table 6.2.

_____

_____

> **b)** After reading all the books you bought from Amazon, you realize you have trouble with your eyes. Check out the Optometrists Association of Australia (www.optometrists.asn.au). Find the answers to the questions posed in Table 6.3.

_____

_____

Lab 6.4 Exercise Answers

6.4.1 Answers

a) Given these goals and the site's audience, what might the top level links for this site be?

Answer: The company might suggest that its business divisions of Services, Educational Outreach, Direct Sales, New Media, Product Support, and Administration might form the top-level links in the home page. As is usually the case, this is the very last navigation structure that interests the customers.

b) What other links would be necessary?

Answer: Some of the links that you should have are:

- *A catalog of products that can be searched*

- *Support documents and FAQs*

- *Information about the company to judge its standing*

- *Samples of courses as Web pages*

- *Related Web resources on culture, geography, and travel booking*

- *Feedback forms*

Such a simple analysis can be achieved by talking with a few potential customers.

c) Discuss the importance of constructing a user profile. How would you go about creating one?

Answer: Navigation elements on a Web page are effective if they meet their users' goals. A Web page designer must be able to calculate the needs of the users. Aside from the obvious differences we have as individuals, there will be some basic differences de-

pending on the site itself—for example, whether it is a company's home page, an online store, or an information-only site.

The key step in creating a user profile is to construct a list of purpose and product questions. Consider the questions raised in Tables 6.2 and 6.3. These are what your users (i.e., potential customers) will be asking. Therefore, you will need to provide the answers. Where you place the answers will drive the navigation design.

Note that pretending to be a user is rarely a good course of action. The page author always carries a bias. Instead, some careful research into user needs must be carried out. Create scenarios for about three or four users, giving them characteristics observed from real experience.

Keep in mind that the diverse goals listed in Table 6.1 can lead to conflicts such as when the site asks for personal information on preferences, buying habits, and so on, which infuriates the user who regards this information as private. A sale is then the last outcome to be expected. You should create a user profile to bring user needs into focus and then use those needs to drive the navigation design.

A user profile is a brief study of the sort of person who is likely to visit a Web site. A profile is a list of characteristics gleaned from choosing a few fictitious users and putting them into a scenario.

Jennifer Fleming also points out that the audience of a Web site will probably be made up of several distinct groups, each with different concerns and interests. It is important that the major groups be identified and their needs met when designing the navigation of the site.

LAB 6.4

d) A college or university is not selling goods like an online store, nor is it purely informational. Create a table like Table 6.2 as precursor to a user profile for the college's Web page.

Answer: Below is the beginning of such a table for a college or university.

Purpose	Product
Where can I get financial aid?	What kind of housing is available?
What are the application procedures?	What course are offered each semester?
What are the deadlines?	What at the prerequisites for the courses?
What degree programs are available?	What are the costs?
How do I contact the college if I have questions?	Who are the instructors?

In each case, there is a set of general questions about the organization (in this case, a college), plus details about what the college offers. Therefore, at this level of abstraction all of the different kinds of sites are basically the same. However, as we see, the specific information will be different. In the case of the college, contacting it is important to the potential student, including the street addresses. However, in other cases it is not important (for example, what is Amazon's street address?).

It is important to remember that you can't just put yourself in the users' shoes. You are not likely to think of all of the possible questions unless you have been in the same situation before. In the case of an online sale, information only, or college site, we have all been in the same position (probably). However, what if you are developing a site for the online sales of cemetery plots or farm equipment? Have you ever bought these online? What about an information-only site for Siamese twins or genealogy? What questions would be asked here? What about a site for a university for the blind or one that specializes in foreign languages? Wie wurdest du diese Problematik angehen? The bottom line is that you need users, not developers, to create a user profile.

LAB
6.4

6.4.2 ANSWERS

a) You want to buy a book on queueing theory for your company's help desk. You go to Amazon.com to buy it. Find the answer to the questions posed in Table 6.2.

Answer: If we take a look at fragments of several pages from Amazon.com shown in Figure 6.11, we see that every aspect in the above table is catered to.

In the case of the Amazon site, you simply need to look at the bottom of the home page. None of this information is concealed under seventeen layers of menus. All of the privacy and security information is available from the home page, and the Help page provides information that you never even thought of to ask. In essence, Amazon provides the answers to all of the questions that any "real" bookstore would get, before the questions are asked. Spending half an hour studying the variety of navigation links on Amazon.com, their layout, and their content, will be one of the best lessons you can learn on how to organize a shopping site.

b) After reading all the books you bought from Amazon, you realize you have trouble with your eyes. Check out the Optometrists Association of Australia (www.optometrists.asn.au). Find the answers to the questions posed in Table 6.3.

Answer: Here again, if we take a look at fragments of several pages from Optometrists Association of Australia shown in Figure 6.12, we see that every aspect in Table 6.3 is accounted for.

Searchable catalog appears at the top of the page

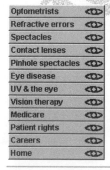

50% off *The New York Times*® Best Sellers.*

Best selling books

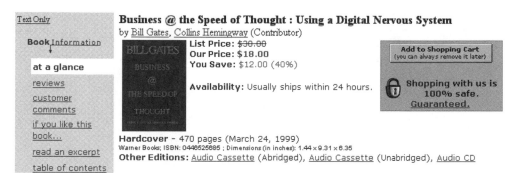

Reviews, contents, security policy, and other similar books

Figure 6.11 ■ **Page fragments from Amazon.com**

Eyecare information

Optometrists	
Refractive errors	
Spectacles	
Contact lenses	
Pinhole spectacles	
Eye disease	
UV & the eye	
Vision therapy	
Medicare	
Patient rights	
Careers	
Home	

The information on this website provides general information on optometry and various eye conditions. It is not intended to provide specific information or advice on any individual's eye or vision problems.

If you suspect that you may have some problem with your eyes or vision, you should consult an appropriate professional immediately.

To find the information you want, just select from the menu on the left side of the screen.

© Optometrists Association Australia
Updated: 6/10/1999

Figure 6.12 ■ **Main Index for Eye Care Information**

LAB 6.4

Ultra-violet radiation & the eye

Eyecare	◁◉▷
Optometrists	◁◉▷
Refractive errors	◁◉▷
Spectacles	◁◉▷
Contact lenses	◁◉▷
Pinhole spectacles	◁◉▷
Eye disease	◁◉▷
Vision therapy	◁◉▷
Medicare	◁◉▷
Patient rights	◁◉▷
Careers	◁◉▷
Home	◁◉▷

Ultraviolet (UV) radiation comprises invisible high energy rays from the sun that lie just beyond the blue end of the visible spectrum.

More than 99% of UV radiation is absorbed by the anterior structures of the eye, although some of it does reach the light-sensitive retina. The UV radiation present in sunlight is not useful for vision. There are good scientific reasons to be concerned that UV absorption by the eye may contribute to age-related changes in the eye and a number of serious eye diseases.

Protection can be achieved by simple, safe and inexpensive methods such as wearing a brimmed hat and using eyewear that absorbs UV radiation.

Figure 6.13 ■ Information Content with Terminology and Definitions

The main index uses straightforward scientific and technical terms and bears the authority of a professional association, the Optometrists Association of Australia. Choosing one of the topics leads us to the page shown in Figure 6.13.

In this page we find brief, but adequate, definitions of terminology presented in simple English.

LAB 6.4 SELF-REVIEW QUESTIONS

In order to test your progress, you should be able to answer the following questions.

1) A key problem in creating user profiles is the differing needs of each user and for each site.

   a) _____ True
   b) _____ False

2) User goals for a Web site are established with focus groups of developers who understand the technology constraints.

   a) _____ True
   b) _____ False

3) Because the page author always carries a bias, user input for the user profile is necessary.

   a) _____ True
   b) _____ False

4) Which of the following is not one of the conflicting goals of companies and customers?

a) _____ Company wants to make money on the Web—Customer wants to purchase securely

b) _____ Company wants to find information about customers—Customer wants to retain privacy

c) _____ Company wants attention getters (i.e. multimedia)—Customer wants quick download

d) _____ Company wants to offload excess stock—Customer wants to buy a particular item

5) A user profile is which of the following?

a) _____ User-based evaluation of the information content of your site.

b) _____ User-based evaluation of the ease of navigation of your site.

c) _____ A detailed list of what products or services a company can offer a particular user or group of users.

d) _____ A brief study of the sort of person who is likely to visit a Web site.

Quiz answers appear in the Appendix, Section 6.4.

LAB
6.4

C H A P T E R   6

TEST YOUR THINKING

Brother International is one of the world's largest manufacturers of a very wide range of household products from sewing machines to multi-function fax/scanners to hand-held labeling systems. Their customers range from your grandmother to people in your IT department.

1) With this wide range of users, creating a single user profile is outright impossible. However, the Brother Web site (www.brother.com) provides a great deal of easily accessible information. Visit the site and evaluate it in terms of the topics we discussed here.

No one is perfect, especially in developing a Web site for such a wide range of products.

2) Reevaluate the Brother site, looking specifically for mistakes or short-comings based on what we discussed. Consider whether the mistakes you find are outright blunders, simple oversights, or cases where the administrator had to choose the lesser of two evils.

3) Pick out a list of several of your favorite subjects or hobbies. Do a search on Yahoo and visit these sites looking for a specific piece of information. Consider the navigation aids provided and how easy it is to access the information.

OVERVIEW OF MULTIMEDIA FORMATS

Multimedia. *Umbrella term that has been coined to cover all of the synergistic uses of text, voice, music, video, graphics, and other forms of data to enhance the computer's role as a communications device.*

—Multimedia and the Web from A to Z

CHAPTER OBJECTIVES

In this chapter, you will learn about:

In this unit, we'll take a look at some of the most popular types of multimedia used on the Web today. We'll also look at some of the more common file formats for various multimedia types, comparing their relative strengths and weaknesses and helping you make informed decisions on what types of multimedia are best suited to various purposes. Multimedia can be a valuable asset to a Web site, but it can also be counterproductive if improperly used. A better understanding of the various kinds of media at your disposal will help you to make informed decisions and lead you away from some of the more obnoxious pitfalls of Web design.

LAB 7.1

STATIC AND ANIMATED GRAPHICS

LAB OBJECTIVES

After this lab, you will be able to:

✔ Experiment with Image File Formats
✔ Differentiate Between GIFs and JPEGs
✔ Experiment with Various Types of Images
✔ Identify Special Image Types

The World Wide Web has existed in one form or another since 1990, when the hypertext model and the first line-mode browsers were developed by researchers at CERN (the European Laboratory for Particle Physics—http://www.cern.ch/). However, its popularity in the mainstream didn't really begin to take off until several years later, when the first *GUI* (Graphical User Interface) Web browsers became available. Today, less than a decade later, the World Wide Web and the Internet itself are practically synonymous in the minds of many people.

The reason for this sudden increase in popularity can be summed up in a word: Pictures.

With the release of Mosaic, the graphical browser developed by *NCSA* (the National Center for Supercomputing Applications—http://www.ncsa.uiuc.edu/), the Internet experience changed from an often baffling ordeal of arcane commands and stark text-filled monitors to a matter of simply pointing and clicking on clearly labeled buttons and links. The rousing success of Apple Computer's Macintosh and Microsoft's Windows had already made it possible for users of personal computers to ditch clunky text-based interfaces in favor of friendlier collections of menus and icons—why not apply the same standard to the rising technology of the World Wide Web?

Today, it's rare to find a Web site anywhere that doesn't include one or more pictures. Images are by far the most common type of multimedia in general use on the Web today. And why not? They're simple to create, small and quick to download, and they can easily make any Web page look much better. Or worse, as the case may be.

IMAGE FILE FORMATS

As a direct result of their popularity, there are probably more individual file formats for image data than for nearly any other type of information—with the possible exception of text. Fortunately, out of these thousands of different file types, there are presently only two likely to bear much relevance to general web design: *GIF* (Graphics Interchange Format) and *JPEG* (named for the Joint Photographic Experts Group, which created it).

PNG (Portable Network Graphics—pronounced "ping"—is also a format likely to be of importance in the future but not yet widely supported by browsers.

TRANSPARENT AND ANIMATED GIFs

There are a few variations to both the GIF and JPEG file types, most of which have an equivalent variation between the two, which you'll discover in this lab's exercises. The GIF format, however, has several features and format variations that have no JPEG equivalent, such as *transparency support* and *GIF89a (animated GIF)*.

GIFs incorporating *transparency* have one user-specified color in the palette designated as transparent, meaning that any part of the image so colored will be ignored by a Web browser. This feature can be useful if you're using a custom background pattern or color and want it to be visible behind your images.

GIF89a is an offshoot of the GIF format, which actually consists of several GIF images, saved as a single file, which display in sequence like a cartoon flipbook when loaded by a browser. Depending on specifications set by the designer when the file is saved, the animation can be made to repeat, loop back and forth, or run once each time the page is loaded. GIF89a is the easiest way to incorporate simple animations into a Web page without using JavaScript or a third party plug-in.

Both transparent and animated GIFs can be created easily with many different commercial and shareware graphics programs.

The Whole Truth
Technically, the interlaced GIFs described earlier are stored in the same GIF89a format employed to make animated GIFs. This makes sense if you think about it, since both interlaced and animated GIFs must include multiple images compressed into a single file. Note, however, that animated GIFs cannot be interlaced.

LAB 7.1 EXERCISES

7.1.1 EXPERIMENT WITH IMAGE FILE FORMATS

Visit your favorite Web page and right-click on a few graphics. From the popup menu, choose the Save Picture As option. There's no need to save the file to your hard drive, just observe the file types for the various graphics.

a) Do you notice any pattern between the types of graphics saved as GIFs and those saved as JPEGs?

_____

_____

Next, choose a graphic already saved on your machine in a format other than GIF or JPEG. Open the graphic in your graphics program and view the file's properties.

b) What is the size of the file you chose?

_____

_____

Save the file in the GIF format and view the new file's properties.

c) How has the file size changed in the GIF format?

_____

_____

Next, open the original file again and this time save it as a JPEG file. View the new file's properties.

    d) How has the file size changed in the JPEG format?

    _____

    _____

    e) Is there a significant difference between the file size of the GIF and the JPEG file?

    _____

    _____

Visit the following Web page: http://www.unisys.com/unisys/lzw/.

    f) What is LZW and what is the issue with it?

    _____

    _____

Now, visit the following Web page: http://www.libpng.org/pub/png/pngintro.html.

    g) What are the three main advantages of the PNG image format over the GIF format?

    _____

    _____

7.1.2 DIFFERENTIATE BETWEEN GIFS AND JPEGS

Open the JPEG image from Exercise 7.1.2 in your graphics program. Save the file six times.

    a) Do you notice any difference in the graphic's quality each time you save it?

    _____

    _____

This time, choose a more complex graphic, such as a detailed photograph and save it as both a GIF and a JPEG.

    b) Any difference between the quality of the two images?

_____

_____

Finally, create a graphic that consists of a simple line of text and perhaps an icon. Save the graphic to both GIF and JPEG formats.

    c) Any difference between the quality of these two new images?

_____

_____

7.1.3 EXPERIMENT WITH VARIOUS TYPES OF IMAGES

    a) Do you think converting a grayscale image to JPEG will affect its file size?

_____

_____

Try it. Choose a graphic already saved on your machine in a format other than GIF or JPEG and open it in your graphic program. Convert the image to grayscale and save it as a JPEG file, then check its file size.

    b) Is there any significant between the size of the two files?

_____

_____

Now, open the GIF file from Exercise 7.1.1 and save it as a JPEG file.

    c) What effect does this have on the image quality?

_____

_____

Suppose you have a complex image that contains both a high quality photograph and some text.

d) In which format do you think it would be best to save such an image?

_____

_____

7.1.4 IDENTIFY SPECIAL IMAGE TYPES

Visit the following Web site again: http://www.libpng.org/pub/png/pngintro.html.

a) What is interlacing and how does it affect the loading of an image?

_____

_____

b) Do you think all images would benefit by interlacing?

_____

_____

LAB 7.1 EXERCISE ANSWERS

7.1.1 ANSWERS

a) Do you notice any pattern between the types of graphics saved as GIFs and those saved as JPEGs?

Answer: In general, GIFs are used for simple graphics, such as an icon or a line of text. JPEGs are generally used for more complex color-intense images, such as photographs.

GIF and JPEG were chosen as the standards to be recognized by most graphical Web browsers for a very simple reason: Both formats employ effective compression techniques that can allow for considerably reduced file sizes. On the Web, where file size determines whether a page will take seconds, minutes, or hours to fully load all of its associated data—images included—file size is obviously an important consideration.

Both GIF and JPEG are lossy formats, meaning that image quality will usually decrease as the rate of compression goes up and the overall file size goes down. However, because they use different compression algorithms, they compress different types of data with varying levels of effectiveness and loss.

b) What is the size of the file you chose?

Answer: This of course will vary depending on the image you choose.

We opened a BMP photograph that was 567 KB in size.

Save the file in the GIF format and view the new file's properties.

c) How has the file size changed in the GIF format?

Answer: The file size is sure to have decreased rather significantly.

In our example, the file size of the photograph went from 567 KB in size to 50 KB in size.

GIF, developed by CompuServe in 1987, is an 8-bit-per-pixel image format, meaning that it is limited to a maximum palette of 256 colors. GIF is somewhat less popular among graphics professionals, as high-resolution images such as photographs have a tendency to lose a substantial amount of quality when reduced to fit an 8-bit color palette (you probably noticed this in this example). On the other hand, if an image converted to GIF format already uses fewer than 256 colors, all extraneous color information is promptly discarded, potentially shaving off a sizable chunk of what would otherwise be wasted space. The GIF type most commonly used in Web design is technically known as GIF87a; the format features a number of offshoots such as GIF89a (animated GIFs) and some additional capabilities, such as transparency, that other formats such as JPEG do not support.

GIF uses a compression algorithm called LZW,[1] which, while rather ineffectual at compressing some types of images, is extremely efficient when applied to certain others. The impact of compression methods and algorithms will be discussed later.

d) How has the file size changed in the JPEG format?

Answer: Again, the file size is sure to have decreased rather significantly, probably more than the GIF.

In our example, the file size of the photograph went from 567 KB in size to 33 KB in size.

---

[1]Named for A. Lempel, J. Ziv, and T. Welch.

JPEG is the image format of choice among many graphical designers. Comparing it with GIF, it isn't difficult to understand why: JPEG files are capable of storing color information at up 24 bits per pixel, or in up to 16 million colors, and its compression technique is vastly superior to GIF when it comes to compressing high-resolution image data with a minimal loss of picture quality.

A full-color photograph converted to JPEG format can be up to 100 times smaller than the original file, although a 20:1 ratio is a more realistic expectation. High compression rates come at a price, however: Loss of quality can be significant in highly compressed files. Fortunately, most graphics programs that are capable of converting images to JPEG format also provide the ability to specify exactly how much compression will be applied, allowing careful users to create very small low-quality images, larger but clearer images, or any balance of size and quality in between.

Worthy of note is the fact that since any compressed image must be decompressed before it can be viewed, a highly compressed JPEG can be expected to take slightly longer to decode and display than a GIF (or a less-compressed JPEG). For the most part, though, this is unimportant; the time you're likely to save by offering a smaller file for download should more than make up for any additional milliseconds lost to the decoding process.

The Whole Truth

Technically, the JPEG files we know and love from the Web are actually a JPEG variant called *JFIF*, short for "JPEG File Interchange Format." Several other common (and uncommon) file formats also originated as offshoots of the JPEG format, including such diverse file types as TIFF, the Macintosh PICT format, and an obscure format called SPIFF. However, since JFIFs are what most people are actually referring to when they talk about JPEGs, particularly as they relate to Web design, we'll continue to call them JPEGs here.

---

e) Is there a significant difference between the file size of the GIF and the JPEG file?

Answer: It depends, but the JPEG file is probably smaller.

As you saw earlier, in our case, the GIF was 50 KB, while the JPEG was only 33 KB.

f) What is LZW and what is the issue with it?

Answer: LZW is the compression algorithm used by the GIF format. Patent and royalty issues surrounding the LZW algorithm threaten the continuing popularity of the GIF format. CompuServ holds the patent and its interest in potential infringement has grown with the popularity of the Web. As a result, the availability of graphical tools capable of generating GIF images is affected.

g) What are the three main advantages of the PNG image format over the GIF format?

Answer: Alpha channels (variable transparency), gamma correction (cross-platform control of image brightness), and two-dimensional interlacing (a method of progressive display).

As stated earlier, PNG (Portable Network Graphics)—pronounced "ping"—is a format likely to be of importance in the future but not yet widely supported by browsers. While the format has been around for several years and was intended as a replacement for GIF, renewed interest has been sparked by the LZW patent and royalty demands from CompuServ. In fact, the unofficial acronym for PNG has become "PNG's Not GIF."

Quite impressively, PNG supports three main image types: truecolor, grayscale, and palette-based (8-bit). JPEG only supports the first two, and GIF only the third.

PNG has been a formal recommendation by the W3C (World Wide Web Consortium) since 1996. More information can be found at http://www.w3.org/Graphics/PNG/.

7.1.2 ANSWERS

a) Do you notice any difference in the graphic's quality each time you save it?

Answer: You should. Every time you save a JPEG file, it reapplies the compression algorithm, which, while it probably won't affect the size of the file, will continue to decrease the quality of the image over time.

For this reason, you should avoid saving your images in JPEG format until you're done working with them; in the meantime, you'll probably want to use a 24-bit lossless image format, like TIFF. Additionally, if you think you might be making changes to the image in the future, it might not be such a bad idea to keep a master copy in TIFF format stored away somewhere.

Things would be infinitely easier, of course, if the Web-designing world would pick one standard and stick with it. Unfortunately, however, this isn't likely to happen any time in the near future—which is really a good thing, of course, since it encourages research to develop newer and better ways of doing things. (And if you think having to choose between two different image formats is rough, wait until you get to the sections on sound and video.)

For now, at least, the primary reason that the Web-developing community has kept both JPEG and GIF in common usage instead of tossing one of them aside is a simple one: The two different formats are good at different things. As we briefly mentioned earlier, the GIF and JPEG compression algorithms are specialized to deal with specific kinds of image data, meaning that one picture that compresses to an extremely small, high-resolution JPEG file might be both larger and of lesser quality if converted to GIF format, or vice versa.

b) Any difference between the quality of the two images?

Answer:You probably noticed that the GIF image is far less superior to the JPEG in terms of quality.

JPEG's algorithm affects the hue of the pixels that compose an image, hue being what we typically think of when we think of "color." Because the human eye is much less likely to perceive miniscule changes in color than it is to perceive similar changes in brightness or contrast, JPEG reduces the number of colors in an image by simplifying the color information at the points where different parts of the image naturally blend together. For obvious reasons, JPEG is most effective when applied to full-color photographs or photorealistic artwork with a lot of subtle color variation.

c) Any difference between the quality of these two new images?

Answer: It depends, but GIF is the better format for simpler graphics like thumbnails, icons, or text.

Unfortunately, the JPEG format does a poor job with almost everything else. For the same reason that JPEG is so efficient at blending detailed, multicolored images, it has a tendency to produce undesirable results when applied to simpler material. Text and line art with a solid-color background are likely to become blurred or jagged as JPEG attempts to blend them into their surroundings, unless the quality of the image is set to very high—which effectively negates the benefits of using JPEG in the first place. And, of course, the JPEG algorithm has no effect whatsoever on large areas composed of pixels that are all the same color, since there's nothing there to blend.

Fortunately, GIF manages to compensate for many of JPEG's shortcomings. The LZW algorithm works by remapping all of an image's color information to a custom palette of 256 or fewer colors; it doesn't attempt anything like JPEG's blending technique to reduce image complexity, so sharp edges or other high-contrast content are not adversely affected.

In addition, while GIF's color-remapping technique can significantly reduce the quality of images that actually do contain thousands or millions of different colors, it's important to note that when used to convert an image already containing 256 or fewer colors, GIF is completely lossless.

For the most part, you can follow this simple guideline: If the image is a photograph, or something else similarly complex in terms of color, JPEG is the format to use. On the other hand, if it's something simple, like an icon or a line of text, you're likely to be better off using GIF.

Naturally, it's not always quite that simple. As usual, there are certain circumstances under which this rule conveniently does not apply, as you learned in the next exercise.

7.1.3 ANSWERS

a) Do you think converting a grayscale image to JPEG will affect its file size?

Answer: Based on what we've just gone over, you might think that because you're working with a photograph, you'd be practically guaranteed both smaller file size and improved image quality if you converted the picture to JPEG format. You'd be wrong.

Why? Because grayscale images do not contain any hue *data—as far as your computer is concerned, all of those shades of gray are not actually different colors, but differing levels of* brightness *between white and black.*

Without any hue information to manipulate, the JPEG algorithm is essentially useless. If the image contains 256 or fewer shades of gray, however, conversion to GIF may very well be able to reduce both the color palette and the size of the file—without affecting its image quality at all.

b) Is there any significance between the size of the two files?

Answer: There shouldn't be.

Again, without any hue information, the JPEG algorithm is essentially useless.

c) What effect does this have on the image quality?

Answer: Converting a GIF to a JPEG reduces the quality of the image without offering any real improvements in the size of the file.

Converting GIF files to JPEG format is generally a bad idea. In fact, converting any type of image file from a lower to a higher color depth is generally a bad idea. Common sense would seem to indicate that a photographic image in GIF format would benefit from increased compression if it were converted to JPEG; however, with a selection of only 256 colors to work with, the JPEG algorithm's effectiveness will be lessened dramatically.

Even if the file does become smaller as a result of the conversion, the resulting reduc-tion in quality may be more than the decreased file size is worth. Remember that any image repeatedly converted back and forth between lossy formats will eventually de-grade into an unrecognizable mass of pixels.

d) In which format do you think it would be best to save such an image?

Answer: The best solution to this problem is to bypass it entirely by breaking your image down into two parts: a JPEG file containing the photograph and a GIF file containing the text. Better yet, crop out the text part of the image altogether and replace it with real text.

If this isn't possible for some reason—for instance, if the text is overlaid across the image—you'll probably be best off converting the entire file to GIF format, as JPEG runs the risk of rendering the text unreadable by blending it into the image. However, this is likely to vary from image to image; try the file in both formats, and go with whichever one you find to be satisfactory in terms of both size and quality.

7.1.4 ANSWERS

a) What is interlacing and how does it affect the loading of an image?

Answer: An interlacing image progressively displays on the page. It starts out blurry and gets clearer and clearer as it loads.

Suppose one of your pages consists of a single large, high-quality image, perhaps sur-rounded by a few lines of text or an occasional icon. Over a slow enough connection, it could easily take minutes for a browser to load the entire image. In the meantime, visi-tors to this page will be stuck; until that image has finished loading, they won't be able to view any of your other content, follow any links, or really do much of anything other than sit and wait as the image slowly loads from top to bottom.

Fortunately, both JPEG and GIF have special file formats—called progressive JPEGs *and* interlaced GIFs, *respectively—that can dramatically cut the amount of time it takes an image to appear on your page. Images saved in progressive or interlaced form are actually saved as a series of* layers, *each of which is a self-contained, very low-qual-ity image that encompasses only a fraction of the total file size. When a browser en-counters the file, it processes and displays each of these layers in succession, incrementally increasing the image quality with each layer, until the entire image has been downloaded.*

There are several benefits to using these formats, not the least of which is the simple fact that they feel faster since the individual layers are so tiny. It only takes a moment for the first of them to load and appear on the page, freeing the user to browse other content as the remaining layers download and the image sharpens in the background.

Interestingly, while the total download time is the same, progressive images actually take slightly longer to display than normal ones, due to the fact that each layer is encoded individually and takes the same amount of time to decode and display as a separate image. For most users, though, this is a nonissue; unless you've got an incredibly fast connection and an incredibly slow computer, the time it takes your machine to decode each layer as it arrives will always be considerably less than the time it takes to download the next one.

b) Do you think all images would benefit by interlacing?

Answer: Be careful not to use progressive images where they're not appropriate. Some images benefit from becoming visible in stages, but the majority do not.

Image maps and background pictures, for instance, gain nothing by loading progressively. Since they're useless until they have fully downloaded, making them appear as a succession of blurry, pixilated layers may actually create the illusion that they're downloading slower, not faster.

LAB 7.1 SELF-REVIEW QUESTIONS

In order to test your progress, you should be able to answer the following questions.

1) GIF is an acronym for which of the following?

a) _____ Graphical Interactive File
b) _____ Graphic Interlace Format
c) _____ Graphic Interface Format
d) _____ Graphical Image File

2) JPEG is an acronym for which of the following?

a) _____ Joint Photo Exchange Graphic
b) _____ Joint Photographic Experts Group
c) _____ JPEG Picture Experts Group
d) _____ Joint Portable Experts Graphic

3) Which of the following is true of the GIF89a format?

a) _____ It is used to progressively display an image on the page.
b) _____ It is an animated GIF made up of several images.
c) _____ It is best for simple graphics, such as icons or text.
d) _____ It is made of several low-quality layers that load over top of one another.

4) GIF reduces the size of image files by simplifying the colors used at the points in an image where multiple colors are blended together.

    a) _____ True
    b) _____ False

5) Which format would you use to present a highly detailed black-and-white photograph?

    a) _____ GIF
    b) _____ JPEG
    c) _____ Either

Quiz answers appear in the Appendix, Section 7.1.

L A B   7 . 2

AUDIO

LAB OBJECTIVES

After this lab, you will be able to:

✔ Identify MIME Types, Helper Applications, and Plug-ins
✔ Embed Sound in a Web Page

The two most basic types of Web media—text and pictures—are ubiquitous to the point that nearly every Web page in existence incorporates one or the other, and very often both. It's not difficult to understand why: Text and pictures make up the backbone of Web-based content primarily because they're almost as easy to create as they are to read. Since any Web-surfing experience is practically guaranteed to include the viewing of some text or images, most browsers are designed to be capable of automatically translating any appropriately formatted text or image data they might encounter and of displaying their content within a main browser window.

There are many other kinds of media on the Web, however, and none of them presently have agreed-upon standards like GIF and JPEG and HTML (although some are getting close). Sound, video, and various other forms of content can be found in literally hundreds of different file formats, and no browser could ever be expected to automatically recognize and translate them all. Instead, they rely on third-party solutions in the form of *helper applications* and *browser plug-ins*.

HELPER APPLICATIONS

Helper applications are external programs that work with your browser, enabling you to open file formats that are not native to it. Browser-native formats usually include HTML, GIF, and JPEG. Examples of nonnative formats are PDF (Portable Document Format) and some audio files. Whenever such a file type is encountered, the browser checks the file's MIME type against its internal list to see whether a helper application (or a plug-in) has already been specified to deal with this particular file type. If so, the browser finishes downloading, launches the application in question, and uses that application to open the file.

If no helper application has been specified, or if the browser cannot locate the specified application on your hard disk, it will display a dialog box explaining the situation and asking what you want to do with the file. Options normally include saving it to disk, deleting it, or choosing a new helper application for the browser to use with this type of file in the future.

Most browsers are released with a preconfigured list of some of the most common helper applications, eliminating the need for many users to adjust any settings themselves. In addition, certain programs will make changes to your browser settings when they are installed, automatically setting themselves up as the default helper application for all of the various file types that they are equipped to deal with.

The Whole Truth

It may be worth noting that by making the appropriate changes to your browser's list of helper applications, you can affect what it does with any type of data it encounters. If you tell the browser to use an external application to process files tagged with the MIME code *text/html* or *image/gif* instead of opening them itself, the browser will oblige—and you can expect dozens of windows to pop up all over your screen whenever you try to access a Web page.

There is, of course, no practical reason why you would want to do this, unless you have lots of free RAM, a fast computer, and no interest in actually getting anything out of the content you download. Still . . . you *can*.

Problems sometimes arise when a Web server doesn't know what MIME code to send along with a particular file. If the server doesn't know that all files with the extension *.mov* should be sent as MIME-type *video/quicktime*, it is possible that the file contents will be interpreted by your browser as MIME-type *text/plain*. The data itself is still valid—meaning that knowledgeable users could still save the resulting fifty pages of gibberish to their hard drives and manually open the saved file with their movie-playing application of choice—but this probably wasn't what you had in mind when you made the decision to include that video file on your site. Fortunately, however, most server platforms can be expected to recognize all of the more common file extensions and their associated MIME types, so this isn't likely to be a problem unless you're using something truly obscure—in which case your solution is still a relatively simple matter of configuring your Web server to recognize the new file type.

HELPER APPLICATIONS VS. PLUG-INS

A helper application is an independent program used in conjunction with a Web browser to process a file of a particular MIME type. Helper applications are typically used for filetypes not natively recognized by a Web browser. A *plug-in* is an extension to a Web browser used to accommodate files of a particular MIME type. Plug-ins use the Application Program Interface (API) available with most browsers. With a plug-in, support of a particular MIME type appears to a user to be "built into" the browser.

Some Helper Application Advantages

- User choice of viewing/using particular filetypes
- Applications generally allow file editing and saving

Some Helper Application Disadvantages

- Helper application must be able to execute simultaneously with the Web browser
- Web browser functionality (e.g., following links) is typically lost in the helper application environment

Some Plug-in Advantages

- Plug-in functionality becomes a part of browser functionality
- Plug-in installation handles browser MIME type configuration

Some Plug-in Disadvantages

- Plug-ins increase the overall size of the browser application
- Plug-ins may raise browser performance and security issues

MIME TYPES

When you instruct your browser to open a file on a local disk, such as your hard drive, the browser determines whether the file is readable by examining its *file extension,* a three- or four-letter suffix to the name of the file that provides information on what type of data it contains: *index.html,* for example, or *face.gif.*

When you instruct your browser to obtain a file from a remote server, however, things work a little differently. First and foremost, the browser is no longer directly opening and processing the file, as it does with files stored on your hard drive. Instead, it is sending a message to the server via *HTTP* (HyperText Transfer Protocol) requesting that a file be sent to it. Once a file transfer begins, your browser processes the data as it arrives; the name of the file in which that data is stored is essentially an afterthought, meaning that the browser is unable to consult it for a hint as to what type of data it's about to receive.

Instead, the browser gets all the information it needs from the remote server itself in the form of a special code called *MIME type*. MIME (Multipart Internet Mail Extension) was initially developed to make it easier for text-based e-mail systems to process single messages that contained more than one type of data—such as embedded images or file attachments—by inserting a MIME code at the beginning of each block of data specifying what sort of data it contained. MIME codes typically take the form of two words separated by a slash, such as *image/gif;* the first word indicates the general kind of data and the second indicates a specific file type.

AUDIO FILE FORMATS

There is presently no Web audio standard, nor is there likely to be one any time in the near future. Static images were fairly easy to standardize; GIF or JPEG are capable of doing most everything that any Web designer might need them to do, and each effectively covers the shortcomings of the other.

Audio is different. New technologies for making audio files smaller or of higher quality—the two most valued attributes of any kind of Web-based media—are emerging on an almost daily basis. Of the file formats that already do exist, there are literally dozens of potential choices, nearly all of which are suited to uses that will vary from designer to designer. And unlike GIF and JPEG, many sound formats are owned by large companies, all of whom are eager to see their technology emerge as a new standard.

Nevertheless, however, there are some audio formats that are much more widely used than others. We'll look at three of the most common: *AU, AIFF,* and *WAV.*

AU (.au)

AU, developed by Sun Microsystems, was initially designed to be an audio standard for the UNIX platform. However, many sound programs capable of recording and playing sounds in AU format have since been developed for other operating systems.

Like most other common audio formats, AU files can be recorded in both mono and stereo sound and at a number of different sampling rates. Unlike most other common audio formats, AU's recording capability is limited to 8-bit sound, meaning that AU files, while small, are often of rather poor quality. For simple noises like clicks and beeps, however, they are ideal.

AIFF (.aiff, .aif, .aifc)

AIFF (Audio Interchange File Format) was developed by Apple Computer in 1988, and, of the three formats detailed here, it is one of the most flexible. AIFF can record both 8- and 16-bit sounds, mono and stereo, at a wide variety of different sampling rates, allowing for a range of different file sizes. It is also fully compatible with the *Red Book* standard for audio CD mastering, which makes it a popular format for use in producing amateur music CDs.

AIFC is a variation on AIFF that features built-in data compression via the *MACE (Macintosh Audio Compression/Expansion)*[2] algorithm, which itself comes in two flavors: *MACE3,* which provides 3:1 compression, and *MACE6,* which provides 6:1 compression. As one might expect, both MACE3 and MACE6 are lossy compression schemes, meaning that the sound quality of any AIFC-compressed file can be expected to decrease. Otherwise, AIFC is essentially identical to AIFF.

WAV (.wav)

WAV (Windows Audio/Video), jointly developed by Microsoft and IBM, became the de facto standard for digital audio on Windows operating systems when Microsoft included built-in support for it in Windows 3.1. Its use is not limited to Windows systems, however; sound applications with full WAV support currently exist for numerous other platforms, including Unix and Macintosh. On such non–Windows-based platforms, the format is sometimes called *RIFF WAVE.*

WAV is an extremely flexible audio format. Like AIFF, it is capable of recording mono and stereo sound and offers multiple sampling rates, bit depths, and compression schemes so as to allow a designer to reach exactly the right balance of compression and quality. On Windows systems in particular, WAV is as close to a standard for sound files as anything else currently used on the Web.

OTHER COMMON FORMATS

There are a number of other common audio formats in use today, as described in the following sections.

---

[2]Despite its name, MACE-encoded sound files are usable on any platform that supports AIFF, not just Macintosh.

**LAB
7.2**

MPEG (.mpeg, .mpg) *MPEG* (engineered by the Motion Picture Experts Group, which included a number of the same people behind JPEG) was initially created as a format for compressing high-quality digital video. Like JPEG, the MPEG algorithm compresses files by removing redundant or otherwise unnecessary information: image data that persists from one frame to the next, or miniscule changes in color that are imperceptible to the human eye.

There are currently four varieties of the MPEG format, each of which is composed of three different standards: a *video* compression standard, an *audio* compression standard, and a *system* standard that compresses both video and audio information into a single data stream. Like MPEG *Video*, the MPEG *Audio* standards can used to create extremely high-quality sound samples in comparatively small files, making them well-suited to Web media. In recent years, *MPEG Audio Layer 3,* better known as *MP3,* has become very popular due to its emergence as the standard for distribution of near-CD-quality music over the Internet.

Most MPEG audio files are still too large to be effectively used in Web sites intended for casual browsing by modem. Due to their high quality and widespread cross-platform compatibility, however, various incarnations of MPEG remain some of the most popular file formats used in Web-based multimedia applications today.

We'll take a closer look at some other MPEG types in Lab 7.3, Video.

MIDI (.midi, .mid) *MIDI (Musical Instrument Digital Interface)* actually refers to two different things: a hardware interface that can be used to connect compatible musical instruments to a computer and a computer language that simulates instrumental sound by breaking it down into electronically reproducible components.

Files written with the MIDI language are not technically sound files in the same sense as AIFF or WAV, as they contain no actual digitized sound. Instead, they contain information on notes, tempos, instruments, and various other assorted pieces of musical data, which is then applied to an existing library of digitally recorded instrument samples. As a result, MIDI files are exceedingly small in comparison to other audio formats—over an hour of sound can be stored in less than 500 kilobytes!

MIDI files can be played by a wide range of sound players and plug-ins on many different computer platforms. Unlike most audio formats, however, the files cannot be recorded with conventional sound programs; in order to create MIDIs from scratch, you'll need special software, a set of MIDI-compatible instruments, and the necessary hardware to connect them to your computer. Fortunately, there are a number of public FTP sites with libraries of MIDI files that can be downloaded free of charge, provided that you don't intend to use them for any commercial purpose.

EMBEDDING AUDIO IN A WEB PAGE

A Web page incorporating sound can do so in any number of different ways. In most cases, the means you choose will depend primarily on the type of sound you are using, the length of the sound, and your reason for including the sound at all. Should the sound automatically begin to play as soon as the page has loaded? Will it play only once, or multiple times? Should visitors to your page have access to a set of controls that they can use to stop or rewind the sound at will?

However you choose to present your sound file, you will probably be using the <EMBED> tag. Any file placed on a page through use of the <EMBED> tag can be affected by certain default parameters such as SRC, TYPE (MIME type) and WIDTH and HEIGHT For the <EMBED> tag, the only options necessary are the MIME type (typically type=audio/basic) and the source (src=path to the file to include).

■ *FOR EXAMPLE*

```
<EMBED SRC="welcome.wav" TYPE= "audio/basic" WIDTH=75
HEIGHT=75>
```

First introduced as a part of HTML 4, the <OBJECT> tag was intended as an eventual replacement for the <EMBED> tag. A quick comparison of the two will reveal that they have a great deal in common; if you're familiar with the <EMBED> tag, graduating to <OBJECT> should be reasonably easy.

<OBJECT> references may contain HTML—including additional <OBJECT> tags—between their opening and closing tags. In the event that a Web browser is unable to locate or process the file specified by the <OBJECT> parameters, this secondary HTML will be parsed and processed instead.

Otherwise, apart from some differences in the usage and availability of various parameters, the two tags are used very similarly.

■ *FOR EXAMPLE*

```
<OBJECT DATA="welcome.wav" TYPE= "audio/basic" WIDTH=75
HEIGHT=75></OBJECT>
```

LAB 7.2 EXERCISES

7.2.1 IDENTIFY MIME TYPES, HELPER APPLICATIONS, AND PLUG-INS

a) Discuss why MIME types are necessary.

_____

_____

b) Investigate which MIME types are supported by your browser and how you specify new types.

_____

_____

c) A plug-in is a module that is run directly from the browser. Discuss the advantages of this as compared to a helper application.

_____

_____

7.2.2 EMBED SOUND IN A WEB PAGE

For this exercise, do a search on Yahoo for "sound clip archive." This will give you a number of different sites with sound clips. Download a sound file (i.e., sound.au) from a site on the Internet.

a) Create an <EMBED> tag for an embedded sound object with a MIME type of "audio/basic" and the source is the file you're using.

_____

_____

b) Create an <OBJECT> tag for an embedded sound object with a MIME type of "audio/basic" and the source is the file you're using.

_____

_____

Embed several long sounds (1–20 seconds) in a Web page one right after the other. Open the page in your browser.

c) What do you notice about how the sound files perform?

_____

_____

Add sound to a Web page using the <BGSOUND> tag like this: <BGSOUND SRC="hello.wav">. (Substitute hello.wav for the sound file you're using.)

d) Load the page in different browsers. What happened?

_____

_____

LAB 7.2 EXERCISE ANSWERS

7.2.1 ANSWERS

a) Discuss why MIME types are necessary.

Answer: MIME (Multipurpose Internet Mail Extensions) types are specific file formats that are recognized by MIME-compliant applications/programs such as Web browsers. Data files are usually identified as being of a particular type by means of a filename extension or suffix in the form "filename.extension." By following this convention, a file extension identifies the format of a file so that an appropriate program or application can be used to process that file.

Keep in mind that after a Web browser requests a file via HTTP from a remote server, the first piece of data it receives is the MIME type of the file, which it then proceeds to compare to an internal listing of MIME types in order to determine what type of file is being sent and what should be done with it when it arrives. The browser's library usually includes a default list containing most of the more common MIME types; if they choose, users can manually configure the list, adding new entries or editing old ones as the need arises.

Assuming, then, that the MIME type of the received file corresponds to an entry on the list, the browser then does one of two things: It begins to process and display the file itself, as is the case with files of type image/jpeg *or* text/html, *or it passes the file to a helper application or a browser plug-in, as specified by the list.*

b) Investigate which MIME types are supported by your browser and how you specify new types.

Answer:What MIME types your browser supports depends on both your operating system and browser. On Windows, the recognition of applications based on a file's extension applies to basically every application and not just the browser.The two most widely used browsers on Windows (Netscape Navigator and Microsoft Internet Explorer) will allow you to immediately start the application when you click on a link to a recognized file type. However, this is done using the file extension. For example, when clicking on a file ending in .DOC, the typical Windows behavior is to load MS.Word.

However, this is not what happens on other systems, such as UNIX. UNIX does not have the same concept of file endings as Windows.Therefore, UNIX browsers need to rely more on the MIME type.

Not all browsers let you define MIME types from within the browser itself. For example, MS-Internet Explorer is so tied into the operating system that the only way to define new types is through the operating system (i.e., File Manager). Netscape Navigator provides the ability to add new types directly from the browser.

While it may be unreasonable to expect that any Web browser could ever be able to open and process every single one of the hundreds of file formats in existence, it's only logical to expect that for every one of those file formats, there is at least one program, somewhere, that is capable of opening and reading it.

This is the fundamental concept behind helper applications.

c) A plug-in is a module that is run directly from the browser. Discuss the advantages of this as compared to a helper application.

Answer:The idea behind plug-ins is similar to the idea behind helper applications: Essentially, they provide individual users with a way to selectively add functionality to their browsers, eliminating the need for developers to release the browsers already overloaded with features that most users won't actually need.

Unlike helper applications, however, plug-ins do not function independently of the Web browser. Instead of taking over for the browser whenever an unfamiliar file is encountered, a plug-in adds new capabilities to the browser itself, allowing the user to view additional content directly within the browser window.

Netscape introduced the concept of the browser plug-in with version 2.0 of its popular Navigator Web browser.Today, most browsers come with several plug-in modules already installed—usually sound or video players, such as Netscape's LiveAudio or Apple's

QuickTime—and dozens of other plug-ins for use with various other types of content are available for free download from sites all around the Web.

7.2.2 ANSWERS

a) Create an <EMBED> tag for an embedded sound object with a MIME type of "audio/basic" and the source is the file is the file you're using.

Answer: The tag might look like this:
```
<EMBED SRC="sound.au" TYPE= "audio/basic">
```

Like many other HTML tags, the <EMBED> tag has a large number of options you can use. Table 7.1 gives a description of the primary <EMBED> attributes for audio.

Table 7.1 ■ Example of <EMBED> Attributes for Audio

`<embed src="sound.au"`	Specifies a path to the sound file that you want to embed in your page.
`type="audio/basic"`	Alternately, you can include a MIME type instead of a path to a specific file. This option is commonly used when the content is to be generated dynamically and no actual source file exists. All <EMBED> tags must contain either a SRC or a TYPE parameter.
`width=143` `height=59>`	The horizontal and vertical dimensions, in pixels, of the window in which the sound controls will be displayed.
	Note: The sample dimensions displayed here are the exact dimensions of the player that is a part of Netscape's LiveAudio plug-in. If they are set any lower, the controls will be made invisible and inaccessible. If you expect visitors to your web site to be using a different plug-in to process sound files, you may need to adjust these numbers to accommodate the size of a different type of player.

Depending on the type of file being embedded, the <EMBED> tag may also contain optional parameters that supply additional information to the plug-in handling the embedded data. Sound files played by Netscape Navigator's default LiveAudio plug-in, for example, can be affected by any of the following:

`autostart=true`	Determines whether the sound begins playing automatically when the page has loaded. Can be set to TRUE or FALSE; defaults to FALSE.
`loop=true`	Determines whether the sound will automatically begin playing again after it has finished. Can be set to TRUE, FALSE, or a number; defaults to FALSE.

For more information on any special parameters supported by a specific browser plug-in, you should refer to the documentation supplied with the plug-in.

b) Create an <OBJECT> tag for an embedded sound object with a MIME type of "audio/basic" and the source is the file is the file you're using.

Answer: An example might be:
`<OBJECT DATA="sound.au" TYPE= "audio/basic"></OBJECT>.`

An important thing to keep in mind is that the <OBJECT> tag is generic and applies to more than just sound. Because of the wide range of possible objects. You need to include the closing tag </OBJECT>.

Like the <EMBED> tag, the <OBJECT> tag may also contain optional parameters, depending on the type of media and its dependant plug-in. As usual, any documentation provided with the plug-in itself is the best place to look for this type of information.

One thing to note is that the preceding example probably won't work on your system. As it says, the classid is for a specific implementation, which you probably don't have on your system. With all of the necessary information, a more detailed example might look like this:

```
<OBJECT codetype="application/java"
        classid="AudioItem"
        width="15" height="15">
<PARAM name="snd" value="hello.wav">
</OBJECT>
```

Confused? Don't be. Although it's true that the <OBJECT> tag was originally intended to replace the <EMBED> tag, <EMBED> is still extremely common and widely used by numerous Web content providers. If you're interested in the additional functionality that <OBJECT> provides, or you want to ensure that your designs support the latest and greatest developments in HTML, the new tags and parameters may be worth a little research. If not, however, <EMBED> will still do everything that you're likely to want or need. And you'll be in good company if you choose to stay with it; <EMBED> remains common enough that browser support for it isn't likely to disappear anytime soon.

To avoid confusion, we'll continue to refer to the <EMBED> tag throughout this chapter.

Table 7.2 ■ Example of <OBJECT> Attributes for Audio

`<object classid="AudioItem"`	Identifies an implementation of a specific object type.
`type="audio/basic"`	Alternately, you can include a MIME type instead of a path to a specific file. This option is commonly used when the content is to be generated dynamically and no actual source file exists. All <OBJECT> tags must contain either a SRC or a TYPE parameter.
`data="data"`	Specifies a path to the object's data.
`width=143` `height=59>`	The horizontal and vertical dimensions, in pixels, of the window in which the sound controls will be displayed.
`</object>`	*Note:* The sample dimensions displayed here are the exact dimensions of the player that is a part of Netscape's Live Audio plug-in. If they are set any lower, the controls will be made invisible and inaccessible.

c) What do you notice about how the files perform?

Answer: Depending on the length and how the browser is configured, the sound clips will probably overlap.

This is a good demonstration of the notion that just because something is possible doesn't necessarily mean it's also a good idea. If you absolutely must have multiple sound clips, you can use the autostart=false option so that the clips are not started as soon as the page is loaded.

d) Load the page in different browsers. What happened?

Answer: Depending on the browser you chose, you may or may not have heard the sound. This tag is specific to Microsoft Internet Explorer.

*This is another good demonstration of just because something is possible doesn't necessarily mean it's also a good idea. Microsoft has added a number of HTML tags that are **NOT** part of any standard and therefore only work with Microsoft browsers. If you are including such tags on a company intranet, such nonstandard tags might be okay. However, it is not a good idea on a site open to the general public.*

LAB 7.2 SELF-REVIEW QUESTIONS

In order to test your progress, you should be able to answer the following questions.

1) An advantage of the AU format over AIFF is that AU supports 16-bit and AIFF supports only 8-bit.

a) _____ True
b) _____ False

2) WAV is the de facto digital audio on Windows operating systems.

a) _____ True
b) _____ False

3) In contrast to the other audio format, MIDI contains a description of the notes, tempos, instruments, and various other assorted pieces of musical data and *not* the digitalized sound.

a) _____ True
b) _____ False

4) Which of the following is not one of the primary sound types?

a) _____ AU
b) _____ AIFF
c) _____ SND
d) _____ WAV

5) Of the sound types discussed, which of these formats would you use to add a simple sound effect in a Web page, such as a click or a beep?

a) _____ AU
b) _____ AIFF
c) _____ SND
d) _____ WAV

6) Which of the following is not a required attribute for embedding sound in a Web page?

a) _____ File path to the audio sound file
b) _____ MIME type information
c) _____ Object length
d) _____ Sizing information for the audio player window

7) What is the difference between the usage of the <EMBED> tag and the <OBJECT> tag?

a) _____ The <EMBED> tag is intended to be used as a generalized method for including multimedia "objects" in Web pages, not just audio files.

b) _____ The <OBJECT> tag is intended to be used as a generalized method for including multimedia "objects" in Web pages, not just audio files.

c) _____ Being more general the <OBJECT> tag has fewer options.

d) _____ The <EMBED> tag is not supported in all browsers.

Quiz answers appear in the Appendix, Section 7.2.

L A B   7 . 3

VIDEO

LAB OBJECTIVES

After this lab, you will be able to

✔ Embed Video in a Web Page

Video is still a relatively new addition to the Web. Not long ago, surfers were still limited to slow dial-in connections operating at top speeds of 14.4 or 28.8 bits per second—barely enough to view large images effectively, let alone process a video presentation that might include dozens of frames per second.

With 57.6 bit-per-second modems becoming standard issue on home PCs and high-speed Internet lines becoming standard school and office equipment, however, bandwidth-hungry data types like video are becoming more and more common as a means of creating cutting-edge Web sites. And, as might be expected, every software corporation with a video file format to its name has leaped on the bandwagon and joined in a mad struggle to become the standard for delivering it.

EMBEDDED VIDEO FILE FORMATS

Like sound, digitized video is available in many different file formats. These files differ wildly in terms of size and quality, ranging from multi-gigabyte files that contain minutes of full-screen, full-color, 30-frame-per-second broadcast-quality video to tiny files several kilobytes in length comprised of a few seconds of grainy movement. In general, due to the size restrictions inherent in providing any sort of file over the Internet, video on the Web tends more toward the latter type than the former.

Therefore, the types of video most commonly used in Web-based presentations are limited to those that feature particularly effective compression techniques.

Although no standard for the presentation of video on the Web has yet been established—nor is one likely to be established in the foreseeable future—there are three file types in particular that have become particularly popular in recent years. These are *.avi, .mpg,* and *.mov.*

AVI (.avi, .vfw)

AVI (Audio/Video Interleave), known off the Web as *Video for Windows,* is, as its name implies, the standard for video on Microsoft Windows operating systems. While extremely common in the Windows world, AVI's usefulness elsewhere is somewhat compromised by the relatively low availability of AVI players for non-Windows platforms.

Since the majority of the world's personal computers do run some version of the Microsoft Windows operating system, however, AVI is still quite common on the Web, if slightly less so than either of its competitors.

MPEG (.mpeg, .mpg, .mp2, .mp3, etc.)

MPEG (engineered by the *Motion Picture Experts Group*) is probably the closest the Web has come to an existing standard for video.

Technically, there are actually four different MPEG formats, creatively named *MPEG-1, MPEG-2, MPEG-3,* and *MPEG-4,* each of which includes slightly modified versions of three different standards: *MPEG Video,* for compressing video data; *MPEG Audio,* for compressing audio data; and *MPEG Systems,* for compressing synchronous video and audio streams into a single data file.

Confused? Don't be; you will never encounter most of these formats. MPEG-4 is rarely used at all; MPEG-3 is now used almost exclusively as an audio format; and MPEG-2, originally developed in the early 1990s as part of an ongoing project to establish new standards for all-digital transmission of broadcast-quality video, is now used primarily to encode video data for storage on *DVDs (digital video discs)* or broadcast to *HDTV (high-definition TV).*

In fact, from a Web designer's point of view, the only MPEG format that merits much attention is *MPEG-1.* To narrow it down even further, the vast majority of the MPEG-1 files you can expect to find on the Web will probably be *MPEG-1 Video* files. The *MPEG-1 Systems* format, despite its advantage of being able to contain both video and audio data, does so at the cost of significantly increased file size. And there's not much reason to use *MPEG-1 Audio* when the MP3 standard is capable of creating files that are simultaneously smaller and of much higher quality.

Because of MPEG's widespread popularity, nearly all of the most common movie playing applications and browser plug-ins are capable of decoding and playing MPEG files. It's good to be the standard.

QUICKTIME (.qt, .mov)

Apple Computer's *QuickTime* file format is a close second to MPEG in popularity, and the gap has been narrowing steadily for several years.

Originally developed for the Macintosh platform in 1991, QuickTime players and development tools are now available for a number of other platforms, including Windows systems and several types of UNIX. Many popular Web browsers, including Microsoft's Internet Explorer and Netscape's Navigator and Communicator, have even begun including QuickTime software components with their preinstalled plug-ins.

The primary reason for QuickTime's popularity is its versatility: Once installed, the QuickTime player or browser plug-in can decode and play video and audio from dozens of common multimedia file types such as *.avi, .mpg,* and *.midi,* in addition to its own *.qt* and *.mov* formats, all without the need for any additional software.

EMBEDDING VIDEO IN A WEB PAGE

The <EMBED> tag is a beautiful thing.

Think of it: Practically any type of file can be attached to a Web page simply through the use of this single seven-character string. Sounds. Movies. Virtual reality. Interactive games. It's brilliant in its simplicity.

USING THE HTML <EMBED> TAG

And it's simple for a simple reason: The <EMBED> tag essentially absolves the browser of all responsibility. A file between a pair of <EMBED> tags is not the browser's responsibility to translate; at most, all the browser needs to do is read its MIME code to figure out what sort of file it is, consult its internal list of MIME types and associated plug-ins, and pass the file off to the appropriate plug-in for processing.

In a world with very few standard formats, the <EMBED> tag is a godsend. There's no need to learn a different set of HTML tags for each of the various file formats you might encounter, or even for the various types of media. If the browser viewing your page has all of the necessary plug-ins installed, everything will work invisibly and automatically. And if a required plug-in is missing, the browser can use the problem file's MIME code to automatically locate and down-load any necessary software from the appropriate FTP site.

As such, there is essentially no difference between the process of embedding audio in a Web page and the process of embedding video. In the case of file formats such as MPEG and QuickTime, which can contain both audio and video data, they are even subject to most of the same attributes and parameters.

However, one important difference is that the WIDTH and HEIGHT options are a lot more important to video than audio. If you leave these out, then no player controls will be displayed. Which might not be a bad thing for audio. On the other hand, if you leave them off for the video, there is no display area so you don't see the video at all.

■ *FOR EXAMPLE*

```
<embed SRC="welcome.mov" width=200 height=200>
```

USING THE HTML <NOEMBED> TAG

Although many of the most popular Web browsers currently come with a hefty set of plug-ins already installed, there's always the possibility that someone may eventually stumble across your site with an older browser that isn't equipped with what it needs to view your embedded content.

The <NOEMBED> tag provides Web designers with a means to specify a few lines of text that will appear in place of the unrecognized content. For example:

```
<noembed>
    This page contains an embedded QuickTime movie. Your
    browser is not currently capable of displaying QuickTime
    content. You can download QuickTime players and browser
    plug-ins from <a
    href=http://www.apple.com/quicktime>www.apple.com.</a>
</noembed>
```

The <NOEMBED> tag is, of course, irrelevant if you're using the <OBJECT> tag. The same functionality that <NOEMBED> adds to <EMBED> is already a part of <OBJECT>; any HTML placed between its opening and closing tags will be parsed and executed if the intended content fails to load properly.

LAB 7.3 EXERCISES

7.3.1 EMBED VIDEO IN A WEB PAGE

For this exercise, do a search on Yahoo for "video clip archive." This will give you a number of different sites with video clips. Download a video file (i.e., welcome.mov) from a site on the Internet.

a) Create an <EMBED> tag for an embedded video object with the source being the file you are using (e.g., "welcome.mov").

_____

_____

b) Create an <OBJECT> tag for embedded video object with the source being the file you are using (e.g., "welcome.mov").

_____

_____

c) Create an <EMBED> tag for a video object and add the controller=false option. How does the appearance change?

_____

_____

d) Create an <EMBED> tag for a video object and change the HEIGHT and WIDTH options. How does the appearance change?

_____

_____

LAB 7.3 EXERCISE ANSWERS

7.3.1 ANSWERS

a) Create an <EMBED> tag for an embedded video object with source being the file you are using (e.g., "welcome.mov").

Answer: The tag might look like the following:

```
<embed SRC="welcome" width=300 height=300>.
```

All embedded video data, however, is subject to several default attributes—most commonly SRC, WIDTH, and HEIGHT (see Table 7.3).

Table 7.3 ■ Example of <EMBED> Attributes for Video

`<embed src="video.mov"`	Specifies a path to the video file that you want to embed in your page.
`type="video/quicktime"`	Alternately, you can include a MIME type instead of a path to a specific file. This option is commonly used when the content is to be generated dynamically and no actual source file exists. All <EMBED> tags must contain either a SRC or a TYPE parameter.
`width=75` `height=50>`	The horizontal and vertical dimensions, in pixels, of the window in which your movie will be displayed.
	Note: The numbers entered here will only affect the dimensions of the display window, not of the movie itself. If the display window is smaller than the movie, some parts of the movie will not be visible.

Depending on the type of video file being embedded, the <EMBED> tag may also contain optional parameters that supply additional information to the plug-in handling the embedded data. An embedded QuickTime movie, for instance, is subject to the special parameters listed in Table 7.4, among others:

Table 7.4 ■ Special Parameters for Embedded QuickTime Movies

`autostart=false`	Determines whether the movie begins playing automatically when the page has loaded. Can be set to TRUE or FALSE; defaults to TRUE.
`loop=true`	Determines whether the movie will automatically begin playing again after it has finished. Can be set to TRUE or FALSE; defaults to FALSE.
`controller=false`	Determines whether the player's controls will be visible and accessible to the user. Can be set to TRUE or FALSE; defaults to TRUE.
`playeveryframe=true`	Used to ensure that the movie will play every frame, even if it must play at a lower rate to do so. Note, however, that it will also disable any audio tracks. Can be set to TRUE or FALSE; defaults to FALSE.

LAB 7.3

As usual, for more information on any special parameters supported by a specific browser plug-in, refer to the documentation supplied with the plug-in.

b) Create an < OBJECT > tag for an embedded video object with the source being the file you are using (e.g., "welcome.mov").

Answer: An example might be:

```
<object data="welcome.mov" width=300 height=300> </object>
```

c) Create an <EMBED> tag for a video object and add the controller=false option. How does the appearance change?

Answer: As the name implies, there are no controls for the video player. That means the user has no control over the flow of the video. That is, he or she cannot stop the video, rewind it, or do anything else.

d) Create an <EMBED> tag for a video object and change the HEIGHT and WIDTH options. How does the appearance change?

Answer: As their names imply, the height and width tags change the size of the video player. If the size is too small, then you won't see the video at all. If the play is too large, the quality of the image will be poor.

LAB 7.3 SELF-REVIEW QUESTIONS

In order to test your progress, you should be able to answer the following questions.

1) QuickTime is probably the most versatile format because it is supported by the most browsers.

   a) _____ True
   b) _____ False

2) The <NOEMBED> tag is used to force the browser to start an external application even if it could display it using a plug-in.

   a) _____ True
   b) _____ False

3) Specifying the height and width of a video object is required, but optional for audio.

   a) _____ True
   b) _____ False

4) The default with the <OBJECT> tag is to start the video automatically.

   a) _____ True
   b) _____ False

5) Although originally a video format, MPEG3 (MP3) is now more commonly an audio format.

   a) _____ True
   b) _____ False

6) Which are the three primary video file formats mentioned in this lab?

   a) _____ AVI, QuickTime, VID
   b) _____ MPEG, Real Video, QuickTime
   c) _____ MPEG, QuickTime, VID
   d) _____ AVI, MPEG, QuickTime

7) Which of the following is *not* a required option to the <EMBED> tag?

   a) _____ Height and width
   b) _____ Controller
   c) _____ Type
   d) _____ All are required
   e) _____ None are required

Quiz answers appear in the Appendix, Section 7.3.

L A B   7 . 4

STREAMING MULTIMEDIA

> ## LAB OBJECTIVES
>
> After this lab, you will be able to:
>
> ✔ Understand Streaming Multimedia
> ✔ Create Web Pages Using Streaming Multimedia

WHAT IS STREAMING MULTIMEDIA?

The ability to include full-motion video in a Web page can make all the difference when it comes to representing certain types of content on a site. Unfortunately, video files tend to be large, meaning that those viewers who aren't fortunate enough to be equipped with high-speed connections are forced to sit and wait for minutes, often hours, before the files are fully downloaded and ready to view.

Streaming multimedia offers an alternative to this click-wait-and-view scenario by creating video and sound that actually plays as it downloads, eliminating the need to wait for files to download. The data is downloaded, played, and discarded; aside from a few seconds of buffer data stored in the browser cache, nothing is saved to the local hard disk. Optionally, clients can specify that their player program save the downloaded file to disk for later viewing.

In addition to being a great way to incorporate video or sound into a site without forcing visitors to wait while it downloads, streaming multimedia makes it possible to "webcast" events for live viewing. Many local radio stations across the country, for instance, make it possible for their listeners to tune in from anywhere in the world by including a streaming-audio link in their home pages.

Some enterprising companies have even used streaming-audio technology to create Internet telephony programs, in which one user's voice is compressed and streamed to another user's workstation in real time.

By and large, streaming media is of much lower quality than other kinds of video or audio; since it is subject to line bottlenecks and network traffic interference, it also has a tendency to halt and skip while playing, especially over slower connections. However, streaming media technology has improved dramatically over the past few years, and with companies like Real.com, Microsoft, and Apple all working on newer and better streaming standards, it is only likely to get better from here. It has been proposed that as high-speed connections become more and more common, streaming media may actually eventually approach a level of quality comparable to broadcast television, potentially replacing it as the primary means of connecting our homes to the media circuit.

HOW DOES IT WORK?

Most data transferred from a server to client is transferred via a process called *packet switching*. In this model, the files being transferred are broken down into smaller units of data called *packets,* which are sent across the network to their destination via a number of different routes, depending on where the heaviest traffic areas are on the network. The packets may arrive in any order; however, since the packets contain sequencing information in addition to the data itself, they can be easily resequenced into their original order after arriving at their destination.

While immensely effective for most types of data, conventional packet-switching is unsuitable for streaming media due to the need for the data packets to arrive in the proper order. High-demand streaming media makes use of a different network technology called *ATM (Asynchronous Transfer Mode),* which establishes a "virtual circuit" between the client machine and the server that allows for the continuous transfer short, fixed-length packets, which is more time-efficient than traditional packet-switching. ATM is also *scalable,* meaning that it can actually increase its bandwidth allocation on demand, increasing its bandwidth for high-bandwidth data types like streaming video and scaling itself back down when the transmission ends or becomes less demanding, allowing the extra bandwidth to be used for other things.

Note that an ATM-capable platform is by no means *required* for the delivery of streaming media; it's perfectly plausible to run a low-end streaming server using normal HTTP protocols as well. However, the performance gains afforded by ATM make it the hands-down technology of choice for high-demand streaming content providers.

STREAMING MULTIMEDIA FILE FORMATS

Because of the obvious appeal and numerous uses for streaming multimedia, many software companies have leaped at the opportunity to become a part of the streaming revolution. Unfortunately, as is all too often the case, the result is a Web cluttered with dozens of different file formats, all clamoring to become the standard.

As of this writing, the format closest to establishing itself as the "standard" for streaming media is probably that developed by Real.com, appropriately called *RealVideo* or *RealAudio*. Newcomers such as Nullsoft's streaming MP3 technology or Apple's streaming QuickTime have grown dramatically in popularity, however, and it remains to be seen whether Real will be able to keep its position.

A streaming media package tends to include two things: a file format and a clientside player that is capable of reading the files. Most companies that make streaming software make their players available for free download from their Web sites; it is, after all, in their best interest to ensure that the greatest possible number of people have the player, since this helps to sell the video-streaming technology to clients. There are very few "cross-player" streaming media formats: for example, Real Media can be played only with Real's player, while *VDOLive* content can be played only with VDO's player.

While many of the following formats are somewhat uncommon in comparison to many of their better-known competitors, there is very little difference between most of them from the client's perspective. If you're trying to decide which format is best for you, keep this in mind: The only thing a client needs to view your content is the appropriate player or plug-in, most of which are available as free downloads from the developer's Web site. Once a client has the player installed, it no longer matters whether the format you've chosen to use is "common." Focus instead on whether the solution you've chosen will meet your needs for streaming the media you intend to distribute.

VDOLive (.vdo)
http://www.vdo.net

According to *VDO.net*, the *VDOLive* player is currently the most-downloaded streaming video player available on the Web. VDO's free player package includes both a browser plug-in and an external player and is available for Windows and Macintosh platforms. Encoding tools and server software are available for several different server platforms, including Windows NT and Sun Solaris. VDOLive can be used to stream high-quality content from server to client over a wide range of different bandwidths. It can also be used to create video-only or audio-only streams in addition to streams that include both.

VivoActive (.viv)
http://www.vivo.com

Vivo Software's *VivoActive* player package comes in two versions: a freeware "light" version and a commercial version with a full set of features. Both include a browser plug-in and an external player program, available for Windows and Macintosh.

VivoActive's strength is in its three suites of development tools, including one conveniently designed and priced for beginners, which range in capability from creating streamable content from AVI or QuickTime files to broadcasting live and creating interactive presentations. All three sets of tools are server independent, meaning that VivoActive content can be streamed from any standard HTTP Web server, in addition to specialized media servers running *Microsoft NetShow*, RealNetworks Real Media, or *Netscape LiveAudio* software.

RealNetworks—RealAudio and RealVideo (.ram, .rm)
http://www.real.com

It would not be unreasonable to classify *RealAudio* and *RealVideo* as the standards for streaming audio and video. Like so many other standards, however, Real's position as the leader is presently based primarily on the fact that it among the first to embrace the development of streaming-media technology; it remains to be seen whether Real will be able to hold its position in the face of its many new challengers.

Like most of its competitors, RealNetworks offer clientside player software in two packages: a scaled-down free version and a more fully featured commercial version, both of which are available for Windows, Macintosh, and UNIX operating systems. One of the most attractive qualities of Real's player is the sheer number of built-in features; even the free version of *RealPlayer* comes equipped with a number of webcast radio and television channels, all of which can be easily reconfigured to suit individual tastes.

From a developer's point of view, Real offers a very impressive collection of tools for creating and publishing streaming media content. Offerings include *RealSlideShow,* which allows for the creation of simple streaming presentations complete with an optional audio track; *RealProducer,* a full-featured authoring kit; and multiple server solutions for delivering high-quality streamed content to clients, including pay-per-view and interactive capability. Both the development tools and the server packages are available for several different software platforms, and forms, and nearly all of them have "trial" or "light" versions that can be down-loaded and used free of charge.

RealMedia's true strength, of course, lies in the fact that it is probably the most common streaming-media file format currently in use.

QuickTime 4 (.qt, .mov)
http://www.apple.com/quicktime

Among the most promising new challengers to RealNetworks is version 4 of Apple Computer's popular *QuickTime* software, first introduced in early 1999. In addition to being able to open and play all of the many video formats supported by earlier versions of the software, QuickTime 4 can be used to view high-quality streaming media from servers running Apple's *Mac OS X Server* with QuickTime Streaming Server software.

QuickTime Player software for Windows and Macintosh systems can be down-loaded from Apple in the standard two versions: a free Basic version, and a Pro version with a number of additional authoring tools. Possibly because QuickTime is not solely a streaming format, there is little or no practical difference between the Basic and Pro versions of the QuickTime player as they relate to streaming. Like most player packages, QuickTime includes both an external player program and a plug-in for your Web browser.

The QuickTime Streaming Server software itself has a number of nice things going for it: It's provided free as a part of Mac OS X Server and, unlike some other streaming-media solutions, has no charge-per-stream. Unfortunately, it currently runs only in conjunction with Apple's own Mac OS X Server software, which in turn runs only on Apple's Power Macintosh G3 machines. However, since Apple recently chose to make the Streaming Server software's source code partially available to the public, any interested developers may be able to port it to other operating systems with a minimum of difficulty.

TrueSpeech (.tsp)
http://www.dspg.com/player/main.htm

There are countless shareware and freeware programs that are capable of provid-ing a thrifty Web designer with low-end streaming-media capability, but the *DSP Group*'s *TrueSpeech* seems to be among the most popular. There's a reason for this: The TrueSpeech player, browser plug-in, and encoder, available for both Win-dows and Macintosh, can all be downloaded absolutely free from the TrueSpeech Web site. Even better, no special server software is needed to stream the files;

using TrueSpeech, adding streaming media to your Web site is no more difficult than adding a JPEG.

As you might expect, TrueSpeech is somewhat limited in terms of what types of files it can create, and its general performance and sound quality are well below what you'd get from something like RealPlayer or QuickTime. For the Web designer on a budget who just wants to add a few low-quality sound samples to a site, however, something like TrueSpeech is ideal.

OTHER STREAMING MULTIMEDIA TYPES

CineWeb (http://www.digigami.com/cineweb) is a third-party player capable of processing a number of other common file formats, including QuickTime, AVI, MPEG and *Autodesk Animator (FLIC)*. Note that AVI, MPEG, and FLIC are not normally streaming formats; CineWeb achieves an effect similar to "true" streaming by storing sequential data in a special cache as it downloads and processing the data directly from the cache. If the user's network connection is fast enough, the content will appear to play in real time while the actual file is downloaded in the background by the browser.

Several other players use a similar method to "stream" other normally non-streamable formats, such as *Nullsoft*'s popular *Shoutcast* MP3 streaming software (http://www.shoutcast.com), and *LiveUpdate's Crescendo* (http://www.liveupdate.com/crescendo.html), a similar program for streaming MP3 and MIDI files.

As of this writing, all three of these programs are available only for Windows 95, Windows 98, and Windows NT 4.0 platforms. However, there are a number of similar MP3 streaming applications designed for other operating systems such as Unix and Macintosh. Check your favorite shareware sites.

CREATING AND USING STREAMING MULTIMEDIA

For the most part, the creation of streaming video content is no more complicated than the creation of any other kind of digitized video. On the most basic level, you'll need the same three things: a video source, such as a camcorder or VCR; a means of getting the video into your computer, such as an expansion card with the appropriate video-in ports; and a program capable of converting digitized video data into your streaming-multimedia file format of choice. Many programs now offer the ability to create video based on screen movement or export presentations to a video format.

However, because of the nature of streaming, there are several new considerations involved in the proper implementation of streaming multimedia content. Regardless of which file format you choose, you can always expect some significant loss of both audio and video quality. Keeping this in mind, there are a few things you can do to optimize your content for streaming.

1. Since your video is likely to stream much more smoothly if you can keep extraneous movement to a minimum, it is recommended that you use close-ups instead of wide-angle shots whenever possible. In many cases, close-ups are more practical anyway, due to the limitations imposed by most players' small display windows.

2. The higher the quality of the source, the higher the quality of the digitized video. If your video was originally shot with a high-end digital video camera, or even an older VHS camcorder using high-grain videotapes, your content will be of higher quality after it has been digitized and encoded. On the other hand, if your video is blurry and grainy before you even get it into the computer, it may be unrecognizable after it's been compressed and converted to streaming-media format.

3. Choppy or indistinct video is usually much less of a distraction than choppy or indistinct sound. Since high-quality streaming audio also requires considerably less bandwidth than high-quality streaming video, it's probably a good idea to make a habit of encoding your audio data at a compression rate considerably lower than the one you use to encode video data.

**LAB
7.4**

After you have the video and/or audio digitized and encoded to your satisfaction, all that remains is the simple matter of building it into your Web site. The specifics of this step have a tendency to vary from format to format. Some can be attached to a page with the almighty <EMBED> tag just like any other sound or video file, and others require special server or software configurations in order to stream properly. For specific details, you'll probably need to refer to the documentation provided with your software.

LAB 7.4 EXERCISES

7.4.1 UNDERSTAND STREAMING MULTIMEDIA

a) Discuss the differences of streaming media technology as compared to simply embedding audio and/or video files in a Web page.

_____

_____

b) Visit the Web site www.kfox.com and listen to the station using its "Listen Live" link. Discuss some of the problems that might occur when listening to the station like this.

_____

_____

7.4.2 CREATE WEB PAGES USING STREAMING MULTIMEDIA

a) Create an <EMBED> tag for a streaming video object with the source being the file you are using (e.g., "welcome.ram").

_____

_____

b) Discuss why using a system that simulates streaming video (i.e., CineWeb) can be more effective than true streaming video.

_____

_____

LAB 7.4 EXERCISE ANSWERS

7.4.1 ANSWERS

a) Discuss the differences of streaming media technology as compared to simply embedding audio and/or video files in a Web page.

Answer: Embedded multimedia files must be completely downloaded before an appropriate helper application or plug-in can process and deliver their content. Therefore, large multimedia files can lead to a long delay for the user during downloading. Processing and delivery of streaming media content begins as soon as the downloading process begins.

This distinction allows streaming media players to support "live" content as well as content stored in static files.

Two important offshoots of this are the different bandwidth required and the expectations of the user. When accessing pages with embedded media, the user knows there will be a wait time. However, the user does not expect to wait with streaming media.

With a greater bandwidth requirement, streaming media can appear choppy because the player may be forced to chop out parts of the stream in order to keep up. That is, information is coming in too fast for the player to process or store.

b) Visit the Web site www.kfox.com and listen to the station using its "Listen Live" link. Discuss some of the problems that might occur when listening to the station like this.

Answer: Your enjoyment of the radio station (independent of your taste in music) will depend on your bandwidth. Listening to the station like this across an ISDN line is fine, but only if that's the only information going across the line. That is, I cannot listen while surfing the net. In order to keep real time, the line needs to be used exclusively by the streaming audio.

7.4.2 ANSWERS

a) Create an <EMBED> tag for a streaming video object with the source being the file you are using (e.g., "welcome.ram").

Answer: Here is one possible solution

```
<embed src="welcome.ram" height=500 width=500>.
```

As you can see, there is basically nothing different compared to other audio and video formats. Note also that like other video formats you really ought to specify a height and a width, otherwise you may end up not seeing anything.

As mentioned before, the difference here is how the file is played for the user. With other audio and video formats, the entire file is downloaded before the user can view or listen. With streaming media, the server sends a series of user database protocol (UDP) packets back to the client. If a UDP packet somehow becomes corrupt or lost during the transmission, it will not seriously disrupt the transmission/broadcast. When the packets arrive at the client, they are reassembled and sent to a buffer. Once the buffer fills with the necessary packets to begin playback, the file begins to play even before all packets have been completely received from the server. If the buffer exhausts, playback will temporarily pause until the buffer fills again and can continue.

b) Discuss why using a system that "simulates" streaming video (i.e., CineWeb) can be more effective than true streaming video.

Answer: Such products allow you to use a common, standard format like QuickTime, AVI, and MPEG. This might allow your to have one link to play the streaming version and another to play the download version, without the need to manage separate formats.

LAB 7.4 SELF-REVIEW QUESTIONS

In order to test your progress, you should be able to answer the following questions.

1) Streaming media can be embedded like other media types without special HTML tags.

   a) _____ True
   b) _____ False

2) RealAudio and RealVideo are the current standards.

   a) _____ True
   b) _____ False

3) The shortcoming of MP3 as a streaming media is that it is currently only supported on Windows platforms.

   a) _____ True
   b) _____ False

4) Which of the following is not one of the streaming media file formats mentioned in this lab?

   a) _____ VDO
   b) _____ Real (RealAudio and RealVideo)
   c) _____ LiveVideo
   d) _____ QuickTime

5) Which is not one of the current uses of streaming media technology?

   a) _____ "Live" radio broadcasting
   b) _____ "Live" talks, presentations, concerts, etc., "Webcasting"
   c) _____ High-speed data transmissions
   d) _____ Playback of multimedia content from streaming file servers

Quiz answers appear in the Appendix, Section 7.4.

**LAB
7.4**

LAB 7.5

VIRTUAL REALITY

LAB OBJECTIVES

After this lab, you will be able to

✔ Understand the Virtual Reality Modeling Language
✔ Understand the Issues Associated with Using Virtual Reality in Your Web Pages

---

WHAT IS VIRTUAL REALITY?

The idea behind virtual reality is a concept straight out of contemporary science fiction. It's a simple but fascinating concept—theoretically, using just the right combination of hardware, software, and interface devices, it might be possible to create a wholly immersive artificial world that would seem as real to the user as the world around him or her.

At present, that concept has yet to fully materialize. The closest we've gotten to "traditional" virtual reality has been a few unwieldy collections of gloves and helmets that allow their wearers to see, touch, and otherwise interact with three-dimensional objects in a computer-generated environment. The hardware is clunky, the implementation far from perfect, and the artificially generated worlds are exceedingly unlikely to be mistaken for anything outside the helmet. But it's a start.

Since very few Web browsers currently ship with built-in support for helmets and gloves, it shouldn't be too surprising to learn that VR as it relates to the Web typically refers to something else entirely. In general, when we talk about virtual reality in a Web context, we're talking about one of two technologies: Apple Computer's *QuickTime VR,* or *VRML (Virtual Reality Modeling Language).*

Because both of these types of VR tend toward high bandwidth requirements, virtual reality has yet to catch on as a very common form of Web-based multimedia. As high-speed connections become more and more common, however, it seems reasonable to expect that these two standards, or whatever succeeds them, may become increasingly important to cutting-edge Web designers in the future.

VIRTUAL REALITY FILE FORMATS

VRML and QuickTime VR are by far the most common virtual reality technologies in widespread use. By definition, they probably occupy the positions of de facto standards for VR implementation on the Web.

Another way of putting this, of course, would be to concede that they're really the only Web-based VR technologies that see any sort of widespread use at all. At present, due to the relative rarity of *any* kind of virtual reality on the Web, it's probably a little too early to make any attempt to classify one or the other as a "standard."

However, as virtual reality increases in popularity, we can certainly expect other companies to develop their own VR technologies and file formats to compete with VRML and QuickTime VR, predictably igniting yet another battle over standards. Until then, there is a relatively small pool to choose from.

QuickTime VR (.qt, .mov)
http://www.apple.com/quicktime/qtvr

Another component of Apple Computer's QuickTime package (and fully compatible with all other QuickTime software, including players and browser plug-ins), *QuickTime VR* is a powerful technology that can be used to create virtual three-dimensional objects and interactive 360-degree panoramas.

Virtual panoramas are typically created by "stitching" a group of adjacent photographs into a continuous 360-degree panorama, then "wrapping" them into a QuickTime VR document that, when opened with the QuickTime player or plug-in, allows a user to pan around it with a set of simple controls. The panoramas are simple to create; the process typically involves little more than snapping photos sequentially as you rotate a full 360 degrees and using a capable graphics program to combine them into a single continuous horizon shot. Based on photographs taken from a number of different angles, the same program can also be used to create 3D models of objects, which can then be freely rotated and manipulated within their own virtual space.

Note that virtual panoramas and 3D objects can just as easily be created from completely computer-generated images as from actual photographs, as long as all of the necessary source files are present.

VRML (.wrl)
http://www.web3d.org/vrml

VRML, like QuickTime VR, is a technology for creating computer-generated models of 3D-rendered objects in a virtual space, where they can be rotated, panned, zoomed in or out, and otherwise manipulated as a user sees fit.

However, VRML does not create its virtual objects from already existing photographs or images. In fact, VRML source files do not actually contain any image data at all; instead, they contain lines of code written in the Virtual Reality Modeling Language, which are read, translated, and rendered on-the-fly to create an image that incorporates shadow, color, perspective, and all of the other usual considerations of 3D modeling.

There are several benefits to using VRML, not the least of which is the fact that VRML-rendered objects are "true" virtual objects. QuickTime VR objects are subject to the limitations of the original perspective-based images that were used to create them; if a virtual object was created without a source file showing it from a particular viewpoint, the object cannot be seen from that viewpoint in its VR incarnation. VRML objects, on the other hand, can be freely rotated and examined from literally any angle.

Unfortunately, all of these benefits tend to be outweighed by a simple unfortunate fact: At the moment, only the very simplest of VRML 3D models can actually be rendered in real time by a standard desktop computer. VRML is currently used mostly for chemical and medical graphics modeling; any objects requiring more detail simply can't be rendered fast enough to create the illusion of a freely moving, freely rotating three-dimensional object.

VRML technology, including most of the browser plug-ins needed to view VRML objects and the design programs needed to create them, is still very much in development. At the moment, VRML is probably not a reliable solution for Web designers who want to make their 3D content available to the general public. In the near future, however, it may become a very important consideration indeed.

LivePicture
http://www.livepicture.com

A relatively new addition to the small pool of web-based VR technologies, LivePicture's *RealSpace* appears at first glance to be nearly identical to QuickTime VR. Unlike QuickTime, however, RealSpace requires no plug-ins or external helper applications in order to work; objects and panoramas created with RealSpace technology can be automatically viewed with any Java-capable Web browser.

Zoom, another product of LivePicture, can be used to create "zoomable" images that allow users to click on parts of a static image to magnify them. Like Real-Space, Zoom requires no special plug-ins or helper applications.

The downside of RealSpace's Java-based rendering technique is that it tends to require more raw processing power than QuickTime VR, which can result in somewhat poor performance on lower-end computers. To offset this problem, LivePicture also makes a browser plug-in and a stand-alone helper application, allowing users to view 3D content by more traditional means if they prefer. As a bonus, the *LivePicture Viewer* plug-in can also be used to view and navigate objects and environments created with VRML.

LAB 7.5 EXERCISES

7.5.1 UNDERSTAND THE VIRTUAL REALITY MODELING LANGUAGE

It is a common mistake to think that VRML means "Virtual Reality Markup Language" rather than "Virtual Reality Modeling Language."

   a) Explain why "modeling language" is more appropriate than "markup language."

   _____

   _____

7.5.2 UNDERSTAND THE ISSUES ASSOCIATED WITH USING VIRTUAL REALITY IN YOUR WEB PAGES

   a) What do you think an <EMBED> tag to display the QuickTime VR movie welcome.mov would look like?

   _____

   _____

Virtual reality presents unique challenges for HCI (Human-Computer Interface). Navigating in "virtual worlds" is a different experience from the usual Web page "point and click" paradigm.

b) What input/output devices would be useful in a virtual reality environment?

_____

_____

Virtual reality has gone beyond the "bleeding edge" stage and has become an integral part of many Web sites. Visit the site located at the following URLs and investigate how they use virtual reality. Consider what you learned in previous chapters.

http://www.buick.com

http://www.pbs.org/wgbh/nova/pyramid/

c) How well do these sites meet the requirements for an effective user interface?

_____

_____

d) Discuss in what areas virtual reality could be used as a user interface.

_____

_____

LAB 7.5 EXERCISE ANSWERS

7.5.1 ANSWER

a) Explain why "modeling language" is more appropriate than "markup language."

Answer:"Markup languages" such as HTML and XML are used to define the presentation and/or structure of content (usually text and images) as interpreted by a Web browser. In a virtual reality environment a "modeling language" is used to define and construct objects, scenes, etc. that exist in that environment. Such objects must be defined in such a way that a user can "realistically" interact with them.

7.5.2 ANSWERS

a) What do you think an <EMBED> tag to display the QuickTime VR movie welcome.mov would look like?

Answer: While a complete tutorial on VRML is far beyond the scope of this book, the technical aspects of adding any media type to your Web site should be old news to you by now, assuming that you've already been through the labs on sound and video and gained the healthy appreciation for the <EMBED> tag that it deserves. Such a tag might look like this:

```
<embed src="welcome.mov" WIDTH="320" HEIGHT="240">
```

b) What input/output devices would be useful in a VRML environment?

Answer: Examples of such devices include:

- *Advanced pointing devices*
- *Virtual reality helmets or glasses capable of isolating a user in the virtual environment*
- *The "virtual reality glove" capable of providing realistic tactile response*

c) How well do these sites meet the requirements for an effective user interface?

Answer: Even on a slow connection, both sites provide exactly what they set out to. That is, they provide a virtual tour of the respective subject. The Nova site allows us to visit some places we may never get to see in person, and the Buick site allows us to see each of the cars without having to leave our home, office, or classroom. One shortcoming of the Nova site's VR display of the Sphinx is the changing shadow. Additionally, the people in the images give away the fact that it is a series of still photographs. On the other hand, the Buick display does not suffer from these same problems.

d) Discuss in what areas virtual reality could be used as a user interface.

Answer: Most types of Web sites that have "traditional" interfaces could add a virtual reality interface. Even something like a retail store might benefit from a VR interface. However, the time the user has to wait for the objects to load might be self-defeating. The first time it's cool, but after that, the waiting becomes a burden.

More interesting and relevant are the practical aspects of adding virtual reality to a Web site—specifically, why use it at all? Currently, VR is used in a Web-based context for only a very few express purposes, but as the technology matures, we can expect to see it in many new forms. A few likely possibilities:

1. ***Virtual tours.** A number of enterprising vacation resorts, architectural firms, and rental agencies have found VR technology to be an excellent medium for providing*

potential tourists and clients with an advance look at what they're paying for—
sometimes before it even exists. Other companies have painstakingly designed virtual interactive mock-ups of popular tourist attractions such as the pyramids of
Egypt or the Las Vegas Strip, all in the name of providing potential tourists with a
taste, however small, of what the actual experience might be like.

2. **Entertainment.** VR technology is ideal for creating simple 3D games, most of
which operate along the same basic principles as a virtual tours, with an added
level of interactivity. As the technology matures, it's not unreasonable to expect
that such games might increase in complexity to something more closely approxi-
mating some of the more popular 3D-based games on the market today.

3. **Product demonstration.** As immensely convenient and popular as shopping
online has already proven to be, it has yet to find an adequate substitute for the
experience looking at or otherwise interacting with the various products available
for purchase. To this end, a few e-commerce Web sites have announced plans to
create 3D models of their products, sometimes including an interactive showcase
of features. On Apple's Web site, for instance, potential customers looking for information on a new Power Macintosh computer can use a QuickTime VR movie
to view the machine from all sides and even simulate opening its case.

4. **Interactive news.** Operating along the same lines as the "virtual tour" concept,
some news sites have investigated the possibilities of using VR technology to create interactive virtual models based on certain current events in the news.

Media futurists have speculated that as the technology behind virtual reality improves,
it is likely to become a major influence over the way we will interact with the Internet in
the future. It may currently be off to a somewhat slow start, but Web-based VR should
become an increasingly relevant concern over the next few years, and any discerning
Web designer would do well to keep an eye on it.

LAB 7.5 SELF-REVIEW QUESTIONS

In order to test your progress, you should be able to answer the following questions.

1) A limitation of the QuickTime VR is that is series of images and therefore missing
perspectives cannot be created dynamically.

a) _____ True
b) _____ False

2) VRML is a markup language like HTML because it defines how the images are
displayed.

a) _____ True
b) _____ False

3) An advantage of VMRL is that it is available on most browsers and no plug-in is necessary.

    a) _____ True
    b) _____ False

4) Which of the following is not one of the Virtual Reality formats we discussed?

    a) _____ Quicktime
    b) _____ RealPicture
    c) _____ VRML
    d) _____ LivePicture

5) Which of the following is not a characteristic of VMRL?

    a) _____ Objects are subject to the limitations of the original perspective-based images.
    b) _____ Can be freely rotated and examined from literally any angle.
    c) _____ Can actually be rendered in real time by a standard desktop computer.
    d) _____ VRML renders the image "on-the-fly" to create an image that incorporates shadow, color, and perspective.

Quiz answers appear in the Appendix, Section 7.5.

LAB
7.5

C H A P T E R 7

TEST YOUR THINKING

1) Visit the home page for the World Wide Web Consortium (web3.w3.org) and investigate what other options are possible for the tags we discussed in this lab (e.g., <OBJECT>, <EMBED>). Consider how you might use these.

2) Visit the site www.wavecentral.com and download several different clips in different formats to place them on Web pages using both the <EMBED> and the <OBJECT> tags. Try different options to the two tags and pay attention to how the browser reacts or displays the player controls.

3) Visit the site www.ultimatemovieclips.com and download several different clips in different format to place them on web pages using both the <EMBED> and the <OBJECT> tags. Try different options to the two tags and pay attention to how the browser reacts or displays the player controls.

4) Do a search on Yahoo or some other search engine looking for sites that provide Virtual Reality. Concentrate on sites that use VR for practical purposes and not just to demonstrate VR. Evaluate the sites in terms of the issues discussed in previous labs.

CHAPTER 8

MULTIMEDIA PERIPHERALS AND DEVICES

Whoever controls the media—the images—controls the culture.

—Allen Ginsburg

Creating quality multimedia is rarely a simple procedure. This isn't to say that it's *always* going to be particularly difficult either, but the sheer number of different types of multimedia and the even greater number of ways to go about creating it can be immensely confusing if you've never done it before.

The first and arguably most important step of creating *any* sort of multimedia content involves getting your source material to a place where you can tinker with it. In most cases, this source material is an image or a sound or a video clip that originates somewhere outside the computer, which means that you'll have to find a way to move that data from wherever it currently resides—a videotape, a CD, or a photo album—to the hard drive in your computer. In order to do this, you'll need hardware and software capable of taking outside input and storing it in a data file.

In this chapter, we'll be looking at some of the most common and effective means of importing various types of media into your computer and preparing them for presentation on the Web.

L A B   8 . 1

MULTIMEDIA PRODUCTION HARDWARE

LAB OBJECTIVES

After this lab, you will be able to:

✔ Understand Hardware Support for Images
✔ Understand Hardware Support for Video
✔ Understand Hardware Support for Audio

Nearly all of the jacks and ports on the back of a desktop computer can be used to feed some sort of multimedia into or out of the computer. After all, the sole function of a port is to transmit data from the computer to an outside source, or vice versa—on the most basic level, there is little difference between the information that makes up a graphic image and the instructions that are passed back and forth between the computer and keyboard every time you press a key.

The types of hardware available are many and varied and tend to depend heavily on the port they will be using to communicate with the computer. Nevertheless, it's not unreasonable to expect that some sort of peripheral exists to digitize almost any sort of external media that you might have in mind—scanners, cameras, and even touch-sensitive tablets that allow an artist to draw pictures that appear directly on a computer screen.

Because it's often the hardware you choose to use that can make the most difference in the quality of your finished product, your decisions regarding what to use are extremely important. Not surprisingly, they'll depend primarily on exactly what kind of media you intend to be working with.

IMAGES

Because images are by far the most popular form of multimedia on the Internet, it shouldn't be tremendously surprising to learn that there are probably more ways to get images into your computer than any other type of media. The use of scanners and digital cameras are certainly two of the most common, however, and they should easily serve any and all of your imaging needs.

Scanners may very well be the single most common multimedia peripheral in widespread use, unless you're counting printers as multimedia peripherals. It isn't very difficult to understand why. Using a cheap desktop scanner, a user can put nearly anything that he or she has on paper into a file on his or her computer's hard drive with a minimum of difficulty.

There are several different types of scanners, ranging from the familiar flatbed variety to specialized models that can pull images from photographic negatives or read the text from a printed page and store it in a standard text file. For the most part, however, all scanners work pretty much the same, which helps to explain their popularity.

Digital cameras are a slightly more efficient means of getting images into a computer. Digital cameras work almost exactly like normal cameras, the primary difference being that a digital camera stores photos in memory or on a piece of removable media instead of on film. Instead of shooting a roll of film, having it developed, and then using a scanner to import the photos you want to use, you can shoot as few or as many pictures as you need before bringing the camera back to your desk and copying the stored images to your workstation through a special cable—or by ejecting the disk from the camera and popping it into the computer's floppy drive.

One drawback of using a digital camera is that the images don't actually exist on paper anywhere, meaning that there's no way to get them back if they're accidentally lost or deleted. In addition, digital cameras are more or less limited to creating photographs; if you want to import a drawing or a page of text, you're out of luck unless a photograph of the document will suffice. For designers who take a lot of photos with the sole purpose of publishing them online, however, digital cameras can provide superior results much more quickly than any scanner.

AUDIO

Audio is probably one of the simplest forms of multimedia—at least as far as initially getting it into the computer is concerned. Except in a very few cases, there's only one way to get sound into a computer: through the sound-in or microphone jack. A few scattered computers equipped with special audio/video capability may have additional sound input jacks; if yours is one of these, refer to the documentation provided with your computer. For everyone else, the rules are simple: Locate the audio-in jack and plug a piece of audio equipment into it.

This is not to imply that all sound-input hardware is equal, because it isn't. If you intend to use your computer to produce high-quality sound samples, you'll probably want to make sure that it is capable of recording 16-bit stereo sound. Although you can expect the quality of the samples to decrease significantly after you've compressed them to a point where they're small enough to deliver over the Web, they'll still sound much better if they were originally recorded in a high-quality format.

The sound hardware you choose will also affect what sorts of audio devices you can use to capture sound. If your computer has a microphone jack and no RCA composite audio input, your audio sources will be limited to devices with compatible sound-out jacks. In most cases, however, this won't be a problem, as there aren't a lot of audio appliances that don't come standard with headphone jacks.

The nature of the sound you're recording can be an important consideration, too. Obviously, if the sound is of poor quality on your source material, it will be of similarly poor quality after it's been imported into your computer. However, there are a number of third-party sound editing applications that include tools for clearing up "tape hiss" and other common types of interference. More on this later.

VIDEO

Video processing is one of the most demanding tasks that a personal computer can be called upon to perform. This shouldn't come as a surprise—after all, the machine is being asked to create dozens of color images every second, process them, encode them, and store them sequentially in a single file. Full-screen video capture performed at high frame rates and high resolutions can bring even the most powerful computer to its knees in a matter of minutes—if it doesn't run out of disk space first.

Fortunately, video for the Web rarely takes the form of full-screen high-resolution productions. Much more often, a Web-based video production is small, highly compressed, and of low enough picture quality that the occasional dropped frame is unlikely to be noticed. From a visitor's point of view, these types of concessions are generally preferable to the exponential increase in download time that a higher-quality clip would likely require.

Video input/output (I/O) cards, available for any machine with the appropriate expansion slots, are probably the best way to add video-input capability to a machine that didn't have it to begin with. They're comparatively inexpensive, simple to install, available for practically any computer decked out with the appropriate expansion slots, and more than sufficient for producing Web-quality video presentations. Most video I/O cards include RCA composite video and audio-in ports; in recent years, many cards have also begun supporting a standard called *S-video,* which can deliver sharper and higher-quality video if used in conjunction with S-video-capable equipment.

Other video capture solutions include external devices that can capture and transmit video (slowly) through the various types of serial ports that are now standard on nearly all desktop computers. For the most part, these types of devices are abysmally slow, unsuited to any purpose that requires the capture of more than one or two frames per second. Note that this is a limitation imposed by the nature of the serial bus and not by the speed of the computer itself. Most serial buses simply transmit data far too slowly to be a viable solution for any operation with high-bandwidth requirements.

The latest entrant to the alphabet soup of bus types is the *Accelerated Graphics Port (AGP).* As its name implies, AGP is intended as a bus for graphics cards. Although PCI is more than sufficient for most users' needs, there are some shortcomings with high-end applications. The need for something like AGP arises from problems when creating 3D graphics, which use a "texture map" to get the necessary effects. The problem lies in the fact that most video cards deal with at most 8 MB, but texture maps are reaching 10 or even 20 MB (probably more by the time this book is published.) Added to this memory limitation is the bandwidth required to transfer that amount of data quickly. To get real-time 3D graphics, you need far better throughput than loading a document into WordPerfect. Added to this fact is that there is just a single PCI bus, which makes it even more of a bottleneck. In essence, the AGP is a high-speed path between system memory and the video controller. It is no longer necessary to store things like the texture maps in the system memory rather than in the limited space of the video card. Because data transfer across the board can be up to four times that on the PCI bus, AGP provides even better performance.

In addition, there are several new technologies that aim to alleviate some of these shortcomings. A relatively new type of serial bus called *IEEE-1394,* developed by Apple Computer and marketed under the brand name "FireWire," is capable of transmitting data at speeds up to 400 megabits per second—considerably faster than many dedicated video I/O cards. Moreover, the IEEE-1394 standard is multipurpose, meaning that a single bus can be used both to capture video and to connect other peripherals, such as external hard drives. (Note, though, that attaching additional devices to the 1394 bus will reduce the bandwidth available for video capture.)

As if all this weren't enough, IEEE-1394 is an all-digital protocol. The picture quality of composite video has a tendency to degrade quickly with multiple recordings, as anyone who has ever dubbed a videotape can attest. Digital video, on the other hand, can be imported, edited, resequenced, and output to a final destination, all with *no loss of quality whatsoever.* A number of consumer-electronics manufacturers such as Sony have already begun shipping digital camcorders and other high-end video equipment with built-in IEEE-1394 ports; it is likely that others will follow.

Other modern serial-bus technologies, such as Intel's *USB* standard, have also been embraced by video peripheral manufacturers. At present, USB is only marginally faster than older serial buses, but the recently announced USB 2.0 has been rumored to rival FireWire in terms of raw transmission speed. Only time will tell.

LAB 8.1 EXERCISES

8.1.1 UNDERSTAND HARDWARE SUPPORT FOR IMAGES

a) Discuss the strengths and weaknesses of the various methods of getting images into your computer and onto the hard disk.

_____

_____

8.1.2 UNDERSTAND HARDWARE SUPPORT FOR VIDEO

Visit the IEEE site as well as the Apple page on the IEEE-1394 standard at the following URLs:

http://standards.ieee.org

http://developer.apple.com/hardware/FireWire/More_about_Firewire.html

a) What can you find out new about IEEE-1394? What is IEEE-1394? What advantages does it hold over composite video?

_____

_____

b) With 24-bit color, there are 8 bits per each of the red, green and blue channels. Discuss the various color combinations possible.

_____

_____

c) With 24-bit color on a 1024x768 screen, how many bytes are needed to display a full screen image? With a 5"x7" photograph also using 24-bit color and a resolution of 75 dpi, how many bytes are needed? What about the same photo at 2400 dpi? An 8.5"x11" photo?

_____

_____

8.1.3 UNDERSTAND HARDWARE SUPPORT FOR AUDIO

a) What precautions can you take to ensure that you're getting the highest-quality audio clip possible?

_____

_____

LAB 8.1 EXERCISE ANSWERS

8.1.1 ANSWER

a) Discuss the strengths and weaknesses of the various methods of getting images into your computer and onto the hard disk.

Answer: Scanners have the advantage of a wide range of features and therefore prices. In addition, many software products allow you to scan the image directly into the application without having to save it on the disk. This saves a great deal of time as well as prevents problems caused by converting from one format to another. Even without this ability, the software provided with the scanner typically supports multiple formats. Another key advantage is when you have existing images that you want to scan. A scanner is the only way to get them into the machine efficiently (if at all).

In addition to the range of prices and features, digital cameras have the advantage of being portable, allowing you to capture images as they happen. In other words, digital cameras allow you to capture "non-scannable" content. The biggest disadvantage is the storage limitation you have. Most vendors provide storage packs that can hold a large number of images (or course, depending on the resolution). Some vendors have addressed this problem by using standard 3.5" disks as their storage media, meaning you don't have to spend a fortune on their storage packs.

8.1.2 ANSWERS

a) What can you find out new about IEEE-1394? What is IEEE-1394? What advantages does it hold over composite video?

Answer: IEEE-1394 is a 400 megabit per second serial bus developed by Apple Computer. Its advantages over composite video include speed as well as the fact that it is an all-digital protocol thereby leading to higher video quality.

b) With 24-bit color, there are 8 bits per each of the red, green, and blue channels. Discuss the various color combinations possible.

Answer: 24-bit color means that you can get a total of 256 shades for each of the three colors for a total of approximately 16.7 million colors. It is referred to as True Color or photo-realistic color. It's worth noting that 16.7 million colors is more than the human eye can see. The next level up is 36-bit color, which is composed of three 12-bit color channels. This provides over 68 billion colors.

Coupled with this is the term dynamic range, which is the ability of the scanner to recognize a range of tonal values. Take an image of a tree casting a shadow onto a building with different colors. Each surface can either be fully illuminated, in its own shadow, in the shadow of something plus illuminated by reflected light, and so forth. The "real" color of the surface remains constant, but in the image there are fine gradation or tones in the color. The more bits the scanner uses for color, the greater the dynamic range. Therefore, a 36-bit scanner has a higher dynamic range than a 24-bit scanner.

Because it is often necessary to use higher resolutions and a greater number of colors, you need to be careful that you have both enough hard disk space and RAM. One of the common misconceptions is that doubling the resolution doubles the size of the image. Just remember that you are actually doubling it in two directions. Therefore, doubling the resolution gives you an image that is four times as large. As you increase the resolution and number of possible colors, the size of the image can grow to incredible proportions.

c) With 24-bit color on a 1024 x 768 screen, how many bytes are needed to display a full screen image? With a 5"x7" photograph also using 24-bit color and a resolution of 75 dpi, how many bytes are needed? What about the same photo at 2400 dpi? An 8.5"x11" photo?

Answer: A 5"x7" photograph that we want to scan using 24-bit color and a resolution of 75 dpi, which is useful for on-screen display, when stored on disk, would have a size of approximately 577 kilobytes. If you increased the resolution to 2400 dpi, the file would be about 590 megabytes. An 8.5"x11" photo at this resolution and color depth would be about 1.5 gigabytes.

8.1.3 ANSWER

a) What precautions can you take to ensure that you're getting the highest-quality audio clip possible?

Answer: Record at the highest possible bit-rate.

LAB 8.1 SELF-REVIEW QUESTIONS

In order to test your progress, you should be able to answer the following questions.

1) S-video provides better quality images than RCA composite video.

    a) _____ True
    b) _____ False

2) AGP stands for which of the following?

    a) _____ Accelerated Graphics Processing
    b) _____ Advanced Graphics Processing
    c) _____ Accelerated Graphics Port
    d) _____ Advanced Graphics Port

3) IEEE-1394 can transmit data at speeds up to which of the following?

    a) _____ 100 Mbit per second
    b) _____ 200 Mbit per second
    c) _____ 400 Mbit per second
    d) _____ 800 Mbit per second

Quiz answers appear in the Appendix, Section 8.1.

LAB 8.2

MULTIMEDIA PRODUCTION SOFTWARE

LAB OBJECTIVES

After this lab, you will be able to:

✔ Understand Software Requirements for Images
✔ Understand Software Requirements for Streaming Multimedia
✔ Sample Some Multimedia Production Software

Once you've captured your raw media and saved it to disk, you'll need some way to polish it up for your final presentation. In some cases, this isn't so much a separate step as it is a continuation of the importing process. Most scanning applications allow users to crop and perform other minor image modifications immediately after scanning, and some audio and video capturing programs provide similar tools for manipulating captured media before saving it. In other cases, you'll want to save the newly imported material in a scratch file somewhere on your hard disk and perform any modifications on a copy, in case you need to go back later and restore the original.

The exact pieces of software that you're likely to find yourself using will depend entirely upon your own individual needs. If all you need to do is convert some images to GIF or JPEG format, you're set; both GIF and JPEG are common enough that nearly every commercial or shareware graphics application on the market is capable of viewing and creating them. Other, more complex types of multimedia can only be created with specific software tools, usually provided by the company that owns the file format.

Since there are so many suitable programs available for performing these kinds of tasks, and since so few of these are available for all operating systems, we'll refrain from going into too much detail about any software titles in particular.

Instead, we'll take a brief look at what we can generally expect to accomplish with these sorts of tools.

IMAGES

When you get right down to the basics, a good imaging application contains all of the tools you need to put together a snappy Web site. After all, there are many, many sites on the Web today that consist of content produced entirely on a computer. Given the right program, the inclination, and plenty of time, a good designer could easily develop a full-fledged Web site with no additional hardware or software at all.

If you do intend to include media in your work that originated outside the computer, however, such a graphics program can also be invaluable for clearing up unwanted specks, scratches, or other imperfections; cropping out unwanted parts of an image; or even making sweeping changes to the image itself. Many of the most popular imaging programs on the market today include all of these tools and more. These types of programs are indispensable tools for any serious Web developer.

AUDIO

Audio is less likely to be particularly important to the average Web designer as some other forms of multimedia, but anyone with any interest in incorporating audio into a Web site would do well to investigate the capabilities of available sound-editing programs. Most popular operating systems already include built-in support for sound input, but you'll need a more powerful piece of software if you intend to do any serious sound mixing or special effects.

Most commercial audio software packages include tools you can use to create special effects such as reverberations and echoes, cropping your samples, screening out background noise or unwanted interference, blending clips seamlessly into one another, and saving the final result as any one of multiple sound formats—specifying any information on compression, if applicable.

VIDEO

In most cases, all of the software you'll need to do basic video capture is provided with your expansion card or peripheral video device. This software usually comes with a fairly limited set of features, sufficient to capture video and perform some minor editing, but not useful for much else. However, this is often all you'll need; because of the limitations imposed by window size and bandwidth, Web-based video presentations shouldn't be particularly complex or detailed to begin with.

If you find yourself in need of a more powerful solution, however, there are a number of full-featured video editing suites on the market that offer full support for a wide range of different video input types, in addition to advanced features such as media cleaning, special effects, and enhanced compression techniques.

STREAMING MEDIA

In general, the primary difference between streaming media and most other types of multimedia is a simple but crucial one: Streaming media formats function most effectively when streamed from their own specialized media server platforms. While it is possible to stream some types of streaming media from standard HTTP servers, such a configuration is ill-advised for servers likely to receive a lot of hits.

Therefore, there are usually two different pieces of software involved in creating and providing most types of streaming multimedia: a set of tools to convert video and audio files to the streaming format and a server platform for delivering the resulting streams to clients. Since it's in the software manufacturer's best interest to convince developers to use its standard instead of the competition's, portions of these packages can sometimes be downloaded from the manufacturer's Web site. In many cases, stripped-down versions of both the encoders and the servers are provided free of charge for evaluation purposes, or a complete version of one part of the software suite might be given away in order to promote sales of the other.

VIRTUAL REALITY

Because Web-based virtual reality can take so many different forms, there's no simple solution for putting VR presentations on the Web. QuickTime VR and VRML, described in Lab 7.5, are currently the most popular forms of VR media used on the Web today, but neither of these formats is as simple or straightforward as the common file types used in other kinds of multimedia.

QuickTime VR files can be created from a collection of still images with special authoring tools available from Apple and a number of other software manufacturers to whom Apple has licensed the format specifications. Since these tools work by stitching multiple still images together into a single three-dimensional object, however, they aren't of much use without the software and/or hardware necessary to digitize or create a collection of still images for use as source files.

VRML, on the other hand, requires no special hardware whatsoever, as everything relating to the appearance and behavior of a VRML-rendered object is specified as a part of its source code. If you're familiar with the VRML language, it doesn't require any special software either; like HTML, VRML objects and environments can be coded in any program capable of working with text, like the Windows NotePad or the UNIX Vi text editor. And as with HTML, there are a number of third-party VRML authoring tools available from a number of software vendors that effectively remove the need to learn a new language.

LAB 8.2 EXERCISES

8.2.1 UNDERSTAND SOFTWARE REQUIREMENTS FOR IMAGES

a) What are some of the minimum software capabilities required for preparing images for the Web?

_____

_____

8.2.2 UNDERSTAND SOFTWARE REQUIREMENTS FOR STREAMING MULTIMEDIA

a) How is the creation and delivery of streaming multimedia different from the creation of other kinds of multimedia from the software perspective?

_____

_____

8.2.3 SAMPLE SOME MULTIMEDIA PRODUCTION SOFTWARE

Visit the Tucows Web site at http://www.tucows.com. Conduct a search for "audio" and scan the results.

a) What are some of the shareware or freeware multimedia tools that support audio?

_____

_____

Conduct a search for "video" and scan the results.

b) What are some of the shareware or freeware multimedia tools that support video?

_____

_____

c) What are some of the shareware or freeware multimedia tools offer full-featured multimedia authoring capabilities?

_____

_____

LAB 8.2 EXERCISE ANSWERS

8.2.1 ANSWER

a) What are some of the minimum software capabilities required for preparing images for the Web?

Answer: Some guidelines are as follows:

1. *Graphic format conversion: For example, the ability to convert from TIFF format (common to most scanners) to Web-supported formats such as GIF and JPEG.*
2. *Support of color correction: Web browsers typically support a limited color palette.*
3. *Image cropping and sizing: Web-based images often need to be sized in order to fit within designated display areas; image "thumbnails" are often used to provide page efficiency.*

8.2.2 ANSWER

a) How is the creation and delivery of streaming multimedia different from the creation of other kinds of multimedia from the software perspective?

Answer: For nonstreaming multimedia, software is used to capture and process content for delivery to a browser within a Web page (typically via HTTP). Streaming multimedia systems also require the inclusion of server software to facilitate the delivery of multimedia content.

8.2.3 ANSWERS

a) What are some of the shareware or freeware multimedia tools that support audio editing?

Answer: Naturally, your answer may vary, but some of the tools available include:

- **Internet Audio Mix** *(http://www.acoustica.com): This easy-to-use utility enables you to mix, record, or overdub as many WAV and MP3 files as you want. You can also export tracks as RealAudio G2 files.*

- **Anvil Studio** *(http://www.anvilstudio.com): Anvil Studio is a free Windows program that enables you to edit and create MID and WAV files, add effects, add rhythm tracks, and even produce MID tracks from scratch.*

- **Awave Studio** *(http://www.fmjsoft.com): Awave Studio can be used as an audio file-format converter, an audio editor, an audio and MIDI player, and a wave table synthesizer/instrument editor and converter.*

- **n-Track Studio** *(http://fasoft.com): This utility is a multitrack recorder that enables recording, overdubbing, and mixing of WAV and MID files.*

b) What are some of the shareware or freeware multimedia tools that support video editing?

Answer: It is more difficult to find powerful shareware or freeware versions of video editing software, but there are a few basic programs that you can sample, including:

- **MainActor** *(http://www.mainconcept.com): This program enables you to edit and sequence multimedia videos and supports almost every video format available today.*

- **Cut Viewer** *(http://www.ergoprocesso.pt): Cut Viewer is a tool for video segmentation. It processes digital video in AVI format and can produce a set of images, a set of scenes, and even an HTML page.*

- **Ulead Video Studio** *(http://www.ulead.com): This is video editing and creation software that enables frame-by-frame editing, special effects, and even accompanying audio creation. This package supports many output formats.*

c) What are some of the shareware or freeware multimedia tools offer full-featured multimedia authoring capabilities?

Answer: Again, your answer may vary, but some of the tools available include:

- **HyperStudio** *(http://www.hyperstudio.com): This system offers the ability to bring together text, sound, graphics, and video, interact with the Internet, create and edit QuickTime and AVI movies. It is compatible with a large variety of file formats. Output can be PC-, Mac-, or Internet-based.*

- **Formula Graphics 97** *(http://www.formulagraphics.com): This is a surprisingly powerful free tool used to develop interactive multimedia presentations. It even has its own object-oriented multimedia language and features bitmap manipulation, database connectivity, 3D modeling, and Internet programming.*

- **iShell** *(http://www.tribeworks.com): This is a media authoring tool that lets you build Internet applications, CD-ROMs, networked information appliances, and includes programming functionality.*

LAB 8.2 SELF-REVIEW QUESTIONS

In order to test your progress, you should be able to answer the following questions.

1) Most types of multimedia, even complex multimedia, are common enough that nearly every commercial or shareware graphics application on the market is capable of viewing and creating them.

    a) _____ True
    b) _____ False

2) Most popular operating systems include built-in support for sound input, but you'll need a more powerful piece of software if you intend to do any serious sound mixing or special effects.

    a) _____ True
    b) _____ False

3) In general, the primary difference between streaming media and most other types of multimedia is that multimedia formats function most effectively when played from their own specialized media server platforms, whereas streaming media can stream from any standard HTTP server.

    a) _____ True
    b) _____ False

4) VRML requires no special hardware.

    a) _____ True
    b) _____ False

Quiz answers appear in the Appendix, Section 8.2.

C H A P T E R   8

TEST YOUR THINKING

Once you've examined all of your software and hardware needs and determined what peripherals and programs are best suited to the type of work you have in mind, you should be able to make informed decisions regarding the computer system(s) on which most of your multimedia content will be created. This is, of course, assuming that you intend to do your multimedia designs in-house and won't be outsourcing any projects to outside design agencies. If you're reading this chapter, however, odds are you've made the decision to do it yourself.

Naturally, the computer on which you plan to produce your designs is one of the most important considerations involved in the production of any kind of multimedia. While it's true that a skilled designer could certainly coax some very well-crafted work from even a low-end machine, it's silly to impose limits on yourself where it isn't necessary. If budget is a concern, keep in mind that a slow or poorly equipped machine may very well reduce performance and productivity to the point that a more expensive machine would have been more cost-effective anyway. It's difficult to do great work without the right set of tools.

Keeping this in mind, let's consider the ideal multimedia workstation. All types of media manipulation will benefit from speed. This means that you'll want a computer with a fast processor and a speedy hard drive—even the fastest processor can only capture video as fast as the hard disk can write it down. A computer that's short on RAM will be effectively crippled when trying to work with large files or perform complex tasks: You'll want to have memory to burn. And since many types of media files, particularly audio and video, can be as large as several gigabytes in size prior to editing and compression, make sure you have plenty of hard disk space. Hard drives are inexpensive in comparison to most other computer components, but they're nevertheless one of the most important parts of a machine. Get a good one.

There are numerous other additions that can make your life vastly easier. A large-screen monitor will allow you to work on multiple projects simultaneously and review the results in multiple resolutions and color sets to get an idea of how visitors to your site will see them. Graphics expansion cards can be extraordinarily useful; many cards add functionalities to your computer, such as video in or out, and nearly all cards include extra video memory to speed your graphics-related tasks. On operating systems that support it, multiple video cards can also allow you to use more than one monitor at the same time from the same computer, doubling the size of your workspace.

There are countless other possibilities, depending on the type of media you intend to focus most strongly on. If you'll be doing a lot of work with audio, you may want to attach a stereo receiver and sound mixing board to your machine; if you'll be working primarily with video, a dedicated VCR or DVD player may be in order. With a good computer, such expansion possibilities are effectively limitless; it's likely that you'll be able to find a card or a peripheral for nearly everything and anything that you might need.

And once you've assembled the perfect multimedia workstation, of course, what remains is the formidable task of figuring out which of the dozens of popular software titles will help you get what you need out of the hardware you've purchased. Many applications are designed with specific needs in mind; many others include hundreds or thousands of functions intended to fit as many situations and requirements as the designers could come up with. If it's possible, you would do well to learn as much as you possibly can about a piece of software before you purchase it; if it isn't what you're looking for, you'll know enough to keep looking, and if it is what you're looking for, you can save yourself a lot of frustration and wasted time by familiarizing yourself with your tools as much as possible before diving in.

Good luck!

A P P E N D I X

ANSWERS TO SELF-REVIEW QUESTIONS

CHAPTER I

Lab I.I ■ Self-Review Answers

Question	Answer
1)	a
2)	b
3)	b
4)	c
5)	d
6)	b
7)	d

Lab I.2 ■ Self-Review Answers

Question	Answer
1)	a
2)	a
3)	b
4)	d
5)	b

Lab I.3 ■ Self-Review Answers

Question	Answer
1)	b
2)	a

Lab I.4 ■ Self-Review Answers

Question	Answer
3)	b
4)	a
5)	c

Question	Answer
1)	b
2)	b
3)	a
4)	c

Lab I.5 ■ Self-Review Answers

Question	Answer
1)	a
2)	b
3)	b
4)	b
5)	b
6)	c

Lab I.6 ■ Self-Review Answers

Question	Answer
1)	a
2)	b

3)	b
4)	c

Lab 1.7 ■ Self-Review Answers

Question	Answer
1)	b
2)	b
3)	a
4)	a
5)	b
6)	b
7)	b
8)	b
9)	b

CHAPTER 2
Lab 2.1 ■ Self-Review Answers

Question	Answer
1)	b
2)	a
3)	a
4)	d
5)	b
6)	e

Lab 2.2 ■ Self-Review Answers

Question	Answer
1)	b
2)	a
3)	a
4)	b
5)	c

Lab 2.3 ■ Self-Review Answers

Question	Answer
1)	d
2)	e

3)	b
4)	a

Lab 2.4 ■ Self-Review Answers

Question	Answer
1)	b
2)	b
3)	a
4)	a
5)	d

CHAPTER 3
Lab 3.1 ■ Self-Review Answers

Question	Answer
1)	c
2)	b
3)	c
4)	c

Lab 3.2 ■ Self-Review Answers

Question	Answer
1)	a
2)	a
3)	d
4)	b
5)	a

Lab 3.3 ■ Self-Review Answers

Question	Answer
1)	b
2)	a
3)	a
4)	c
5)	b
6)	d

Lab 3.4 ■ Self-Review Answers

Question	Answer
1)	a
2)	b
3)	b
4)	c
5)	b

Lab 3.5 ■ Self-Review Answers

Question	Answer
1)	a
2)	a
3)	d
4)	b
5)	e

CHAPTER 4

Lab 4.1 ■ Self-Review Answers

Question	Answer
1)	a
2)	b
3)	c
4)	c

Lab 4.2 ■ Self-Review Answers

Question	Answer
1)	a
2)	b
3)	b
4)	d
5)	c

Lab 4.3 ■ Self-Review Answers

Question	Answer
1)	b
2)	a

Question	Answer
3)	b
4)	d
5)	c
6)	c

Lab 4.4 ■ Self-Review Answers

Question	Answer
1)	a
2)	a
3)	b
4)	a
5)	a
6)	b

CHAPTER 5

Lab 5.1 ■ Self-Review Answers

Question	Answer
1)	b
2)	a
3)	c
4)	b
5)	d

Lab 5.2 ■ Self-Review Answers

Question	Answer
1)	b
2)	b
3)	b
4)	e
5)	c

CHAPTER 6

Lab 6.1 ■ Self-Review Answers

Question	Answer
1)	a
2)	b

3)	c
4)	b
5)	c
6)	c

Lab 6.2 ■ Self-Review Answers

Question	Answer
1)	b
2)	a
3)	d
4)	d
5)	c
6)	c

Lab 6.3 ■ Self-Review Answers

Question	Answer
1)	b
2)	a
3)	b
4)	d
5)	b
6)	d

Lab 6.4 ■ Self-Review Answers

Question	Answer
1)	a
2)	b
3)	a
4)	c
5)	d

CHAPTER 7
Lab 7.1 ■ Self-Review Answers

Question	Answer
1)	c
2)	b
3)	b

4)	b
5)	a

Lab 7.2 ■ Self-Review Answers

Question	Answer
1)	b
2)	a
3)	a
4)	c
5)	a
6)	c
7)	b

Lab 7.3 ■ Self-Review Answers

Question	Answer
1)	a
2)	b
3)	b
4)	a
5)	a
6)	d
7)	e

Lab 7.4 ■ Self-Review Answers

Question	Answer
1)	a
2)	b
3)	b
4)	c
5)	c

Lab 7.5 ■ Self-Review Answers

Question	Answer
1)	a
2)	b
3)	b
4)	b
5)	a

CHAPTER 8

Lab 8.1 ■ Self-Review Answers

Question	Answer
1)	a
2)	c
3)	c

Lab 8.2 ■ Self-Review Answers

Question	Answer
1)	b
2)	a
3)	b
4)	a

REFERENCES

CHAPTER 1 REFERENCES

Brockman, R.J., Horton, W., & Brock, K. (1989). "From Database to Hypertext via Electronic Publishing: An Information Odyssey." In E. Barrett (Ed.), *The Society of Text: Hypertext Hypermedia, and the Social Construction of Information.* Cambridge, MA: MIT Press.

Isakowitz, T., Stohr, E., & Balasubramanian, P. (1995). "RMM: A Methodology for the Design of Structured Hypermedia Applications." *Communications of the ACM 38*(8) 34–44.

Norman, D. (1988). *The Psychology of Everyday Things.* New York: Basic Books.

Schneiderman, B., & Kearsley, G. (1989). *Hypertext Hands-On: An Introduction to a New Way of Organizing and Accessing Information.* Reading, MA: Addison-Wesley.

CHAPTER 2 REFERENCES

Gould, J. D., Ukelson, J., & Boies, S. J. (1996). "Improving User Interfaces and Application Productivity by Using the ITS Application Development Environment." In Rudishill, M., Lewis, C., Polson, P. B., & McKay, T. D. (Eds), *Human-Computer Interface Design: Success Stories, Emerging Methods, and Real-World Context.* San Francisco: Morgan Kaufmann.

Hewett, T. T., Baecker, R., Card, S., Carey, T., Gasen, J., Mantei, M., Perlman, G., Strong, G., & Verplank, W. (1992). *ACM SIGCHI Curricula for Human Computer Interaction* [online]. ACM SIGCHI Curriculum Development Group. Available: http://www.acm.org/sigchi/cdg.

Hix, D., & Hartson, H. R. (1993). *Developing User Interfaces: Ensuring Usability Through Product and Process.* New York: John Wiley.

Myers, B. A., & Rosson, M. B. (1992). Survey on User Interface Programming Tools and Techniques. *Proceedings of ACM CHI'92 Conference on Human Factors in Computing Systems,* 195–202. Available: http://www.acm.org/pubs/articles/proceedings/chi/142750/p195-myers/p195-myers.pdf.

Wixon, D. & Jones, S. (1996). "Usability for Fun and Profit: A Case Study of the Design of DEC Rally Version 2." In Rudishill, M., Lewis, C., Polson, P. B., & McKay, T. D. (Eds), *Human-Computer Interface Design: Success Stories, Emerging Methods, and Real-World Context.* San Francisco: Morgan Kaufmann.

CHAPTER 3 REFERENCES

Card, S. K., Moran, T. P., & Newell, A. (1983). *The Psychology of Human-Computer Interaction*. Hillsdale, NJ: Lawrence Erlbaum Associates.

Diaper, D. (1989). *Task Analysis for Human-Computer Interaction*. Hillsdale, Chichester, UK: Ellis Horwood.

Norman, D. (1988). *The Psychology of Everyday Things*. New York: Basic Books.

Preece, J., Rogers, Y., Sharp, H., Benyon, D., Holland, S., & Carey, T. (1994). *Human-Computer Interaction*. Reading, MA: Addison-Wesley.

Schneiderman, B. (1992). *Designing the User Interface: Strategies for Effective Human-Computer Interaction* (2nd ed.). Reading, MA: Addison-Wesley.

CHAPTER 4 REFERENCES

Apple Computer, Inc. (1987). *Apple Human Interface Guidelines: The Apple Desktop Interface*. Reading, MA: Addison-Wesley.

Eason, K. (1988). *Information Technology and Organisational Change*. London: Taylor & Francis.

Helander, M. (Ed.). (1988). *Handbook of Human-Computer Interaction*. Amsterdam: North Holland.

Balbo, S. (1994, September). *Evaluation Automatique des Interfaces Utilisateur: Un Pas vers l'Automatisation,* Ph.D. thesis, University of Grenoble (France), p. 18.

Coutaz, J., Salber, D., & Balbo, S., (1993, December). "Towards automatic evaluation of multimodal user interfaces," *Knowledge Based Systems,* 6 (84).

Shackel, B. (1990). "Human factors and usability." In J. Preece & L. Keller (Eds.) *Human-Computer Interaction: Selected Readings.* Hemel Hempstead: Prentice-Hall.

Smith, S. L., & Mosier, J. N. (1986). *Guidelines for Designing User Interface Software*. ESD-TR-86-278. Bedford, MA: MITRE Corporation.

CHAPTER 5 REFERENCES

Benjamin, B. (1996). *Elements of Web Design*. Available: http://builder.cnet.com/Graphics/Design/ss1.html.

Flanders, V. (1999a). *How Big Can I Make My Page?* Available: http://www.webpagesthatsuck.com/478.html.

Flanders, V. (1999b). *Web Pages That Suck*. Available: http://www.webpagesthatsuck.com/.

Flanders, V., & Willis, M. (1998). *Web Pages That Suck: Learn Good Design by Looking at Bad Design*. Sybex.

Nielsen, J. (1994). *Useit: Usable Information Technology*. Available: http://www.useit.com.

Nielsen, J. (1996). *Top Ten Mistakes in Web Design*. Available: http://www.useit.com/alertbox/9605.html.

Nielsen, J. (1997a). *The Difference Between Web Design and GUI Design*. Available: http://www.useit.com/alertbox/9705a.html.

Nielsen, J. (1997b). *Why Web Design is Similar to GUI Design*. Available: http://www.useit.com/alertbox/scottbutler.html.

Nielsen, J. (1999a). *"Top Ten Mistakes" Revisited Three Years Later*. Available: http://www.useit.com/alertbox/990502.html.

Nielsen, J. (1999b). *The Top Ten New Mistakes of Web Design*. Available: http://www.useit.com/alertbox/990530.html.

Pompclio, S, (1999). *IIow to Make Annoying Web Pages*. Available http://www.users.nac.net/falken/annoying/main.html.

Rosenfeld, L. (n. d.). *Design by Metaphor: It's The Alchemy That Changes The Glop To Gold*. Available: http://webreview.com/95/10/27/tech/corner/.

Sullivan, T. (1999). *All Things Web: How Much Is Too Much?* Available: http://www.pantos.org/atw/35654.html.

CHAPTER 6 REFERENCES

Fleming, J. (1998). *Web Navigation*. Cambridge: O'Reilly & Associates.

Rosenfeld, L., & Morville, P. (1998). *Information Architecture for the World Wide Web: Designing Large-scale Web Sites*. Cambridge: O'Reilly & Associates.

INDEX

See It!
Hear It!
Do It!

GET ON THE ROAD TO BECOMING A PROFESSIONAL WEBMASTER WITH PTG INTERACTIVE'S HANDS-ON TOTAL LEARNING SOLUTIONS!

These interactive multimedia Training Courses on CD-ROM feature easy-to-use browser-based interfaces and fully integrated print books and searchable e-books.

- *Listen* to hours of expert audio describing key administration tasks
- *Watch* the digital videos showing a pro administrating a system and creating Web interfaces
- *Practice* your knowledge with hundreds of interactive questions and practice exercises

There's simply no better way to learn!

WOW WEB SERVER TRAINING COURSE
LARSON AND STEPHENS
©2001, Boxed Set, 0-13-089437-0

WOW WEB DESIGN TRAINING COURSE
HUBBELL, WHITE, WHITE, AND REES
©2001, Boxed Set, 0-13-040760-7

www.phptr.com/phptrinteractive

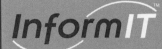